D0374006

German

Phrasebook & Dictionary

Acknowledgments
Product Editor Bruce Evans
Language Writers Gunter Muehl, Birgit Jordan, Mario Kaiser
Cover Image Researcher Naomi Parker

Thanks
James Hardy, Sandie Kestell, Campbell McKenzie, Angela Tinson,
Juan Winata

Published by Lonely Planet Global Limited
CRN 554153

7th Edition – September 2018
ISBN 978 1 78657 452 7
Text © Lonely Planet 2018
Cover Image Bernkastel-Kues town centre. Maurizio
Rellini/4Corners ©

Printed in China   10 9 8 7 6 5 4 3 2 1

Contact lonelyplanet.com/contact

MIX
Paper from
responsible sources
FSC™ C021741

Look out for the following icons throughout the book:

 'Shortcut' Phrase
Easy-to-remember alternative to the full phrase

 Q&A Pair
'Question-and-answer' pair – we suggest a response to the question asked

 Look For
Phrases you may see on signs, menus etc

 Listen For
Phrases you may hear from officials, locals etc

 Language Tip
An insight into the foreign language

 Culture Tip
An insight into the local culture

How to read the phrases:

- Coloured words and phrases throughout the book are phonetic guides to help you pronounce the foreign language.
- Lists of phrases with tinted background are options you can choose to complete the phrase above them.

These abbreviations will help you choose the right words and phrases in this book:

f	feminine	**pl**	plural
inf	informal	**pol**	polite
m	masculine	**sg**	singular
n	neuter		

Contents

PAGE 187

Menu Decoder
Dishes and ingredients explained –
order with confidence and try new foods.

PAGE 197

Two-Way Dictionary
Quick reference vocabulary guide –
3500 words to help you communicate.

INTRO German
Deutsch doytch

Who Speaks German?

OFFICIAL LANGUAGE

**GERMANY
AUSTRIA
LIECHTENSTEIN
BELGIUM
SWITZERLAND
LUXEMBOURG**

Why Bother

Don't be put off by the fact that German tends to join words together to express a single notion – it's not hard to tell parts of words, and you'll have fun recognising 'the Football World Cup qualifying match' hidden within *Fussballweltmeister-schaftsqualifikationsspiel*!

Distinctive Sounds

The ü (pronounced as 'e' with rounded lips), plus the throaty kh (like in the Scottish *loch* or the name Bach) and r (a bit like gargling).

100 MILLION
speak German as their
first language

80 MILLION
speak German as their
second language

German in the World

It's not usually described
as romantic, but its role in
science has long been rec-
ognised, and the German
language lays claim to some
of the most famous works
ever printed – just think
of the influence of Goethe,
Nietzsche, Freud and Einstein.

German in Germany

Each year the *Gesellschaft
für deutsche Sprache* (Society
for German Language) pub-
lishes an *Unwort des Jahres*
(Unword of the Year) and
several runners-up – usually
unloved words that domi-
nated the media that year.
The 2017 'unword' was
Alternative Fakten ('alternative facts').

False Friends

Warning: many German
words look like English
words but have a different
meaning altogether, eg *Chef*
shef is boss, not chef (which
is *Koch* kokh in German).

Language Family

West Germanic – close
relatives include English,
Dutch, Afrikaans, Frisian
and Yiddish.

Must-Know Grammar

German words can have a
number of different endings,
depending on their role in
the sentence. There's also a
formal and informal word
for 'you' (*Sie* zee and *du* doo
respectively).

Donations to English

Numerous – you may recognise *kindergarten*, *kitsch*, *waltz*,
hamburger, *poodle* ...

5 Phrases to Learn Before You Go

1 **Do you accept credit cards?**
Nehmen Sie Kreditkarten?
nay·men zee kre·*deet*·kar·ten

Cash is still king in Germany, so don't assume you'll be able to pay by credit card – it's best to enquire first.

---

2 **Which beer would you recommend?**
Welches Bier empfehlen Sie?
vel·khes beer emp·*fay*·len zee

Who better to ask for advice on beer than the Germans, whether at a beer garden, hall, cellar or on a brewery tour?

---

3 **Can I get this without meat?**
Kann ich das ohne Fleisch bekommen?
kan ikh das *aw*·ne flaish be·*ko*·men

In the land of *Wurst* and *Schnitzel* it may be difficult to find a variety of vegetarian meals, especially in smaller towns.

---

4 **A (non)smoking table, please.**
Einen (Nicht)rauchertisch, bitte.
ai·nen (*nikht*·)row·kher·tish *bi*·te

Germany and Austria have only partial smoking bans, so you may want to choose where to sit in cafes, bars and restaurants.

---

5 **Do you run original versions?**
Spielen auch Originalversionen?
shpee·len owkh o·ri·gi·*nahl*·fer·zi·*aw*·nen

German cinemas usually run movies dubbed into German – look for a cinema that runs subtitled original versions.

10 Phrases to Sound Like a Local

Hey!	**Hey!**	hei
Great!	**Toll!**	tol
Cool!	**Spitze!**	*shpi*·tse
No problem.	**Kein Problem.**	kain pro·*blaym*
Sure.	**Klar!**	klahr
Maybe.	**Vielleicht.**	fi·*laikht*
No way!	**Auf keinen Fall!**	owf *kai*·nen fal
It's OK.	**Alles klar.**	*a*·les klahr
What a pity!	**Schade!**	*shah*·de
Doesn't matter.	**Macht nichts.**	makht nikhts

ABOUT German

Pronunciation

Vowel Sounds

As in English, vowels can be pronounced short or long, to give different meanings (compare 'ship' and 'sheep'). Vowels are pronounced crisply and cleanly with your mouth tenser than in English, eg *Tee* (tea) is pronounced tay, not *tay*·ee.

SYMBOL	ENGLISH EQUIVALENT	GERMAN EXAMPLE	TRANSLITERATION
a	run	hat	hat
ah	rather	habe	*hah*·be
ai	aisle	mein	main
air	hair	Bär	bair
aw	saw	Boot	bawt
ay	say	leben	*lay*·ben
e	red	Bett, Männer	bet, *me*·ner
ee	bee	fliegen	*flee*·gen
er	teacher	schön	shern
i	bit	mit	mit
o	pot	Koffer	*ko*·fer
oo	moon	Schuhe	*shoo*·e
ow	house	Haus	hows
oy	boy	Leute, Häuser	*loy*·te, *hoy*·zer
u	foot	unter	*un*·ter
û	ee with rounded lips	zurück	tsu·*rûk*

Consonant Sounds

All German consonant sounds exist in English, except for the kh and r sounds, so all you need is a little practice.

SYMBOL	ENGLISH EQUIVALENT	GERMAN EXAMPLE	TRANSLITERATION
b	big	Bett	bet
ch	chili	Tschüss	chüs
d	din	dein	dain
f	fun	vier	feer
g	go	gehen	*gay·en*
h	hit	helfen	*hel·fen*
k	kick	kein	kain
kh	Bach	Sprache	*shprah·khe*
l	loud	laut	lowt
m	man	Mann	man
n	no	nein	nain
ng	sing	singen	*zing·en*
p	pig	Preis	prais
r	run	Reise	*rai·ze*
s	so	heiß	hais
sh	show	schön	shern
t	tin	Tag	tahk
ts	hits	Zeit	tsait
v	van	wohnen	*vaw·nen*
y	yes	ja	ya
z	zoo	sitzen	*zi·tsen*
zh	pleasure	Garage	*ga·rah·zhe*

The kh sound is generally like the 'ch' in 'Bach' or the Scottish *loch*, pronounced at the back of the throat. After the vowels e and i it's pronounced more forward in your mouth, almost like a sh sound. A kh sound, however, will always get you by. In this book we've used one symbol for both sounds to simplify things.

The r sound is pronounced at the back of the throat, almost like saying a g sound, but with some friction – a bit like gargling.

Word Stress

Stress in German is straightforward – almost all native German words are pronounced with stress on the first syllable. There are just a couple of things to watch out for.

Some prefixes aren't stressed, like *ver-* in the verb *verstehen* fer·*shtay*·en (understand). Also, words borrowed from other languages keep their original stress, like *Organisation* or·ga·ni·sa·*tsyawn* (organisation) and *Student* shtu·*dent* (student) and therefore may have the stress on a different syllable than in English.

While these are handy rules of thumb, you can always rely on our coloured pronunciation guides which show the stressed syllable in italics.

Intonation

German intonation is quite similar to that of English. If you're asking a question, your voice goes up at the end, just like in English: *Bist du fertig?* bist du *fer*·tikh (Are you ready?) or *Tee?* tay (Tea?). If you start with a question word, however, your voice falls, also like in English: *Woher kommst du?* vo·*hair* komst du (Where are you from?).

Note that, like in English, a rise in intonation can indicate that the speaker hasn't finished. For example, if someone asks you where you're from, you can say *Melbourne ... eine Stadt ... in Australien mel*·bawn ... *ai*·ne shtat ... in ow·*stra*·li·en (Melbourne ... a city ... in Australia), rising on the first two parts, and everyone will wait with bated breath!

Reading & Writing

The relationship between German sounds and the characters that represent them in writing is consistent, so once you become familiar with them, you should be able to pronounce a new word without a hitch. The examples in the tables on pages 10 and 11 show the correspondence between the sounds (in the first column) and how they're typically spelt (in the third column). However, there are a few points worth noting:

» The letter *ß* stands for *ss* (but the rules for whether you use *ß* or *ss* are even confusing to Germans themselves, so you can just ignore these!).

» The letters *sp* and *st* at the start of a word are pronounced like shp and sht, eg *Sport* (sport) is pronounced shport.

» Final *d*, *g*, and *b* are 'unvoiced', ie pronounced more like t, k and p, eg *Geld* (money) is pronounced gelt.

Don't be intimidated by the length of some German words. Unlike English, which often uses a number of separate words to express a single notion, German tends to join words together. After a while you'll start to recognise parts of words and understand longer words. For example, *Haupt-* howpt means 'main', so *Hauptpost* howpt·post means 'main post office', and *Hauptstadt* howpt·shtat is 'main city', ie 'capital'

~ GERMAN ALPHABET ~

A a ah	**B b** bay	**C c** tsay
D d day	**E e** ay	**F f** ef
G g gay	**H h** hah	**I i** ee
J j yot	**K k** kah	**L l** el
M m em	**N n** en	**O o** aw
P p pay	**Q q** koo	**R r** er
S s es	**T t** tay	**U u** oo
V v fow	**W w** vay	**X x** iks
Y y *üp*·si·lon	**Z z** tset	

ABOUT GERMAN

Grammar

This chapter is designed to explain the main grammatical structures you need to make your own sentences. Look under each heading – listed in alphabetical order – for information on functions which these grammatical categories express in a sentence. For example, demonstratives are used for giving instructions. A glossary of grammatical terms is included at the end of the chapter to help you.

Adjectives & Adverbs

Describing People/Things • Doing Things

Adjectives don't change their form if they come after 'be' in a sentence. However, if they come before a noun, adjectives have either 'strong' endings (if used without an article) or 'weak' endings (if used with an article). Strong endings change to match the gender, number and case of the noun, but weak endings don't indicate this. See also **articles**, **case**, **gender** and **plurals**.

My meal is cold.	Mein Essen ist kalt.
	(lit: my-nom-n-sg meal is cold)
	~~main~~ e·sen ist kalt
	mine
cold meal	kaltes Essen (lit: cold-nom-n-sg meal)
	kal·tes e·sen
the cold meal	das kalte Essen
	(lit: the-nom-n-sg cold meal)
	das *kal*·te e·sen

	~ WEAK ENDINGS ~				~ STRONG ENDINGS ~			
	m sg	f sg	n sg	pl	m sg	f sg	n sg	pl
nom	-e	-e	-e	-en	-er	-e	-es	-e
acc	-en	-e	-e	-en	-en	-e	-es	-e
dat	-en	-en	-en	-en	-em	-er	-em	-en
gen	-en	-en	-en	-en	-en	-er	-en	-er

Most adjectives in German can also be used as adverbs in their basic form (with no endings), and they usually come towards the end of the sentence.

a quiet restaurant	ein ruhiges Restaurant (lit: a-nom-n-sg quiet-nom-n-sg restaurant) ain roo·ikh·es res·to·rang
Keep quiet!	Sei ruhig! (lit: be quiet) zai roo·ikh

Articles

Naming People/Things

German has various forms of both the definite article (ie 'the' in English) and the indefinite article (ie 'a' or 'an' in English), depending on the gender, number and case of the noun (see **case**, **gender** and **plurals**). If you just use the nominative (dictionary form), you'll still be understood.

~ DEFINITE ARTICLE ('THE') ~

	m sg	f sg	n sg	pl
nom	der dair	die dee	das das	die dee
acc	den dayn	die dee	das das	die dee
dat	dem daym	der dair	dem daym	den dayn
gen	des des	der dair	des des	der dair

~ INDEFINITE ARTICLE ('A/AN') ~

	m sg	f sg	n sg	pl
nom	ein ain	eine *ai*·ne	ein ain	keine * *kai*·ne
acc	einen *ai*·nen	eine *ai*·ne	ein ain	keine *kai*·ne
dat	einem *ai*·nem	einer *ai*·ner	einem *ai*·nem	keinen *kai*·nen
gen	eines *ai*·nes	einer *ai*·ner	eines *ai*·nes	keiner *kai*·ner

*kein kain is the negative indefinite article meaning 'no'

Be

Describing People/Things • Making Statements

Just like in English, the verb *sein* zain (be) has different forms depending on the subject of the sentence. For information on negative forms, see **negatives**.

~ SEIN (BE) – PRESENT TENSE ~

I	am	ich	bin	ikh	bin
you sg inf	**are**	du	bist	doo	bist
you sg pol	**are**	Sie	sind	zee	zind
he/she/it	**is**	er/sie/es	ist	air/zee/es	ist
we	**are**	wir	sind	veer	zind
you pl inf	**are**	ihr	seid	eer	zait
you pl pol	**are**	Sie	sind	zee	zind
they	**are**	sie	sind	zee	zind

Case

Doing Things • Giving Instructions • Indicating Location • Naming People/Things • Possessing

German has a system of four cases (shown through word endings) which are used to indicate the 'role' of certain words in a sentence and their relationship to other words (ie whether it's the subject, direct or indirect object). Pronouns, adjectives and articles all take different endings for case, while nouns take case endings only in a few instances – a noun's case is generally indicated by the article or adjective accompanying it (see **adjectives & adverbs** and **articles**).

The word lists, **menu decoder** and **dictionaries** in this book provide words in the nominative case – you can just use this case, even if another case would be grammatically correct in a sentence, and you'll still be understood. The main functions of the four cases in German are explained following. See also **prepositions**.

– CASE –

NOMINATIVE nom – shows the subject of a sentence	
The tour guide is handsome.	Der Reiseführer ist schön. (lit: the-nom tour-guide-nom is handsome) dair rai·ze·fü·rer ist shern

ACCUSATIVE acc – shows the direct object of a sentence	
I love the tour guide.	Ich liebe den Reiseführer. (lit: I love the-acc tour-guide-acc) ikh lee·be dayn rai·ze·fü·rer

DATIVE dat – shows the indirect object of a sentence	
I gave my ticket to the tour guide.	Ich habe dem Reiseführer meine Fahrkarte gegeben. (lit: I have the-dat tour-guide-dat my-acc ticket-acc given) ikh hah·be daym rai·ze·fü·rer mai·ne fahr·kar·te ge·gay·ben

GENITIVE gen – shows possession	
What's the tour guide's name?	Wie ist der Name des Reiseführers? (lit: how is the-nom name-nom the-gen tour-guide-gen) vee ist dair nah·me des rai·ze·fü·rers

Demonstratives

Giving Instructions • Indicating Location •
Pointing Things Out

The easiest way to point something out in German is to use *das ist* das ist (this/that is) and *das sind* das zint (these/those are).

That's my bag; those are her suitcases.
Das ist meine Tasche; das sind ihre Koffer.
(lit: that is my-**nom-f-sg** bag those are her-**nom-m-pl** suitcases)
das ist *mai*·ne *ta*·she das zint *ee*·re *ko*·fer

The demonstrative *dieser dee*·zer (this) changes to match the noun's gender, number and case (see **case**, **gender** and **plurals**). The table below shows all the forms – as you can see, they follow the same pattern as the definite article (see **articles**).

~ DEMONSTRATIVES ~

	m sg	f sg	n sg	pl
nom	dieser *dee*·zer	diese *dee*·ze	dieses *dee*·zes	diese *dee*·ze
acc	diesen *dee*·zen	diese *dee*·ze	dieses *dee*·zes	diese *dee*·ze
dat	diesem *dee*·zem	dieser *dee*·zer	diesem *dee*·zem	diesen *dee*·zen
gen	dieses *dee*·zes	dieser *dee*·zer	dieses *dee*·zes	dieser *dee*·zer

Gender

Naming People/Things

In German, all nouns (words which denote a thing, person or idea) have masculine, feminine or neuter gender. You can recognise the noun's gender by the article, demonstrative, possessive or any other adjective accompanying the noun, as they change form to agree with the noun's gender (see **adjectives & adverbs**, **articles**, **demonstratives**, **possessives**). The gender of words is also indicated in the dictionary, but here are some general rules:

» nouns ending in *-er*, *-ig* or *-ing* are generally masculine
» nouns ending in *-in*, *-heit* or *-keit* are generally feminine
» nouns which refer to young people and animals are neuter

The gender of words is indicated with m (masculine), f (feminine) and n (neuter) throughout this phrasebook where relevant. See also the box **M Before F**, page 131.

Have

Possessing

Possession can be indicated in various ways in German (see also **possessives**). One way is with the verb *haben* hah·ben (have), shown below. For negative forms, see **negatives**.

~ HABEN (HAVE) – PRESENT TENSE ~

I	**have**	ich	habe	ikh	*hah·be*
you sg inf	**have**	du	hast	doo	hast
you sg pol	**have**	Sie	haben	zee	*hah·ben*
he/she/it	**has**	er/sie/es	hat	air/zee/es	hat
we	**have**	wir	haben	veer	*hah·ben*
you pl inf	**have**	ihr	habt	eer	hapt
you pl pol	**have**	Sie	haben	zee	*hah·ben*
they	**have**	sie	haben	zee	*hah·ben*

Negatives

Negating

To make a negative statement in German, just add the word *nicht* nikht (not) after the verb, or after the object if included.

I don't smoke.	Ich rauche nicht.
	(lit: I smoke not)
	ikh *row*·khe nikht
I don't love you.	Ich liebe dich nicht.
	(lit: I love you-acc-sg-inf not)
	ikh *lee*·be dikh nikht

In sentences with the indefinite article *ein* ain (a/an) or no article, the negative article *kein* kain is used instead of *nicht*.

I see a taxi.	Ich sehe ein Taxi.
	(lit: I see a-acc-n-sg taxi)
	ikh *zay*·e ain *tak*·si
I don't see a taxi.	Ich sehe kein Taxi.
	(lit: I see no-acc-n-sg taxi)
	ikh *zay*·e kain *tak*·si

Personal Pronouns

Making Statements • Naming People/Things

Personal pronouns ('I', 'you' etc) change their form in German for person, number and case (see **case**). It's similar in English, which has 'I' and 'me' as the subject and object pronouns.

There are two forms of the second-person singular pronoun (ie 'you') in German. Use the polite form *Sie* zee when talking to anyone you don't know well, and the informal forms *du* du (singular) and *ihr* eer (plural) only with people you know well or who are younger than you. Phrases in this book use the form of 'you' that is appropriate to the situation. Where both forms are used, they are indicated by pol and inf.

~ PERSONAL PRONOUNS ~

	nom		acc		dat		gen	
I	ich	ikh	mich	mikh	mir	meer	meiner	*mei*·ner
you sg inf	du	du	dich	dikh	dir	deer	deiner	*dai*·ner
you sg pol	Sie	zee	Sie	zee	Ihnen	ee·nen	Ihrer	ee·rer
he	er	air	ihn	een	ihm	eem	seiner	*zai*·ner
she	sie	zoo	sie	zoo	ihr	eer	ihrer	ee·rer
it	es	es	es	es	ihm	eem	seiner	*zai*·ner
we	wir	veer	uns	uns	uns	uns	unser	*un*·zer
you pl inf	ihr	eer	euch	oykh	euch	oykh	euer	o·yer
you pl pol	Sie	zee	Sie	zee	Ihnen	ee·nen	Ihrer	ee·rer
they	sie	zee	sie	zee	ihnen	ee·nen	ihrer	ee·rer

Plurals

Naming People/Things

The most common ways of forming plurals in German:

» no plural endings and often an umlaut added over the vowel, mostly for masculine nouns ending in a consonant: *Spiegel* shpee·gel (mirror), *Spiegel* shpee·gel (mirrors); *Boden* baw·den (soil), *Böden* ber·den (soils)

» adding -e and often an umlaut over the vowel for nouns ending in a consonant, mostly single-syllable masculine nouns: *Tag* tahk (day), *Tage* tah·ge (days); *Zug* tsook (train), *Züge* tsoo·ge (trains)

» adding *-er* and often an umlaut over the vowel, mostly for single-syllable neuter nouns: *Bild* bilt (picture), *Bilder* bil·der (pictures); *Blatt* blat (leaf), *Blätter* ble·ter (leaves)

» adding *-s* to all nouns ending in a vowel, except those ending in *-e*, and to English loanwords: *Auto* ow·to (car), *Autos* ow·tos (cars); *Park* park (park), *Parks* parks (parks)

» adding *-n* to nouns ending in *-e*, and adding *-en* to almost all feminine nouns: *Junge* yung·e (boy), *Jungen* yung·en (boys); *Frau* frow (woman), *Frauen* frow·en (women)

Possessives

Possessing

A common way of indicating possession is by using possessive adjectives before the noun they refer to. Like other adjectives, they agree with the noun in gender, number and case (see also **case**, **gender** and **plurals**). The table below shows only the nominative case, singular forms; for other cases and for plural see **demonstratives**, as they follow the same pattern.

~ POSSESSIVE ADJECTIVES ~

	m sg		f sg		n sg	
my	mein	main	meine	*mai*·ne	mein	main
your sg inf	dein	dain	deine	*dai*·ne	dein	dain
your sg pl	Ihr	eer	Ihre	ee·re	Ihr	eer
his	sein	zain	seine	zai·ne	sein	zain
her	ihr	eer	ihre	ee·re	ihr	eer
its	sein	zain	seine	zai·ne	sein	zain
our	unser	*un*·zer	unsere	*un*·ze·re	unser	*un*·zer
your pl inf	euer	o·yer	eure	oy·re	euer	o·yer
your pl pol	Ihr	eer	Ihre	ee·re	Ihr	eer
their	ihr	eer	ihre	ee·re	ihr	eer

Prepositions

Giving Instructions • Indicating Location •
Pointing Things Out

Like English, German uses prepositions to explain where
things are in time or space. All prepositions in German require
the noun to be in a certain case (see **case**), most frequently the
dative.

~ PREPOSITIONS ~

after	nach	nakh	**from**	von	fon
at (time)	um	urn	**in (place)**	in	in
before	vor	fawr	**to**	zu	tsoo

Questions

Asking Questions • Negating

The easiest way of forming 'yes/no' questions is to add *nicht
wahr* nikht var (literally 'not true') to the end of a statement,
similar to 'isn't it?' in English. You can also turn a statement
into a question by putting the verb before the subject of the
sentence.

The hotel is nearby, isn't it?	Das Hotel ist nahe, nicht wahr? (lit: the-nom-n-sg hotel is near not true) das ho·*tel* ist *nah*·e nikht var
Is the hotel nearby?	Ist das Hotel nahe? (lit: is the-nom-n-sg hotel near) ist das ho·*tel nah*·e

As in English, there are question words (see the table on p24)
for more specific questions. They go at the start of the sentence,
followed by the verb.

ABOUT GERMAN   GRAMMAR

~ QUESTION WORDS ~

how	wie	vee	**where**	wo	vaw
what	was	vas	**who**	wer	vair
when	wann	van	**why**	warum	va·*rum*

Verbs

Doing Things

Most German verbs are regular, with the infinitive ending in
-*(e)n*. Tenses are formed by adding various endings for each
person to the verb stem (the dictionary form without the -*(e)n*).
See also **be**, **have** and **negatives**.

~ PRESENT TENSE – SAGEN (SAY) ~

I	say	ich	sage	ikh	*zah·*ge
you sg inf	say	du	sagst	doo	zahkst
you sg pol	say	Sie	sagen	zee	*zah·*gen
he/she/it	says	er/sie/es	sagt	air/zee/es	zahkt
we	say	wir	sagen	veer	*zah·*gen
you pl inf	say	ihr	sagt	eer	zahkt
you pl pol	say	Sie	sagen	zee	*zah·*gen
they	say	sie	sagen	zee	*zah·*gen

~ PAST TENSE – SAGEN (SAY) ~

I	said	ich	sagte	ikh	*zahk·*te
you sg inf	said	du	sagtest	doo	*zahk·*test
you sg pol	said	Sie	sagten	zee	*zahk·*ten
he/she/it	said	er/sie/es	sagte	air/zee/es	*zahk·*te
we	said	wir	sagten	veer	*zahk·*ten
you pl inf	said	ihr	sagtet	eer	*zahk·*tet
you pl pol	said	Sie	sagten	zee	*zahk·*ten
they	said	sie	sagten	zee	*zahk·*ten

For the future tense, use the construction '*werden* + infinitive' (like 'going to ...' in English). The verb *werden* vair·den (lit: 'become') changes form for each person as shown in the table below.

| I'm going to travel to Berlin. | Ich werde nach Berlin fahren. (lit: I am-going-to to Berlin travel) ikh *vair*·de nakh ber·*leen fah*·ren |

~ FUTURE TENSE ~

I	am going to	ich	werde	ikh	*vair*·de
you sg inf	are going to	du	wirst	doo	virst
you sg pol	are going to	Sie	werden	zee	*vair*·den
he/she/it	is going to	er/sie/es	wird	air/zee/es	virt
we	are going to	wir	werden	veer	*vair*·den
you pl inf	are going to	ihr	werdet	eer	*vair*·det
you pl pol	are going to	Sie	werden	zee	*vair*·den
they	are going to	sie	werden	zee	*vair*·den

Word Order

Making Statements

In a straightforward German statement, the verb is the second element, usually following the subject of the sentence. So, if the sentence starts with an adverb such as 'tomorrow', the order of the subject and the verb is reversed to keep the verb as the second element. See also **negatives** and **questions**.

| I'm going to Berlin. | Ich gehe nach Berlin. (lit: I go to Berlin) ikh *gay*·e nakh ber·*leen* |
| **Tomorrow I'm going to Berlin.** | Morgen gehe ich nach Berlin. (lit: tomorrow go I to Berlin) *mawr*·gen *gay*·e ikh nakh ber·*leen* |

ABOUT GERMAN GRAMMAR

~ GRAMMAR GLOSSARY ~

adjective	a word that describes something – 'German beer is up there with the world's **best**'
adverb	a word that explains how an action is done – 'it **supposedly** doesn't give you a hangover'
article	the words 'a', 'an' and 'the'
case (marking)	word ending which tells us the role of a thing or person in the sentence
demonstrative	a word that means 'this' or 'that'
direct object	the thing or person in the sentence that has the action directed to it – 'most visitors just drink **it**'
gender	classification of *nouns* into classes (like masculine, feminine and neuter), requiring other words (eg *adjectives*) to belong to the same class
indirect object	the person or thing in the sentence that is the recipient of the action – 'others go to **breweries**'
infinitive	dictionary form of a *verb* – '**to learn** about beer'
noun	a thing, person or idea – 'and its **production**'
number	whether a word is singular or plural – '**breweries** use four **ingredients**: **malt**, **yeast**, **hops**, **water**'
personal pronoun	a word that means 'I', 'you' etc
possessive adjective	a word that means 'my', 'your' etc
possessive pronoun	a word that means 'mine', 'yours' etc
preposition	a word like 'for' or 'before' in English
subject	the thing or person in the sentence that does the action – '**monasteries** still produce beer too'
tense	form of a *verb* that tells you whether the action is in the present, past or future – eg 'drink' (present), 'drank' (past), 'will drink' (future)
verb	a word that tells you what action happened – 'many people **visit** them on brewery tours'
verb stem	part of a *verb* that doesn't change – eg '**tast**e' in '**tast**ing' and '**tast**ed'

Basics

Understanding

KEY PHRASES

Do you speak English?	Sprechen Sie Englisch? pol	*shpre*·khen zee *eng*·lish
	Sprichst du Englisch? inf	shprikhst doo *eng*·lish
I don't understand.	Ich verstehe nicht.	ikh fer·*shtay*·e nikht
What does ... mean?	Was bedeutet ...?	vas be·*doy*·tet...

Q **Do you speak English?**	Sprechen Sie Englisch? pol *shpre*·khen zee *eng*·lish Sprichst du Englisch? inf shprikhst doo *eng*·lish
Q **Does anyone speak English?**	Spricht hier jemand Englisch? shprikht heer *yay*·mant *eng*·lish
A **I speak a little (German).**	Ich spreche ein bisschen (Deutsch). ikh *shpre*·khe ain *bis*·khen (doytsh)
Q **Do you understand (me)?**	Verstehen Sie (mich)? fer·*shtay*·en zee (mikh)
A **I (don't) understand.**	Ich verstehe (nicht). ikh fer·*shtay*·e (nikht)
I'd like to practise German.	Ich möchte Deutsch üben. ikh *merkh*·te (doytsh) *ü*·ben

LANGUAGE TIP

Being Polite

There are two forms of the second-person singular pronoun 'you'. Use the polite form *Sie* zee with anyone you don't know well, and only use the informal form *du* doo with people you know very well. All the phrases in this chapter use *Sie* unless indicated otherwise.

What does 'Kugel' mean?	Was bedeutet 'Kugel'? vas be·*doy*·tet *koo*·gel
How do you pronounce this?	Wie spricht man dieses Wort aus? vee shprikht man *dee*·zes vort ows
How do you say 'ticket' in German?	Wie sagt man 'ticket' auf Deutsch? vee zagt man *ti*·ket owf doytsh
How do you write 'Schweiz'?	Wie schreibt man 'Schweiz'? vee shraipt man shvaits
Could you please repeat that?	Könnten Sie das bitte wiederholen? *kern*·ten zee das *bi*·te vee·der·*haw*·len
Could you please write it down?	Könnten Sie das bitte aufschreiben? *kern*·ten zee das *bi*·te owf·*shrai*·ben
Could you please speak more slowly?	Könnten Sie bitte langsamer sprechen? *kern*·ten zee *bi*·te *lang*·za·mer *shpre*·khen

| ✂ | **Slowly, please!** | Langsamer, bitte! | *lang*·za·mer *bi*·te |

Numbers & Amounts

KEY PHRASES

| How much? | Wieviel? | vee-*feel* |
| How many? | Wie viele? | vee *fee*-le |

Cardinal Numbers

0	null	nul
1	eins	ains
2	zwei	tsvai
3	drei	drai
4	vier	feer
5	fünf	fünf
6	sechs	zeks
7	sieben	*zee*-ben
8	acht	akht
9	neun	noyn
10	zehn	tsayn
11	elf	elf
12	zwölf	zverlf
13	dreizehn	*drai*-tsayn
14	vierzehn	*feer*-tsayn
15	fünfzehn	*fünf*-tsayn
16	sechzehn	*zeks*-tsayn
17	siebzehn	*zeep*-tsayn
18	achtzehn	*akht*-tsayn
19	neunzehn	*noyn*-tsayn
20	zwanzig	*tsvan*-tsikh

21	einundzwanzig	*ain*·unt·tsvan·tsikh
22	zwoiundzwanzig	*tsvai*·unt·tsvan·tsikh
30	dreißig	*drai*·tsikh
40	vierzig	*feer*·tsikh
50	fünfzig	*fünf*·tsikh
60	sechzig	*zekh*·tsikh
70	siebzig	*zeep*·tsikh
80	achtzig	*akht*·tsikh
90	neunzig	*noyn*·tsikh
100	hundert	*hun*·dert
1000	tausend	*tow*·sent
1,000,000	eine Million	*ai*·ne mil·*yawn*

Ordinal Numbers

1st	erste	*ers*·te
2nd	zweite	*tsvai*·te
3rd	dritte	*dri*·te

Amounts

How much?	Wieviel?	vee·*feel*
How many?	Wie viele?	vee·*fee*·le
a quarter	ein Viertel	ain *fir*·tel
a third	ein Drittel	ain *dri*·tel
a half	eine Hälfte	*ai*·ne *helf*·te
all/none	alles/nichts	*a*·les/nikhts
less/more	weniger/mehr	*vay*·ni·ger/mair
(just) a little	(nur) ein bisschen	(noor) ain *bis*·khen
much/a lot	viel	feel
some/many	einige/viele	*ai*·ni·ge/*fee*·le

For other useful amounts, see **self-catering** (p181).

BASICS **TIME & DATES**

Time & Dates

KEY PHRASES

What time is it?	Wie spät ist es?	vee shpayt ist es
At what time?	Um wie viel Uhr?	um vee feel oor
What date?	Welches Datum?	*vel*·khes *dah*·tum

Telling the Time

To denote the time between noon and midnight, use *nachmittags* *nahkh*·mi·tahks for times between noon and 6pm, and *abends* *ah*·bents for times from 6pm to midnight.

Q What time is it?	Wie spät ist es? vee shpayt ist es
A It's (10) o'clock.	Es ist (zehn) Uhr. es ist (tsayn) oor
Quarter past (one).	Viertel nach (eins). *fir*·tel nahkh (ains)
Twenty past (one).	Zwanzig nach (eins). *tsvan*·tsikh nahkh (ains)
Half past one.	Halb zwei. (lit: half two) halp tsvai
Twenty to (one).	Zwanzig vor (eins). *tsvan*·tsikh fawr (ains)
Quarter to (one).	Viertel vor (eins). *fir*·tel fawr (ains)
It's 2.12pm.	Es ist 14:12. es ist *feer*·tsayn oor tsverlf

Q At what time?	Um wie viel Uhr? *um vee feel oor*	
A At ...	Um ... *um ...*	
am	vormittags *fawr·mi·tahks*	
pm	nachmittags/abends *nahkh·mi·tahks/ah·bents*	

The Calendar

Monday	Montag m	*mawn·tahk*
Tuesday	Dienstag m	*deens·tahk*
Wednesday	Mittwoch m	*mit·vokh*
Thursday	Donnerstag m	*do·ners·tahk*
Friday	Freitag m	*frai·tahk*
Saturday	Samstag m	*zams·tahk*
Sunday	Sonntag m	*zon·tahk*
January	Januar m	*yan·u·ahr*
February	Februar m	*fay·bru·ahr*
March	März m	*merts*
April	April m	*a·pril*
May	Mai m	*mai*
June	Juni m	*yoo·ni*
July	Juli m	*yoo·li*
August	August m	*ow·gust*
September	September m	*zep·tem·ber*
October	Oktober m	*ok·taw·ber*
November	November m	*no·vem·ber*
December	Dezember m	*de·tsem·ber*

BASICS

TIME & DATES

summer	Sommer m	*zo*·mer
autumn/fall	Herbst m	herpst
winter	Winter m	*vin*·ter
spring	Frühling m	*frü*·ling

What date?	Welches Datum?	*vel*·khes *dah*·tum
Q What date is it today?	Der Wievielte ist heute?	dair *vee*·feel·te ist *hoy*·te
A It's (18 October) today.	Heute ist (der 18 Oktober).	*hoy*·te ist (dair *akh*·tsayn·te ok·*taw*·ber)

Present

now	jetzt	yetst
right now	jetzt gerade	yetst ge·*rah*·de
today	heute	*hoy*·te
tonight	heute Abend	*hoy*·te *ah*·bent
this afternoon	heute Nachmittag	*hoy*·te *nahkh*·mi·tahk
this morning	heute Morgen	*hoy*·te *mor*·gen
this week	diese Woche	*dee*·ze *vo*·khe
this month	diesen Monat	*dee*·zen *maw*·nat
this year	dieses Jahr	*dee*·zes yahr

Past

| day before yesterday | vorgestern | *fawr*·ges·tern |
| last night | vergangene Nacht | fer·*gang*·e·ne nakht |

last week	letzte Woche	*lets*·te *vo*·khe
last month	letzten Monat	*lets*·ten *maw*·nat
last year	letztes Jahr	*lets*·tes yahr
since (May)	seit (Mai)	zait (mai)
a while ago	vor einer Weile	fawr *ai*·ner *vai*·le
(half an) hour ago	vor (einer halben) Stunde	fawr (*ai*·ner *hal*·ben) *shtun*·de
(three) days ago	vor (drei) Tagen	fawr (drai) *tah*·gen
(five) years ago	vor (fünf) Jahren	fawr (fünf) *yah*·ren
yesterday	gestern	*ges*·tern
yesterday afternoon	gestern Nachmittag	*ges*·tern *nahkh*·mi·tahk
yesterday evening	gestern Abend	*ges*·tern *ah*·bent
yesterday morning	gestern Morgen	*ges*·tern *mor*·gen

Future

day after tomorrow	übermorgen	*ü*·ber·mor·gen
in (six) days	in (sechs) Tagen	in (zeks) *tah*·gen
in (five) minutes	in (fünf) Minuten	in (fünf) mi·*noo*·ten
next month	nächsten Monat	*naykhs*·ten *maw*·nat
next week	nächste Woche	*naykhs*·te *vo*·khe
next year	nächstes Jahr	*naykhs*·tes yahr
tomorrow	morgen	*mor*·gen
tomorrow afternoon	morgen Nachmittag	*mor*·gen *nahkh*·mi·tahk

BASICS | **TIME & DATES**

tomorrow evening	morgen Abend	*mor*·gen *ah*·bent
tomorrow morning	morgen früh	*mor*·gen frü
until (June)	bis (Juni)	bis (*yoo*·ni)
within a month	in einem Monat	in *ai*·nem *maw*·nat
within an hour	in einer Stunde	in *ai*·ner *shtun*·de

During the Day

It's early.	Es ist früh.	es ist frü
It's late.	Es ist spät.	es ist shpayt
afternoon	Nachmittag m	*nahkh*·mi·tahk
dawn	Dämmerung f	*de*·me·rung
day	Tag m	tahk
evening	Abend m	*ah*·bent
midday	Mittag m	*mi*·tahk
midnight	Mitternacht f	*mi*·ter·nakht
morning	Morgen m	*mor*·gen
night	Nacht f	nakht
noon	Mittag m	*mi*·tahk
sunrise	Sonnenaufgang m	*zo*·nen·owf·gang
sunset	Sonnenuntergang m	*zo*·nen·un·ter·gang

Practical

PRACTICAL TRANSPORT

Transport

KEY PHRASES

What time's the next bus?	Wann fährt der nächste Bus?	van fairt dair *naykhs*·te bus
A ticket to (Berlin).	Eine Fahrkarte nach (Berlin).	*ai*·ne *fahr*·kar·te nahhk (ber·*leen*)
Can you tell me when we get to (Kiel)?	Könnten Sie mir bitte sagen, wann wir in (Kiel) ankommen?	*kern*·ten zee meer *bi*·te *zah*·gen van veer in (keel) *an*·ko·men
Please take me to (this address).	Bitte bringen Sie mich zu (dieser Adresse).	*bi*·te *bring*·en zee mikh tsoo (*dee*·zer a·*dre*·se)

Getting Around

What time does the boat/ plane leave?	Wann fährt das Boot/ Flugzeug ab? van fairt das bawt/ *flook*·tsoyk ap
What time does the bus/ train leave?	Wann fährt der Bus/Zug ab? van fairt dair bus/tsook ap
What time does it arrive?	Wann kommt es an? van komt es an
What time's the first bus?	Wann fährt der erste Bus? van fairt dair *ers*·te bus
What time's the last bus?	Wann fährt der letzte Bus? van fairt dair *lets*·te bus
What time's the next bus?	Wann fährt der nächste Bus? van fairt dair *naykhs*·te bus

🔊 LISTEN FOR

Es ist ausgebucht.	es ist *ows*·ge·bookht It's full.
... ist gestrichen.	... ist ge·*shtri*·khen The ... is cancelled.
... hat Verspätung ...	... hat fer·*shpay*·tung The ... is delayed.
Dieser Halt ist ...	*dee*·zer halt ist ... This stop is ...
Der nächste Halt ist ...	dair *nairkh* ste halt ist ... The next stop is ...

How long will it be delayed?	Wie viel Verspätung wird es haben? vee feel fer·*shpay*·tung virt es *hah*·ben
Is this seat free?	Ist dieser Platz frei? ist *dee*·zer plats frai
✂ **Is it free?** Ist hier frei? ist heer frai	
That's my seat.	Dieses ist mein Platz. *dee*·zes ist main plats
Can you tell me when we get to (Kiel)?	Könnten Sie mir bitte sagen, wann wir in (Kiel) ankommen? *kern*·ten zee meer *bi*·te *zah*·gen van veer in (keel) *an*·ko·men
I want to get off here.	Ich möchte hier aussteigen. ikh *merkh*·te heer *ows*·shtai·gen

| Can we get there by public transport? | Können wir mit öffentlichen Verkehrsmitteln dahin kommen? *ker*·nen veer mit *er*·fent·li·khen fair·*kairs*·mi·teln dah·*hin ko*·men |
| I'd prefer to walk there. | Ich gehe lieber zu Fuß dahin. ikh *gay*·e *lee*·ber tsoo foos dah·*hin* |

Buying Tickets

Where can I buy a ticket?	Wo kann ich eine Fahrkarte kaufen? vaw kan ikh *ai*·ne *fahr*·kar·te *kow*·fen
Do I need to book?	Muss ich einen Platz reservieren lassen? mus ikh *ai*·nen plats re·zer·*vee*·ren *la*·sen
A ... ticket to (Berlin).	Eine ... nach (Berlin). *ai*·ne ... nahkh (ber·*leen*)

1st-class	Fahrkarte erster Klasse	*fahr*·kar·te *ers*·ter *kla*·se
2nd-class	Fahrkarte zweiter Klasse	*fahr*·kar·te *tsvai*·ter *kla*·se
child's	Kinderfahrkarte	*kin*·der·fahr·kar·te
one-way	einfache Fahrkarte	*ain*·fa·khe *fahr*·kar·te
return	Rückfahrkarte	*rük*·fahr·kar·te
student's	Studentenfahrkarte	shtu·*den*·ten· fahr·kar·te

Buying a Ticket

 ## What time is the next ...?

Wann fährt der/das nächste ... ab? m/n
van fairt dair/das *naykhs*·te ... ap

 boat
Boot n
bawl

 bus
Bus m
bus

 train
Zug m
tsook

 ## One ... ticket, please.

Eine .... bitte.
ai·ne ... bi·te

 one-way
einfache Fahrkarte
ain·fa·khe *fahr*·kar·te

 return
Rückfahrkarte
rük·fahr·kar·te

 ## I'd like a/an ... seat.

Ich hätte gern einen ...,
ikh *he*·te gern *ai*·nen ...

aisle
Platz am Gang
plats am gang

window
Fensterplatz
fens·ter·plats

 ## Which platform does it depart from?

Auf welchem Bahnsteig fährt es ab?
owf *vel*·khem *bahn*·shtaik fairt es ap

Two (return tickets), please.	Zwei (Rückfahrkarten) bitte. tsvai (*rük*·fahr·kar·ten) *bi*·te
I'd like an aisle seat.	Ich hätte gern einen Platz am Gang. ikh *he*·te gern *ai*·nen plats am gang
I'd like a window seat.	Ich hätte gern einen Fensterplatz. ikh *he*·te gern *ai*·nen *fens*·ter·plats
How long does the trip take?	Wie lange dauert die Fahrt? vee *lang*·e *dow*·ert dee fahrt
Is it a direct route?	Ist es eine direkte Verbindung? ist es *ai*·ne di·*rek*·te fer·*bin*·dung
Can I get a stand-by ticket?	Kann ich ein Standby-Ticket bekommen? kan ikh ain stend·*bai*·ti·ket be·*ko*·men
day ticket	Tageskarte f *tah*·ges·kar·te
weekly ticket	Wochenkarte f *vo*·khen·kar·te
ticket for multiple trips	Mehrfachfahrkarte f *mair*·fakh·fahr·kar·te
I'd like to ... my ticket, please.	Ich möchte meine Fahrkarte bitte ... ikh *merkh*·te *mai*·ne *fahr*·kar·te *bi*·te ...

cancel	zurückgeben	tsu·*rük*·gay·ben
change	ändern lassen	*en*·dern *la*·sen
collect	abholen	ab·*ho*·len
confirm	bestätigen lassen	be·*shtay*·ti·gen *la*·sen

LANGUAGE TIP

Ticket Types

German distinguishes between different types of journeys, depending on the transport used: *Fahrt* fahrt for a journey by road or rail; *Flug* flook for a journey by plane. This distinction is reflected in the names of the tickets used for these journeys: *Fahrkarte fahr*·kar·te for a train/bus/underground ticket; *Flugticket flook*·ti·ket for a plane ticket. This chapter uses *Fahrkarte*, so make sure you use the appropriate word when buying tickets.

Luggage

My luggage has been damaged.	Mein Gepäck ist beschädigt. main ge·*pek* ist be·*shay*·dikht
My luggage has been stolen.	Mein Gepäck ist gestohlen worden. main ge·*pek* ist ge·*shtaw*·len *vor*·den
My luggage hasn't arrived.	Mein Gepäck ist nicht angekommen. main ge·*pek* ist nikht *an*·ge·ko·men
I'd like a luggage locker.	Ich hätte gern ein Gepäckschließfach. ikh *he*·te gern ain ge·*pek*·shlees·fakh

Bus

Which bus goes to (Cologne)?	Welcher Bus fährt nach (Köln)? *vel*·kher bus fairt nakh (kerln)
Which bus goes to (the station)?	Welcher Bus fährt (zum Bahnhof)? *vel*·kher bus fairt (tsum *bahn*·hawf)

> **LANGUAGE TIP**
> **Talking about Destinations**
> German uses two different words for the English word 'to'. With place names, use *nach* nakh, eg 'to Salzburg' is *nach Salzburg* nakh *zalts*·boorg. For all other destinations, use *zum/zur/zum* tsum/tsur/ tsum with masculine/feminine/neuter nouns. For example, 'to the station' is *zum Bahnhof* m tsum *bahn*·hawf; 'to the youth hostel' is *zur Jugendherberge* f tsur *yoo*·gent·her·ber·ge; and 'to the city centre' is *zum Stadtzentrum* n tsum *shtat*·tsen·trum.

Bus number ...	Bus Nummer ... bus *nu*·mer ...
Where's the bus stop?	Wo ist die Bushaltestelle? vo ist dee *bus*·hal·te·shte·le
What's the next stop?	Welches ist der nächste Halt? *vel*·khes ist dair *naykh*·ste halt
I'd like to get off (at Alexanderplatz).	Ich möchte (am Alexanderplatz) aussteigen. ikh *merkh*·te (am a·lek·*san*·der·plats) *ows*·shtai·gen

For bus numbers, see **numbers & amounts** (p30).

Train

What station is this?	Welcher Bahnhof ist das? *vel*·kher *bahn*·hawf ist das
What's the next station?	Welches ist der nächste Bahnhof? *vel*·khes ist dair *naykhs*·te *bahn*·hawf

Where's the nearest metro station?	Wo ist der nächste U-Bahnhof? vaw ist dair *naykhs*·te oo·bahn·hawf
Which line goes to (Potsdamer Platz)?	Welche Linie geht zum (Potsdamer Platz)? *vel*·khe *lee*·ni·e gayt tsum (pots·*dah*·mer plats)
Does this train stop at (Freiburg)?	Hält dieser Zug in (Freiburg)? helt *dee*·zer tsook in (*frai*·boorg)
Do I need to change trains?	Muss ich umsteigen? mus ikh *um*·shtai·gen

Ich möchte ein Auto mieten.
ikh *merkh*·te ain ow·to *mee*·ten
I'd like to hire a car.

Which carriage is 1st class?	Welcher Wagen ist erste Klasse? *vel*·kher *vah*·gen ist *ers*·te *kla*·se
Which carriage is for Munich?	Welcher Wagen geht nach München? *vel*·kher *vah*·gen gayt nahkh *mün*·khen
underground	U-Bahn f *oo*·bahn
underground station	U-Bahnhof m *oo*·bahn·hawf
urban railway	S-Bahn f *es*·bahn

Boat

Are there life jackets?	Gibt es Schwimmwesten? gipt es *shvim*·ves·ten
What's the sea like today?	Wie ist das Meer heute? vee ist das mair *hoy*·te
I feel seasick.	Ich bin seekrank. ikh bin *zay*·krangk

Taxi

I'd like a taxi at (9am).	Ich hätte gern ein Taxi für (neun Uhr). ikh *he*·te gern ain *tak*·si für (noyn oor)
Where's the taxi stand?	Wo ist der Taxenstand? vaw ist dair *tak*·sen·shtant
Are you available?	Sind Sie frei? zint zee frai

How much is it to ...?	Was kostet es bis ...?	
	vas *kos*·tet es bis ...	
Please take me to (this address).	Bitte bringen Sie mich zu (dieser Adresse).	
	bi·te *bring*·en zee mikh tsoo (*dee*·zer a·*dre*·se)	
✂ **To ...**	Zu ...	tsoo ...
Please slow down.	Fahren Sie bitte langsamer.	
	fah·ren zee *bi*·te *lang*·za·mer	
Please wait here.	Bitte warten Sie hier.	
	bi·te var·ten zee heer	
Stop at the corner.	Halten Sie an der Ecke.	
	hal·ten zee an dair *e*·ke	
Stop here.	Halten Sie hier.	
	hal·ten zee heer	

For more phrases, see **directions** (p53) and **money & banking** (p86).

PRACTICAL TRANSPORT

Car & Motorbike

I'd like to hire a/an ...	Ich möchte ein ... mieten.	
	ikh *merkh*·te ain ... *mee*·ten	

4WD	Allradfahrzeug	*al*·raht·fahr·tsoyk
automatic	Fahrzeug mit Automatik	*fahr*·tsoyk mit ow·to·*mah*·tik
car	Auto	*ow*·to
manual	Fahrzeug mit Schaltung	*fahr*·tsoyk mit *shal*·tung
motorbike	Motorrad	*maw*·tor·raht

How much is it per day/week?	Wie viel kostet es pro Tag/Woche?	
	vee feel *kos*·tet es praw tahk/*vo*·khe	

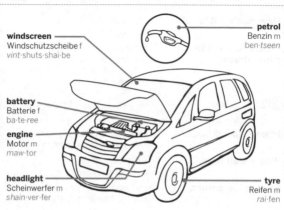

petrol
Benzin m
ben·*tseen*

windscreen
Windschutzscheibe f
vint·shuts·shai·be

battery
Batterie f
ba·te·*ree*

engine
Motor m
maw·tor

headlight
Scheinwerfer m
shain·ver·fer

tyre
Reifen m
rai·fen

Does that include insurance/mileage?	Ist eine Versicherung/ Kilometerzahl inbegriffen? ist *ai*·ne fer·*zi*·khe·rung/ kee·lo·*may*·ter·tsahl *in*·be·gri·fen
Does this road go to ...?	Führt diese Straße nach ...? fürt *dee*·ze *shtrah*·se nahkh ...
What's the speed limit?	Was ist die Höchstgeschwindigkeit? vas ist dee *herkhst*·ge·shvin·dikh·kait
(How long) Can I park here?	(Wie lange) Kann ich hier parken? (vee *lang*·e) kan ikh heer *par*·ken
Where do I pay?	Wo muss ich bezahlen? vaw mus ikh be·*tsah*·len

🔍 LOOK FOR

Einfahrt	*ain*·fahrt	Entrance
Ausfahrt	*ows*·fahrt	Exit
Einfahrt Verboten	*ain*·fahrt fer·*baw*·ten	No Entry
Einbahnstraße	*ain*·bahn·shtrah·se	One Way
Parkverbot	*park*·fer·bawt	No Parking
Stopp	shtop	Stop
Mautstelle	*mowt*·shte·le	Toll

Where's a petrol station?	Wo ist eine Tankstelle? vaw ist ai·ne *tangk*·shte·le
I need a mechanic.	Ich brauche einen Mechaniker. ikh *brow*·khe ai·nen me·*khah*·ni·ker
My car/motorbike has broken down (at ...).	Ich habe (in ...) eine Panne mit meinem Auto/Motorrad. ikh *hah*·be (in ...) ai·ne *pa*·ne mit *mai*·nem ow·to/ *maw*·tor·raht
I had an accident.	Ich hatte einen Unfall. ikh *ha*·te ai·nen *un*·fal
I have a flat tyre.	Ich habe eine Reifenpanne. ikh *hah*·be ai·ne *rai*·fen·pa·ne
I've run out of petrol.	Ich habe kein Benzin mehr. ikh *hah*·be kain ben·*tseen* mair
Can you fix it?	Können Sie es reparieren? *ker*·nen zee es re·pa·*ree*·ren

PRACTICAL TRANSPORT

PRACTICAL TRANSPORT

Bicycle

Where can I hire a bicycle?	Wo kann ich ein Fahrrad mieten? vaw kan ikh ain *fahr*·raht *mee*·ten
How much is it per day?	Wie viel kostet es für einen Tag? vee feel *kos*·tet es für *ai*·nen tahk
How much is it per hour?	Wie viel kostet es für eine Stunde? vee feel *kos*·tet es für *ai*·ne *shtun*·de
Where can I buy a secondhand bike?	Wo kann ich ein gebrauchtes Fahrrad kaufen? vaw kan ikh ain ge·*browkh*·tes *fahr*·raht *kow*·fen
I have a puncture.	Ich habe einen Platten. ikh *hah*·be *ai*·nen *pla*·ten
I'd like to have my bicycle repaired.	Ich möchte mein Fahrrad reparieren lassen. ikh *merkh*·te main *fahr*·raht re·pa·*ree*·ren *la*·sen
Can I take my bike on the train?	Kann ich mein Fahrrad im Zug mitnehmen? kan ikh main *fahr*·raht im tsook *mit*·nay·men
Can we get there by bike?	Können wir mit dem Fahrrad dahin kommen? *ker*·nen veer mit daym *fahr*·raht dah·hin *ko*·men
Are there cycling paths?	Gibt es Fahrradwege? geept es *fahr*·raht·vay·ge
Is there bicycle parking?	Gibt es Fahrrad-Parkplätze? geept es *fahr*·raht·park·ple·tse

For phrases on disabled access, see **senior & disabled travellers** (p97).

Border Crossing

KEY PHRASES

I'm here for (four) days.	Ich bin hier für (vier) Tage.	ikh bin heer für (feer) tah·ge
I'm staying at the ...	Ich wohne im ...	ikh vaw·ne im ...
I have nothing to declare.	Ich habe nichts zu verzollen.	ikh hah·be nikhts tsoo fer·tso·len

Passport Control

I'm here ...		Ich bin hier ... ikh bin heer ...

in transit	auf der Durchreise	owf dair durkh·rai·ze
on business	auf Geschäftsreise	owf ge·shefts·rai·ze
on holiday	im Urlaub	im oor·lowp
to study	zum Studieren	tsum shtu·dee·ren

I'm here for (four) days.	Ich bin hier für (vier) Tage. ikh bin heer für (feer) tah·ge
I'm here for (three) weeks.	Ich bin hier für (drei) Wochen. ikh bin heer für (drai) vo·khen
I'm here for (two) months.	Ich bin hier für (zwei) Monate. ikh bin heer für (tsvai) maw·na·te

| I'm going to (Salzburg). | Ich gehe nach (Salzburg). ikh *gay*·e nahkh (*zalts*·burg) |
| I'm staying at the ... | Ich wohne im ... ikh *vaw*·ne im ... |

At Customs

I have nothing to declare.	Ich habe nichts zu verzollen. ikh *hah*·be nikhts tsoo fer·*tso*·len
I have something to declare.	Ich habe etwas zu verzollen. ikh *hah*·be *et*·vas tsoo fer·*tso*·len
I didn't know I had to declare it.	Ich wusste nicht, dass ich das verzollen muss. ikh *vus*·te nikht das ikh das fer·*tso*·len mus
That's (not) mine.	Das ist (nicht) meins. das ist (nikht) mains

For phrases on payments and receipts, see **money & banking** (p86).

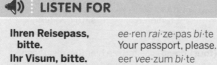

◀)) LISTEN FOR

Ihren Reisepass, bitte.	*ee*·ren *rai*·ze·pas *bi*·te Your passport, please.
Ihr Visum, bitte.	eer *vee*·zum *bi*·te Your visa, please.
Reisen Sie allein?	*rai*·zen zee a·*lain* Are you travelling on your own?
Reisen Sie in einer Gruppe?	*rai*·zen zee in *ai*·ner *gru*·pe Are you travelling in a group?
Reisen Sie mit Ihrer Familie?	*rai*·zen zee mit *ee*·rer fa·*mee*·li·e Are you travelling with your family?

Directions

KEY PHRASES

Where's (a bank)?	Wo ist (eine Bank)?	vaw ist (ai·ne bangk)
What's the address?	Wie ist die Adresse?	vee ist dee a·dre·se
How far is it?	Wie weit ist es?	vee vait ist es

Where's (a bank)?	Wo ist (eine Bank)? vaw ist (ai·ne bangk)
I'm looking for (the cathedral).	Ich suche (den Dom). ikh zoo·khe (dayn dawm)
How can I get there?	Wie kann ich da hinkommen? vee kan ikh dah hin·ko·men
Can you show me (on the map)?	Können Sie es mir (auf der Karte) zeigen? ker·nen zee es meer (owf dair kar·te) tsai·gen
What's the address?	Wie ist die Adresse? vee ist dee a·dre·se
Turn left/right.	Biegen Sie links/rechts ab. bee·gen zee links/rekhts ap
Turn at the corner.	Biegen Sie an der Ecke ab. bee·gen zee an dair e·ke ap
Turn at the traffic lights.	Biegen Sie bei der Ampel ab. bee·gen zee bai dair am·pel ap

It's ...	Es ist ...	es ist ...

behind ...	hinter ...	*hin·ter ...*
far away	weit weg	vait vek
here	hier	heer
in front of ...	vor ...	fawr ...
left	links	lingks
near	nahe	*nah·e*
next to ...	neben ...	*nay·ben ...*
on the corner	an der Ecke	an dair *e·ke*
opposite ...	gegenüber ...	gay·gen·*ü·ber ...*
right	rechts	rekhts
straight ahead	geradeaus	ge·rah·de·*ows*
there	dort	dort

north/south	Norden m/Süden m *nor·den/zü·den*
east/west	Osten m/Westen m *os·ten/ves·ten*
How far is it?	Wie weit ist es? vee *vait* ist es
by bus	mit dem Bus mit daym *bus*
by taxi	mit dem Taxi mit daym *tak·si*
by train	mit dem Zug mit daym *tsook*
on foot	zu Fuß tsoo *foos*

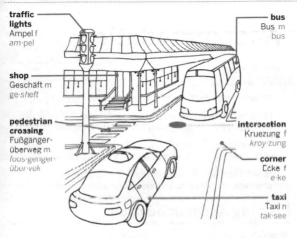

traffic lights
Ampel f
am·pel

shop
Geschäft m
ge·sheft

pedestrian crossing
Fußgängerüberweg m
foos·genger· über·vek

bus
Bus m
bus

intersection
Kreuzung f
kroy·zung

corner
Ecke f
e·ke

taxi
Taxi n
tak·see

PRACTICAL DIRECTIONS

It's (10) metres.	Es ist (10) Meter entfernt. *es ist (tsayn) may·ter ent·fernt*
It's (five) minutes.	Es ist (fünf) Minuten entfernt. *es ist (fünf) mi·noo·ten ent·fernt*
avenue	Allee f *a·lay*
lane	Gasse f *ga·se*
square	Platz m *plats*
street	Straße/Weg f/m *shtrah·se/vayk*

Accommodation

KEY PHRASES

Where's a hotel?	Wo ist ein Hotel?	vaw ist ain ho·*tel*
How much is it per night?	Wie viel kostet es pro Nacht?	vee feel *kos*·tet es praw nakht
Is breakfast included?	Ist das Frühstück inklusive?	ist das *frü*·shtük in·kloo·*zee*·ve
What time is checkout?	Wann muss ich auschecken?	van mus ikh *ows*·che·ken

Finding Accommodation

Where's a/an ...?	Wo ist ...? vaw ist ...	
bed & breakfast	eine Pension	*ai*·ne pahng·*zyawn*
camping ground	ein Camping-platz	ain *kem*·ping·plats
guesthouse	eine Pension	*ai*·ne pahng·*zyawn*
hotel	ein Hotel	ain ho·*tel*
youth hostel	eine Jugendherberge	*ai*·ne yoo·gent·her·ber·ge

Can you recommend somewhere (cheap/ nearby)?	Können Sie etwas (Billiges/ in der Nähe) empfehlen? *ker*·nen zee *et*·vas (*bi*·li·ges/ in dair *nay*·e) emp·*fay*·len

For responses, see **directions** (p53).

🔊 LISTEN FOR

Es tut mir Leid, wir haben keine Zimmer frei.	es toot meer lait veer *hah*·ben *kai*·ne *tsi*·mer frai	I'm sorry, we're full.
Für wie viele Nächte?	für vee *fee*·le *nekh*·te	For how many nights?

Booking Ahead & Checking In

I'd like to book a room, please.	Ich möchte bitte ein Zimmer reservieren. ikh *merkh*·te *bi*·te ain *tsi*·mer re·zer·*vee*·ren
✂ **Are there rooms?**	Gibt es freie Zimmer? gipt es *fra*·ye *tsi*·mer
I have a reservation.	Ich habe eine Reservierung. ikh *hah*·be *ai*·ne re·zer·*vee*·rung
For (three) nights/weeks.	Für (drei) Nächte/Wochen. für (drai) *nekh*·te/*vo*·khen
From (July 2) to (July 6).	Vom (2. Juli) bis zum (6. Juli). vom (*tsvai*·ten *yoo*·li) bis tsum (*zeks*·ten *yoo*·li)
Is breakfast included?	Ist das Frühstück inklusive? ist das *frü*·shtük in·kloo·*zee*·ve
Is there wireless internet access here?	Gibt es hier einen WLAN-Zugang? geept es heer *ai*·nen *vay*·lahn·tsoo·gang

How much is it per night/person?	Wie viel kostet es pro Nacht/Person? *vee feel kos·tet es praw nakht/per·zawn*
How much is it per week?	Wie viel kostet es pro Woche? *vee feel kos·tet es praw vo·khe*
Do you have a double room?	Haben Sie ein Doppelzimmer mit einem Doppelbett? *hah·ben zee ain do·pel·tsi·mer mit ai·nem do·pel·bet*

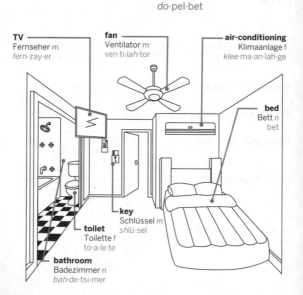

TV
Fernseher m
fern·zay·er

fan
Ventilator m
ven·ti·lah·tor

air-conditioning
Klimaanlage f
klee·ma·an·lah·ge

bed
Bett n
bet

key
Schlüssel m
shlü·sel

toilet
Toilette f
to·a·le·te

bathroom
Badezimmer n
bah·de·tsi·mer

Finding a Room

Do you have a ... room?
Haben Sie ein ...?
hah·ben zee ain ...

 double
Doppelzimmer
do·pel·tsi·mer

 single
Einzelzimmer
ain·tsel·tsi·mer

How much is it per ...?
Wie viel kostet es pro ...?
vee feel kos·tet es praw ...

night
Nacht
nakht

person
Person
per·*zawn*

Is breakfast included?
Ist das Frühstück inklusive?
ist das *frü*·shtük in·kloo·zee·ve

Can I see the room?
Kann ich es sehen?
kan ikh es *zay*·en

 I'll take it.
Ich nehme es.
ikh *nay*·me es

 I won't take it.
Ich nehme es nicht.
ikh *nay*·me es nikht

Do you have a single room?	Haben Sie ein Einzelzimmer? *hah*·ben zee ain *ain*·tsel·tsi·mer
Do you have a twin room?	Haben Sie ein Doppelzimmer mit zwei Einzelbetten? *hah*·ben zee ain *do*·pel·tsi·mer mit tsvai ain·tsel·be·ten
Can I see it?	Kann ich es sehen? kan ikh es *zay*·en
It's fine. I'll take it.	Es ist gut, ich nehme es. es ist goot ikh *nay*·me es

For methods of payment, see **money & banking** (p86).

Requests & Queries

When/Where is breakfast served?	Wann/Wo gibt es Frühstück? van/vaw gipt es *frü*·shtük
Please wake me at (seven).	Bitte wecken Sie mich um (sieben) Uhr. *bi*·te ve·ken zee mikh um (zee·ben) oor
There's no need to change my sheets/towels.	Sie brauchen meine Bettwäsche/Handtücher nicht zu wechseln. zee *brow*·khen *mai*·ne *bet*·ve·she/*han*·tü·kher nikht tsoo *ve*·kseln
Can I use (the internet)?	Kann ich (das Internet) benutzen? kan ikh (das *in*·ter·net) be·*nu*·tsen
Can I use (the laundry)?	Kann ich (eine Waschmaschine) benutzen? kan ikh (*ai*·ne *vash*·ma·shee·ne) be·*nu*·tsen

Do you have a ...?	Haben Sie ...? *hah*·ben zee ...

laundry **service**	einen Wäscheservice	*ai*·nen *ve*·she·ser·vis
lift/elevator	einen Aufzug	*ai*·nen *owf*·tsook
safe	einen Safe	*ai*·nen sayf
swimming **pool**	ein Schwimmbad	ain *shvim*·baht

Do you arrange tours here?	Arrangieren Sie hier Touren? a·rang·*zhee*·ren zee heer *too*·ren
Can I leave a message for **someone?**	Kann ich eine Nachricht für jemanden hinterlassen? kan ikh *ai*·ne *nahkh*·rikht für *yay*·man·den hin·ter·*la*·sen
Is there a message for me?	Haben Sie eine Nachricht für mich? *hah*·ben zee *ai*·ne *nahkh*·rikht für mikh
Can I get another ...?	Kann ich noch einen/eine/ein ... bekommen? m/f/n kan ikh nokh *ai*·nen/*ai*·ne/ain ... be·*ko*·men

blanket	Decke f	*de*·ke
pillow	Kopfkissen n	*kopf*·ki·sen
pillowcase	Kopfkissen bezug m	*kopf*·ki·sen be·tsook
towel	Handtuch n	*hant*·tookh

Could I have my key, please?	Könnte ich bitte meinen Schlüssel haben?	*kern*·te ikh *bi*·te *mai*·nen *shlü*·sel *hah*·ben
Could I have a receipt, please?	Könnte ich bitte eine Quittung haben?	*kern*·te ikh *bi*·te *ai*·ne *kvi*·tung *hah*·ben
I'm locked out of my room.	Ich habe mich aus meinem Zimmer ausgesperrt.	ikh *hah*·be mikh ows *mai*·nem *tsi*·mer ows·ge·shpert
There's no hot water.	Es gibt kein warmes Wasser.	es geept kain *var*·mes *va*·ser
This (sheet) isn't clean.	Dieses (Bettlaken) ist nicht sauber.	*dee*·zes (*bet*·lah·ken) ist nikht *zow*·ber
It's too ...	Es ist zu ...	es ist tsoo ...

cold	kalt	kalt
dark	dunkel	*dung*·kel
light/bright	hell	hel
noisy	laut	lowt
small	klein	klain

The ... doesn't work.	... funktioniert nicht.	... fungk·tsyaw·*neert* nikht

air-conditioning	Die Klimaanlage	dee *klee*·ma·an·lah·ge
fan	Der Ventilator	dair ven·ti·*lah*·tor
heater	Das Heizgerät	das *haits*·ge·rayt
toilet	Die Toilette	dee to·a·*le*·te

Answering the Door

Who is it?	Wer ist da? *vair ist dah*
Just a moment.	Einen Augenblick, bitte! *ai·nen ow·gen·blik bi·te*
Come in.	Herein! *he·rain*
Come back later, please.	Kommen Sie bitte später noch einmal. *ko·men zee bi·te shpay·ter nokh ain·mahl*

Checking Out

What time is checkout?	Wann muss ich auschecken? *van mus ikh ows·che·ken*
How much extra to stay until (six o'clock)?	Was kostet es extra, wenn ich bis (sechs Uhr) bleiben möchte? *vas kos·tet es eks·tra ven ikh bis (zeks oor) blai·ben merkh·te*
I'm leaving now.	Ich reise jetzt ab. *ikh rai·ze yetst ap*
Can you call a taxi for me (for 11 o'clock)?	Können Sie mir (für 11 Uhr) ein Taxi rufen? *ker·nen zee meer (für elf oor) ain tak·si roo·fen*
Can I leave my bags here until (tonight)?	Kann ich meine Taschen bis (heute Abend) hier lassen? *kan ikh mai·ne ta·shen bis (hoy·te ah·bent) heer la·sen*

Could I have my deposit, please?	Könnte ich bitte meine Anzahlung haben? *kern·te ikh bi·te mai·ne an·tsah·lung hah·ben*
Could I have my passport, please?	Könnte ich bitte meinen Pass haben? *kern·te ikh bi·te mai·nen pas hah·ben*
Could I have my valuables, please?	Könnte ich bitte meine Wertsachen haben? *kern·te ikh bi·te mai·ne vert·za·khen hah·ben*
I had a great stay, thank you.	Es hat mir hier sehr gut gefallen. *es hat meer heer zair goot ge·fa·len*
I'll recommend it to my friends.	Ich werde Sie weiterempfehlen. *ikh ver·de zee vai·ter·emp·fay·len*

Camping

Can I camp here?	Kann ich hier zelten? *kan ikh heer tsel·ten*
Where's the nearest camp site?	Wo ist der nächste Zeltplatz? *vaw ist dair naykhs·te tselt·plats*
Do you have ...?	Haben Sie ...? *hah·ben zee ...*

electricity	Strom	*shtrawm*
shower facilities	Duschen	*doo·shen*
a site	einen Stellplatz	*ai·nen shtel·plats*
tents for hire	Zelte zu vermieten	*tsel·te tsoo fer·mee·ten*

Is the water drinkable?	Kann man das Wasser trinken?
	kan man das *va*·ser *tring*·ken
Who do I ask to stay here?	Wen muss ich fragen, wenn ich hier zelten möchte?
	vayn mus ikh *frah*·gen ven ikh heer *tsel*·ten *merkh*·te
How much do you charge ...?	Wie viel berechnen Sie ...?
	vee feel be·*rekh*·nen zee ...

for a car	für ein Auto	für ain *ow*·to
for a caravan	für einen Wohnwagen	für *ai*·nen *vawn*·vah·gen
for a tent	für ein Zelt	für ain tselt
per person	pro Person	praw per·*zawn*

gas cylinder	Gasflasche f
	gahs·fla·she
mallet	Holzhammer m
	holts·ha·mer
peg	Hering m
	hay·ring
rope	Seil n
	zail
sleeping bag	Schlafsack m
	shlahf·zak
spade	Spaten m
	shpah·ten
tent	Zelt n
	tselt
torch (flashlight)	Taschenlampe f
	ta·shen·lam·pe

Renting

I'm here about the ... for rent.	Ich komme wegen des/der/des zu vermietenden ... m/f/n ikh *ko*·me *vay*·gen des/dair/des tsoo fer·*mee*·ten·den ...

apartment	Appartement n	a·*part*·ment
cabin	Hütte f	*hü*·te
holiday apartment	Ferienwohnung f	*fay*·ri·en·vaw·nung
house	Haus n	hows
room	Zimmer n	*tsi*·mer
villa	Villa f	*vi*·la

furnished	möbliert mer·*bleert*
partly furnished	teilmöbliert *tail*·mer·bleert
unfurnished	unmöbliert *un*·mer·bleert
Do you have a/an ... for rent?	Haben Sie ... zu vermieten? *hah*·ben zee ... tsoo fer·*mee*·ten
How much is it for (one) week?	Was kostet es für (eine) Woche? vas *kos*·tet es für (*ai*·ne) *vo*·khe
How much is it for (two) months?	Was kostet es für (zwei) Monate? vas *kos*·tet es für (tsvai) *maw*·na·te

I want to rent it from (July 2) to (July 6).	Ich möchte es vom (2. Juli) bis zum (6. Juli) mieten. ikh *merkh*·te es fom (*tsvai*·ten *yoo*·li) bis tsum (*zeks*·ten *yoo*·li) *mee*·ten
How many rooms does it have?	Wie viele Zimmer hat es? vee *fee*·le *tsi*·mer hat es
Is there a bond?	Gibt es eine Kaution? gipt es *ai*·ne kow·*tsyawn*
Are bills extra?	Kommen noch Nebenkosten dazu? ko·men nokh *nay*·ben·kos·ten da·*tsoo*
Who is my contact person?	Wer ist meine Kontaktperson? vair ist *mai*·ne kon·*takt*·per·zawn

Wann muss ich auschecken?
van mus ikh *ows*·che·ken
What time is checkout?

Staying with Locals

Can I stay at your place?	Kann ich bei Ihnen/dir übernachten? pol/inf kan ikh bai *ee*·nen/deer ü·ber·*nakh*·ten
I have my own sleeping bag.	Ich habe meinen eigenen Schlafsack. ikh *hah*·be *mai*·nen *ai*·ge·nen *shlahf*·zak
Is there anything I can do to help?	Kann ich Ihnen/dir irgendwie helfen? pol/inf kan ikh *ee*·nen/deer *ir*·gent·vee *hel*·fen
Can I bring anything for the meal?	Kann ich etwas für das Essen mitbringen? kan ikh et·vas für das *e*·sen *mit*·bring·en
Can I do the dishes?	Kann ich abwaschen? kan ikh *ap*·va·shen
Can I set/clear the table?	Kann ich den Tisch decken/abräumen? kan ikh dayn tish *de*·ken/*ap*·roy·men
Thanks for your hospitality.	Vielen Dank für Ihre/deine Gastfreundschaft. pol/inf *fee*·len dangk für *ee*·re/*dai*·ne *gast*·froynt·shaft

To compliment your host's cooking, see **eating out** (p170).

Shopping

KEY PHRASES

I'd like to buy ...	Ich möchte ... kaufen.	ikh *merkh*·te ... *kow*·fen
Can I look at it?	Können Sie es mir zeigen?	*ker*·nen zee es meer *tsai*·gen
Can I try it on?	Kann ich es anprobieren?	kan ikh es *an*·pro·bee·ren
How much is this?	Wie viel kostet das?	vee feel *kos*·tet das

Looking For ...

Where's (a/the supermarket)?	Wo ist (ein/der Supermarkt)? vaw ist (ain/dair zoo·per·markt)
Where can I buy (locally produced goods/ souvenirs)?	Wo kann ich (örtlich produzierte Waren/ Andenken) kaufen? vaw kan ikh (*ert*·likh pro·du·*tseer*·te *vah*·ren/ *an*·deng·ken) *kow*·fen

For phrases on getting there, see **directions** (p53), and for additional shops and services, see the **dictionary**.

Making a Purchase

I'd like to buy ...	Ich möchte ... kaufen. ikh *merkh*·te ... *kow*·fen
I'm just looking.	Ich schaue mich nur um. ikh *show*·e mikh noor um

🔊 LISTEN FOR

Kann ich Ihnen helfen?	kan ikh *ee*·nen *hel*·fen Can I help you?
Möchten Sie noch etwas?	*merkh*·ten zee nokh *et*·vas Would you like anything else?
Nein, (haben wir) leider nicht.	nain (*hah*·ben veer) *lai*·der nikht No, we don't have any.

What is this made of?	Woraus ist das gemacht? vaw·*rows* ist das ge·*makht*
How much is this?	Wie viel kostet das? vee feel *kos*·tet das

✂ How much?	Das kostet?	das *kos*·tet

Can you write down the price?	Können Sie den Preis aufschreiben? *ker*·nen zee dayn prais *owf*·shrai·ben
Do you have any others?	Haben Sie noch andere? *hah*·ben zee nokh *an*·de·re
Can I look at it?	Können Sie es mir zeigen? *ker*·nen zee es meer *tsai*·gen
Do you accept credit/debit cards?	Nehmen Sie Kreditkarten/Debitkarten? *nay*·men zee kre·*deet*·kar·ten/*day*·bit·kar·ten
Could I have a bag, please?	Könnte ich eine Tüte bekommen? *kern*·te ikh *ai*·ne *tü*·te be·*ko*·men

Making a Purchase

 I'd like to buy ...
Ich möchte ... kaufen.
ikh merkh·te ... kow·fen

 How much is it?
Wie viel kostet das?
vee feel kos·tet das

— OR —

 Can you write down the price?
Können Sie den Preis aufschreiben?
ker·nen zee dayn prais owf·shrai·ben

 Do you accept credit cards?
Nehmen Sie Kreditkarten?
nay·men zee kre·deet·kar·ten

 Could I have a ..., please?
Könnte ich eine ... bekommen?
kern·te ikh ai·ne ... be·ko·men

 receipt
Quittung
kvi·tung

 bag
Tüte
tü·te

| **Could I have a receipt, please?** | Könnte ich eine Quittung bekommen? |
| | *kern*·te ikh *ai*·ne *kvi*·tung be·*ko*·men |

| ✂ **Receipt, please.** | Eine Quittung, bitte. | *ai*·ne *kvi*·tung *bi*·te |

| **Could I have it wrapped, please?** | Könnte ich es eingepackt bekommen? |
| | *kern*·te ikh es *ain*·ge·pakt be·*ko*·men |

| **I don't need a bag, thanks.** | Ich brauche keine Tüte, danke. |
| | ikh *brow*·khe *kai*·ne *tü*·te *dang*·ke |

| **Does it have a guarantee?** | Gibt es darauf Garantie? |
| | gipt es da·*rowf* ga·ran·*tee* |

| **Can I have it sent overseas?** | Kann ich es ins Ausland verschicken lassen? |
| | kan ikh es ins *ows*·lant fer·*shi*·ken *la*·sen |

| **Can I pick it up later?** | Kann ich es später abholen? |
| | kan ikh es *shpay*·ter *ap*·haw·len |

| **It's faulty/broken.** | Es ist fehlerhaft/kaputt. |
| | es ist *fay*·ler·haft/ka·*put* |

| **I'd like my change, please.** | Ich möchte bitte mein Wechselgeld. |
| | ikh *merkh*·te *bi*·te main *vek*·sel·gelt |

| **I'd like my money back, please.** | Ich möchte bitte mein Geld zurückhaben. |
| | ikh *merkh*·te *bi*·te main gelt tsu·*rük*·hah·ben |

🔊 LISTEN FOR

Ausverkauf m	*ows*·fer·kowf	sale
Nepp m	nep	rip-off
Schnäppchen n	*shnep*·khen	bargain
Sonderangebote n pl	*zon*·der·an·ge·baw·te	specials

I'd like to return this, please.	Ich möchte bitte dieses zurückgeben. ikh *merkh*·te *bi*·te dee·zes tsu·*rük*·gay·ben

Bargaining

That's too expensive.	Das ist zu teuer. das ist tsoo *toy*·er
Can you lower the price?	Können Sie mit dem Preis heruntergehen? *ker*·nen zee mit dem prais he·*run*·ter·gay·en
Do you have something cheaper?	Haben Sie etwas Billigeres? *hah*·ben zee et·vas *bi*·li·ge·res
I'll give you ...	Ich gebe Ihnen ... ikh *gay*·be *ee*·nen ...

Books & Reading

Is there a/an (English-language) section?	Gibt es eine Abteilung (für englische Bücher)? gipt es *ai*·ne ap·*tai*·lung (für *eng*·li·she *bü*·kher)
Is there a/an (English-language) bookshop?	Gibt es einen Buchladen (für englische Bücher)? gipt es *ai*·nen *bookh*·lah·den (für *eng*·li·she *bü*·kher)

Do you have Lonely Planet guidebooks?	Haben Sie Lonely-Planet-Reiseführer? *hah·ben zee lohn·li·ple·net·rai·ze·fü·rer*
I'm looking for something by (Hermann Hesse).	Ich suche nach etwas von (Hermann Hesse). *ikh zoo·khe nahkh et·vas fon (her·man he·se)*

Clothes

Can I try it on?	Kann ich es anprobieren? *kan ikh es an·pro·bee·ren*
My size is ...	Ich habe Größe ... *ikh hah·be grer·se ...*
It doesn't fit.	Es passt nicht. *es past nikht*
small/medium/large	klein/mittelgroß/groß *klain/mi·tel·graws/graws*

For clothes items see the **dictionary**, and for sizes see **numbers & amounts** (p30).

Music & DVD

I'd like a CD.	Ich hätte gern eine CD. *ikh he·te gern ai·ne tsay·day*
I'd like a DVD.	Ich hätte gern eine DVD. *ikh he·te gern ai·ne day·fow·day*
I'd like headphones.	Ich hätte gern Kopfhörer. *ikh he·te gern kopf·her·rer*
What's their best recording?	Was ist ihre beste CD? *vas ist ee·re bes·te tsay·day*
Can I listen to this?	Kann ich mir das anhören? *kan ikh meer das an·her·ren*

Will this work on any DVD player?	Funktioniert die auf jedem DVD-Player? fungk·tsyaw·*neert* dee owf *yay*·dem day·fow·*day*·play·er
What region is this DVD for?	Für welche Region ist diese DVD? für *vel*·khe re·*gyawn* ist *dee*·ze day·fow·*day*

Video & Photography

Can you print digital photos?	Können Sie digitale Fotos drucken? *ker*·nen zee dee·gee·*tah*·le *faw*·tos dru·ken

---

> ## *Kann ich es anprobieren?*
> kan ikh es *an*·pro·bee·ren
> ### *Can I try it on?*

Can you develop this film?	Können Sie diesen Film entwickeln? *ker·nen zee dee·zen film ent·vi·keln*
Can you transfer my photos from camera to CD?	Können Sie Fotos von meiner Kamera auf CD brennen? *ker·nen zee faw·tos fon mai·ner ka·me·ra owf tsay·day bre·nen*
Do you have (batteries) for this camera?	Haben Sie (Akkus) für diese Kamera? *hah·ben zee (a·koos) für dee·ze ka·me·ra*
Do you have (memory cards) for this camera?	Haben Sie (Speicherkarten) für diese Kamera? *hah·ben zee (shpai·kher·kar·ten) für dee·ze ka·me·ra*
I need a ... film for this camera.	Ich brauche einen ... für diese Kamera. *ikh brow·khe ai·nen ... für dee·ze ka·me·ra*

B&W	Schwarzweißfilm	shvarts·*vais*·film
colour	Farbfilm	*farp*·film
slide	Diafilm	*dee·a*·film
(200) speed	(200)-ASA-Film	(*tsvai*·hun·dert)·*ah*·za·film

How much is it to develop this film?	Was kostet es, diesen Film entwickeln zu lassen? *vas kos·tet es dee·zen film ent·vi·keln tsoo la·sen*

CULTURE TIP: Souvenirs

Austria	chocolates (*Pralinen* n pl pra·lee·nen), fruit brandies (*Obstler* m awpst·ler)
Bavarian Forest	crystal glassware (*Kristallglas* n kris·tal·glahs)
Harz Mountains	puppets (*Puppe* f pu·pe), marionettes (*Marionette* f ma·ri·o·ne·te), glassware (*Glaswaren* pl glahs·vah·ren)
Lübeck	marzipan (*Marzipan* n mar·tsi·pahn)
Meissen	modern and antique porcelain (*Porzellan* n por·tse·lahn)
Nuremberg	tin toys (*Blechspielzeug* n blekh·shpeel·tsoyk), gingerbread (*Lebkuchen* m layp·koo·khen)
Rhine and Moselle Rivers	white wines (*Weißwein* m vais·vain)
Rothenburg ob der Tauber	wooden toys (*Holzspielzeug* n holts·shpeel·tsoyk), Christmas decorations (*Weihnachtsschmuck* m vai·nakhts·shmuk)
Switzerland	cuckoo clocks (*Kuckucksuhr* f ku·kuks·oor), chocolate (*Schokolade* f sho·ko·lah·de), cow bells (*Kuhglocke* f koo·glo·ke)
The Black Forest	cuckoo clocks, dolls (*Puppe* f pu·pe), fruit brandies
Thuringia	wooden figures (*Holzfigur* f holts·fi·goor), Christmas decorations

I need a cable to connect my camera to a computer.	Ich brauche ein Kabel, um meine Kamera an einem Computer anzuschließen. ikh brow·khe ain kah·bel um mai·ne ka·me·ra an ai·nem kom·pyoo·ter an·tsoo·shlee·sen

I need a passport photo taken.	Ich möchte ein Passfoto machen lassen.
	ikh *merkh*·te ain *pas*·faw·to *ma*·khen *la*·sen
I need a cable to recharge this battery.	Ich brauche ein Ladekabel für diesen Akku.
	ikh *brow*·khe ain *lah*·de·kah·bel für dee·zen a·koo
digital camera	Digitalkamera f
	dee·gee·*tahl*·kah·me·ra
disposable camera	Wegwerfkamera f
	vek·verf·kah·me·ra

Repairs

Can I have my ... repaired here?	Kann ich hier mein ... reparieren lassen?
	kan ikh heer main ... re·pa·*ree*·ren *la*·sen
When will my shoes be ready?	Wann sind meine Schuhe fertig?
	van zint *mai*·ne *shoo*·e *fer*·tikh
When will my backpack be ready?	Wann ist mein Rucksack fertig?
	van ist main *ruk*·zak *fer*·tikh
When will my camera be ready?	Wann ist meine Kamera fertig?
	van ist *mai*·ne *ka*·me·ra *fer*·tikh
When will my (sun)glasses be ready?	Wann ist meine (Sonnen) Brille fertig?
	van ist *mai*·ne (*zo*·nen·)*bri*·le *fer*·tikh

Communications

KEY PHRASES

Where's the local internet cafe?	Wo ist hier ein Internet-Café?	vaw ist heer ain *in·ter·net·ka·fay*
I'd like to check my email.	Ich möchte meine E-Mails checken.	ikh *merkh·te mai·ne ee·mayls che·ken*
I'd like a SIM card for your network.	Ich hätte gern eine SIM-Karte für Ihr Netz.	ikh *he·te* gern *ai·ne zim·kar·te* für eer nets

Post Office

I want to send a parcel.	Ich möchte ein Paket senden. ikh *merkh·te* ain pa·*kayt* zen·den
I want to send a postcard.	Ich möchte eine Postkarte senden. ikh *merkh·te ai·ne post·kar·te* zen·den
I want to buy an envelope.	Ich möchte einen Umschlag kaufen. ikh *merkh·te ai·nen um·shlahk kow·fen*
I want to buy a stamp.	Ich möchte eine Briefmarke kaufen. ikh *merkh·te ai·ne breef·mar·ke kow·fen*

PRACTICAL COMMUNICATIONS

🔊 LISTEN FOR

Einschreiben n	*ain*·shrai·ben	registered mail
Expresspost f	eks·*pres*·post	express mail
Inlands-	*in*·lants·	domestic
international	in·ter·na·tsyo·*nahl*	international
Luftpost f	*luft*·post	airmail
Postfach n	*post*·fakh	PO box
Postleitzahl f	*post*·lait·tsahl	postcode
Schiffspost f	*shifs*·post	sea mail
zerbrechlich	tser·*brekh*·likh	fragile
Zollerklärung f	*tsol*·er·klair·rung	customs declaration

Please send it by (airmail) to ...	Bitte schicken Sie das per (Luftpost) nach ... *bi*·te *shi*·ken zee das per (*luft*·post) nahkh ...
It contains ...	Es enthält ... es ent·*helt* ...
Where's the poste restante section?	Wo ist der Schalter für postlagernde Briefe? vaw ist dair *shal*·ter für *post*·lah·gern·de *bree*·fe
Is there any mail for me?	Ist Post für mich da? ist post für mikh dah

Phone

❓ What's your phone number?	Wie ist Ihre/deine Telefonnummer? **pol/inf** vee ist *ee*·re/*dai*·ne te·le·*fawn*·nu·mer
🅰 The number is ...	Die Nummer ist ... dee *nu*·mer ist ...

LANGUAGE TIP

Phone Numbers

To avoid confusion with *drei* drai (three) on the phone, Germans use *zwo* tsvoo instead of *zwei* tsvai, for 'two' (see also **numbers & amounts**, p30).

Where's the nearest public phone?	Wo ist das nächste öffentliche Telefon? vaw ist das *naykhs*·te er·fent·li·khe te·le·*fawn*
I want to buy a phone card.	Ich möchte eine Telefonkarte kaufen. ikh *merkh*·te *ai*·ne te·le·*fawn*·kar·te *kow*·fen
Do you have international prepaid phone cards?	Haben Sie internationale Prepaid-Telefonkarten? *hah*·ben zee in·ter·na·tsyo·*nah*·le pree·payd· tay·lay·fawn·kar·ten
I want to make a call to (Singapore).	Ich möchte nach (Singapur) telefonieren. ikh *merkh*·te nahkh (*zing*·a·poor) te·le·fo·*nee*·ren
I want to make a local call.	Ich möchte ein Ortsgespräch führen. ikh *merkh*·te ain *orts*·gesh·prairkh *fü*·ren
I want to make a reverse charges/collect call.	Ich möchte ein R-Gespräch führen. ikh *merkh*·te ain *air*·ge·shpraykh *fü*·ren
How much is a (three)-minute call?	Wie viel kostet ein (drei)-minutiges Gespräch? vee feel *kos*·tet ain (drai)· *mi*·noo·ti·ges ge·*shpraykh*

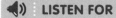

PRACTICAL COMMUNICATIONS

🔊 LISTEN FOR

Tut mir Leid, Sie haben die falsche Nummer.	toot meer lait zee *hah*·ben dee *fal*·she *nu*·mer Sorry, wrong number.
Wer ist am Apparat?	vair ist am a·pa·*raht* Who's calling?
Mit wem möchten Sie sprechen?	mit vaym *merkh*·ten zee *shpre*·khen Who do you want to speak to?
Einen Augenblick, bitte.	*ai*·nen ow·gen·*blik bi*·te One moment, please.
Es tut mir Leid, (er/sie) ist nicht hier.	es toot meer lait (air/zee) ist nikht heer I'm sorry, (he/she) is not here.

I'd like to know the number for ...	Ich möchte gerne die Nummer für ... wissen. ikh *merkh*·te gern dee *nu*·mer für ... *vi*·sen
Can I look at a phone book?	Haben Sie ein Telefonbuch? *hah*·ben zee ain tay·lay·*fawn*·bookh
What's the area/country code for ...?	Was ist die Vorwahl für ...? vas ist dee *fawr*·vahl für ...
It's engaged.	Es ist besetzt. es ist be·*zetst*
The connection's bad.	Die Verbindung ist schlecht. dee fer·*bin*·dung ist shlekht
I've been cut off.	Ich bin unterbrochen worden. ikh bin un·ter·*bro*·khen *vor*·den
Can I speak to ...?	Kann ich mit ... sprechen? kan ikh mit ... *shpre*·khen

Can I leave a message?	Kann ich eine Nachricht hinterlassen? kan ikh *ai*·ne *nahkh*·rikht hin·ter·*la*·sen
My number is ...	Meine Nummer ist ... *mai*·ne *nu*·mer ist ...
Please tell him/her I called.	Bitte sagen Sie ihm/ihr, dass ich angerufen habe. *bi*·te *zah*·gen zee eem/eer das ikh *an*·ge·roo·fen *hah*·be
I'll call back later.	Ich rufe später nochmal an. ikh *roo*·fe *shpay*·ter *nokh*·mahl an
What time should I call?	Wann kann ich am besten anrufen? van kan ikh am *bes*·ten *an*·roo·fen

Mobile/Cell Phone

I'd like a/an ...	Ich hätte gern ... ikh *he*·te gern ...	
charger for my phone	ein Ladegerät für mein Handy	ain *lah*·de·ge·rayt für main *hen*·di
mobile/cell phone for hire	ein Miethandy	ain *meet*·hen·di
prepaid mobile/ cell phone	ein Handy mit Prepaidkarte	ain *hen*·di mit *pree*·payd·kar·te
prepaid recharge card	eine Karte mit Prepaid-Guthaben	*ai*·ne *kar*·te mit pree·payd·*goot*·hah·ben
SIM card for your network	eine SIM-Karte für Ihr Netz	*ai*·ne *zim*·kar·te für eer nets

| **What are the rates?** | Wie hoch sind die Gebühren? vee hawkh zint dee ge·*bü*·ren |

The Internet

Where's the local internet cafe?	Wo ist hier ein Internet-Café? vaw ist heer ain *in*·ter·net·ka·fay
Is there wireless internet access here?	Gibt es hier einen WLAN-Zugang? geept es heer *ai*·nen *vay*·lahn·tsoo·gang
Can I connect my laptop here?	Kann ich meinen Laptop hier anschließen? kan ikh *mai*·nen *lep*·top heer *an*·shlee·sen
How much per hour/ page?	Was kostet es pro Stunde/ Seite? vas *kos*·tet es praw *shtun*·de/ *zai*·te
I'd like to ...	Ich möchte ... ikh *merkh*·te ...

burn a CD	eine CD brennen	*ai*·ne tse de *bre*·nen
check my email	meine E-Mails checken	*mai*·ne *ee*·mayls *che*·ken
download my photos	meine Fotos herunterladen	*mai*·ne *faw*·tos he·*run*·ter·lah·den
use a printer	einen Drucker benutzen	*ai*·nen *dru*·ker be·*nu*·tsen
use a scanner	einen Scanner benutzen	*ai*·nen *ske*·ner be·*nu*·tsen
use Skype	Skype benutzen	skaip be·*nu*·tsen

Do you have PCs/Macs?	Haben Sie PCs/Macs? *hah*·ben zee pay·*tsays*/meks	
Do you have headphones (with a microphone)?	Haben Sie Kopfhörer (mit einem Mikrofon)? *hah*·ben zee *kopf*·her·rer (mit *ai*·nem *mee*·kro·fawn)	
How do I log on?	Wie logge ich mich ein? vee *law*·ge ikh mikh ain	
What's the password?	Wie lautet das Passwort? vee *low*·tet das *pas*·vort	
Can I connect my ... to this computer?	Kann ich ... an diesen Computer anschließen? kan ikh ... an *dee*·zen kom·*pyoo*·ter *an*·shlee·sen	

camera	meine Kamera	*mai*·ne *kah*·me·ra
iPhone	mein iPhone	main *ai*·fawn
iPod	meinen iPod	*mai*·nen *ai*·pod
media player (MP3)	meinen MP3-Player	*mai*·nen om pay *drai* play·er
USB flash drive (memory stick)	meinen USB-Stick	*mai*·nen oo·es·*bay*·shtik

It's crashed.	Es ist abgestürzt. es ist *ap*·ge·shtürtst
I've finished.	Ich bin fertig. ikh bin *fer*·tikh

Money & Banking

KEY PHRASES

How much is it?	Wie viel kostet es?	vee feel *kos*·tet es
Where's the nearest ATM?	Wo ist der nächste Geldautomat?	vaw ist dair *naykhs*·te *gelt*·ow·to·maht
What's the exchange rate?	Wie ist der Wechselkurs?	vee ist dair *vek*·sel·kurs

Paying the Bill

Q How much is it?	Wie viel kostet es? vee feel *kos*·tet es
A It's free.	Das ist umsonst. das ist um·*zonst*
A It costs (30) euros.	Das kostet (30) Euro. das *kos*·tet (*drai*·tsikh) *oy*·ro
Can you write down the price?	Können Sie den Preis aufschreiben? *ker*·nen zee dayn prais *owf*·shrai·ben
There's a mistake in the bill.	Da ist ein Fehler in der Rechnung. dah ist ain *fay*·ler in dair *rekh*·nung
Do you accept credit/ debit cards?	Nehmen Sie Kreditkarten/ Debitkarten? *nay*·men zee kre·*deet*·kar·ten/ *day*·bit·kar·ten

I'd like my change, please.	Ich möchte bitte mein Wechselgeld.
	ikh *merkh*·te *bi*·te main *vek*·sel·gelt
I'd like a receipt, please.	Ich möchte bitte eine Quittung.
	ikh *merkh*·te *bi*·te *ai*·ne *kvi*·tung
I'd like a refund, please.	Ich möchte bitte mein Geld zurückhaben.
	ikh *merkh*·te *bi*·te main gelt tsu·*rük*·hah·ben

At the Bank

Where's the nearest ATM?	Wo ist der nächste Geldautomat?
	vaw ist dair *naykhs*·te *gelt*·ow·to·maht
Where's the nearest foreign exchange office?	Wo ist die nächste Geldwechselstube?
	vaw ist dee *naykhs*·te *gelt*·vek·sel·shtoo·be

PRACTICAL

MONEY & BANKING

🔊 LISTEN FOR

Kann ich bitte einen Ausweis sehen?	kan ikh *bi*·te *ai*·nen *ows*·vais *zay*·en
	Can I see some ID, please?
Bitte unterschreiben Sie hier.	*bi*·te un·ter·*shrai*·ben zee heer
	Please sign here.
Es gibt da ein Problem mit Ihrem Konto.	es gipt dah ain pro·*blaym* mit *ee*·rem *kon*·to
	There's a problem with your account.
Ihr Konto ist überzogen.	eer *kon*·to ist ü·ber·*tsaw*·gen
	You're overdrawn.

What time does the bank open?	Wann macht die Bank auf?
	van makht dee bangk owf
Where can I ...?	Wo kann ich ...?
	vaw kan ikh ...
I'd like to ...	Ich möchte ...
	ikh *merkh*·te ...

arrange a transfer	einen Transfer tätigen	*ai*·nen trans·*fer* *tay*·ti·gen
cash a cheque	einen Scheck einlösen	*ai*·nen shek *ain*·ler·zen
change money	Geld umtauschen	gelt *um*·tow·shen
change travellers cheques	Reisechecks einlösen	*rai*·ze·sheks *ain*·ler·zen
get a cash advance	eine Barauszahlung	*ai*·ne *bahr*·ows·tsah·lung
get change for this note	diesen Schein wechseln	*dee*·zen shain *vek*·seln
withdraw money	Geld abheben	gelt *ap*·hay·ben

What's the exchange rate?	Wie ist der Wechselkurs?
	vee ist dair *vek*·sel·kurs
What's the charge for that?	Wie hoch sind die Gebühren dafür?
	vee hawkh zint dee ge·*bü*·ren da·*für*
What's the commission?	Wie hoch ist die Kommission?
	vee hawkh ist dee ko·mi·*syawn*
The ATM took my card.	Der Geldautomat hat meine Karte einbehalten.
	dair *gelt*·ow·to·maht hat *mai*·ne *kar*·te *ain*·be·hal·ten

LANGUAGE TIP

Currencies

Talking about prices is really easy in German because you don't need to add a plural ending to the currency. Twenty dollars is simply *zwanzig Dollar* tsvan·tsikh *do*·lahr. Some more international currencies to get you started: Euro m *oy*·ro (euro); Pfund n pfunt (pound); Rubel m *roo*·bel (ruble).

I've forgotten my PIN.	Ich habe meine Geheimnummer vergessen. ikh *hah*·be *mai*·ne ge·*haim*·nu·mer fer·*ge*·sen
Can I use my credit card to withdraw money?	Kann ich mit meiner Kreditkarte Geld abheben? kan ikh mit *mai*·ner kre·*deet*·kar·te gelt *ap*·hay·ben
Has my money arrived yet?	Ist mein Geld schon angekommen? ist main gelt shawn *an*·ge·ko·men
How long will it take to arrive?	Wie lange dauert es, bis es da ist? vee *lang*·e *dow*·ert es bis es dah ist

PRACTICAL BUSINESS

Business

KEY PHRASES

I'm attending a conference.	Ich nehme an einer Konferenz teil.	ikh *nay*·me an *ai*·ner kon·fe·*rents* tail
I have an appointment with ...	Ich habe einen Termin bei ...	ikh *hah*·be *ai*·nen ter·*meen* bai ...
Can I have your business card?	Kann ich Ihre/ deine Karte bekommen? **pol/inf**	kan ikh *ee*·re/ *dai*·ne *kar*·te be·*ko*·men

I'm attending a conference.	Ich nehme an einer Konferenz teil. ikh *nay*·me an *ai*·ner kon·fe·*rents* tail
I'm attending a course/meeting.	Ich nehme an einem Kurs/ Meeting teil. ikh *nay*·me an *ai*·nem kurs/ *mee*·ting tail
I'm visiting a trade fair.	Ich besuche eine Messe. ikh be·*zoo*·khe *ai*·ne *me*·se
I'm here for (three) days/weeks.	Ich bin für (drei) Tage/Wochen hier. ikh bin für (drai) *tah*·ge/*vo*·khen heer
I'm with my colleague.	Ich bin mit meinem Kollegen hier. m ikh bin mit *mai*·nem ko·*lay*·gen heer Ich bin mit meiner Kollegin hier. f ikh bin mit *mai*·ner ko·*lay*·gin heer

PRACTICAL BUSINESS

CULTURE TIP

Body Language
Shaking hands is customary for both men and women in Germany, Austria and Switzerland. Always give a firm handshake and look people in the eye. Never keep your other hand in your pocket, as this is considered impolite.

I'm alone.	Ich bin allein. *ikh bin a·lain*
I'm staying at ...	Ich wohne im ... *ikh vaw·ne im ...*
I have an appointment with ...	Ich habe einen Termin bei ... *ikh hah·be ai·nen ter·meen bai ...*
Q Can I have your business card?	Kann ich Ihre/deine Karte bekommen? pol/inf *kan ikh ee·re/dai·ne kar·te be·ko·men*
A Here's my business card.	Hier ist meine Karte. *heer ist mai·ne kar·te*
That went very well.	Das war sehr gut. *das vahr zair goot*
Thank you for your time.	Danke für Ihre/deine Zeit. pol/inf *dang·ke für ee·re/dai·ne tsait*
Thank you for your interest.	Danke für Ihr/dein Interesse. pol/inf *dang·ke für eer/dain in·te·re·se*
Shall we go for a drink/meal?	Sollen wir noch etwas trinken/essen gehen? *zo·len veer nokh et·vas tring·ken/e·sen gay·en*

See also the box **titles & addressing people** (p104).

Sightseeing

KEY PHRASES

I'd like a guide.	Ich hätte gern einen Reiseführer.	ikh *he*·te gern *ai*·nen *rai*·ze·fü·rer
Can I take photographs?	Kann ich fotografieren?	kan ikh fo·to·gra·*fee*·ren
What time does it open?	Wann macht es auf?	van makht es owf
I'd like to see ...	Ich möchte ... sehen.	ikh *merkh*·te ... *zay*·en

Requests & Queries

I'd like an audio set.	Ich hätte gern einen Audioführer. ikh *he*·te gern *ai*·nen *ow*·di·o·fü·rer
I'd like a guide.	Ich hätte gern einen Reiseführer. ikh *he*·te gern *ai*·nen *rai*·ze·fü·rer
I'd like a (local) map.	Ich hätte gern eine Karte (von hier). ikh *he*·te gern *ai*·ne *kar*·te (fon heer)
Do you have information on (historical) sights?	Haben Sie Informationen über (historische) Sehenswürdigkeiten? *hah*·ben zee in·for·ma·*tsyaw*·nen *ü*·ber (his·*taw*·ri·she) *zay*·ens·vür·dikh·kai·ten

I'd like to see ...	Ich möchte ... sehen.
	ikh *merkh* te ... *zay*·en
What's that?	Was ist das?
	vas ist das
How old is it?	Wie alt ist es?
	vee alt ist es
Can I take photographs (of you)?	Kann ich (Sie/du) fotografieren? pol/inf
	kan ikh (zee/doo) fo·to·gra·*fee*·ren
Could you take a photograph of me?	Könnten Sie ein Foto von mir machen?
	kern·ten zee ain *faw*·to fon meer ma lihen

Kann ich fotografieren?
kan ikh fo·to·gra·*fee*·ren
Can I take photographs?

Getting In

What time does it open/close?	Wann macht es auf/zu? *van makht es owf/tsoo*
Q **What's the admission charge?**	Was kostet der Eintritt? *vas kos·tet dair ain·trit*
A **It costs ...**	Er kostet ... *air kos·tet ...*
Is there a discount for ...?	Gibt es eine Ermäßigung für ...? *gipt es ai·ne er·may·si·gung für ...*

children	Kinder	*kin·der*
families	Familien	*fa·mee·li·en*
groups	Gruppen	*gru·pen*
older people	Senioren	*zay·nyaw·ren*
students	Studenten	*shtu·den·ten*

Galleries & Museums

Q **What kind of art are you interested in?**	Für welche Art von Kunst interessieren Sie sich? **pol** *für vel·khe art fon kunst in·tre·see·ren zee zikh* Für welche Art von Kunst interessierst du dich? **inf** *für vel·khe art fon kunst in·tre·seerst doo dikh*
A **I'm interested in ...**	Ich interessiere mich für ... *ikh in·tre·see·re mikh für ...*
A **I like the works of ...**	Ich mag die Arbeiten von ... *ikh mahk dee ar·bai·ten fon ...*
Q **What's in the collection?**	Was gibt es in der Sammlung? *vas gipt es in dair zam·lung*

A It's a/an ... exhibition.	Es ist eine ...-Ausstellung. es ist *ai*·ne ...·*ows*·shte·lung
It reminds me of ...	Es erinnert mich an ... es er·*i*·nert mikh an ...

Tours

Are there (organised) walking tours?	Gibt es (organisierte) Wandertouren? geept es (or·ga·ni·*zeer*·te) *van*·der·too·ren
I'd like to do cooking/ language classes.	Ich würde gerne eine Kochkurs/Sprachkurs machen. ikh *vür*·de gern *ai*·ne *kokh*·kurs/*shprahkh*·kurs *ma*·khen
Can you recommend a ...?	Können Sie ein ... empfehlen? *ker*·nen zee ain ... emp·*fay*·len
When's the next ...?	Wann ist der/die nächste ...? m/f van ist dair/dee *naykhs*·te ...

boat trip	Bootsrundfahrt f	*bawts*·runt·fahrt
day trip	Tagesausflug m	*tah*·ges·ows·flook
excursion	Ausflug m	*ows*·flook
tour	Tour f	toor

Is (accommodation) included?	Ist (die Unterkunft) inbegriffen? ist (dee *un*·ter·kunft) *in*·be·gri·fen
Is (food) included?	Ist (das Essen) inbegriffen? ist (das *e*·sen) *in*·be·gri·fen

PRACTICAL SIGHTSEEING

PRACTICAL SIGHTSEEING

🔍 LOOK FOR

Ausgang	ows·gang	Exit
Damen	dah·men	Women
Eingang	ain·gang	Entrance
Geschlossen	ge·shlo·sen	Closed
Heiß	hais	Hot
Herren	hair·en	Men
Kalt	kalt	Cold
Kein Zutritt	kain tsu·trit	No Entry
Offen	o·fen	Open
Rauchen	row·khen	No Smoking
Verboten	fer·baw·ten	
Toiletten (WC)	to·a·le·ten (vee·tsee)	Toilets
Verboten	fer·baw·ten	Prohibited

Is (transport) included?	Ist (die Beförderung) inbegriffen? ist (dee be·fer·de·rung) in·be·gri·fen
How long is the tour?	Wie lange dauert die Führung? vee lang·e dow·ert dee fü·rung
Do I need to take ... with me?	Muss ich ... mitnehmen? mus ikh ... mit·nay·men
Q What time should we be back?	Wann sollen wir zurück sein? van zo·len veer tsu·rük zain
A Be back here at (10) o'clock.	Seien Sie um (zehn) Uhr zurück. zai·en zee um (tsayn) oor tsu·rük
I've lost my group.	Ich habe meine Gruppe verloren. ikh hah·be mai·ne gru·pe fer·law·ren

Senior & Disabled Travellers

KEY PHRASES

I need assistance.	Ich brauche Hilfe.	ikh *brow*·khe *hil*·fe
Is there wheel-chair access?	Gibt es eine Rollstuhlrampe?	gipt es *ai*·ne *rol*·shtool·ram·pe
Are there toilets for people with a disability?	Gibt es Toiletten für Behinderte?	gipt es to·a·*le*·ten für be·*hin*·der·te

I have a disability.	Ich bin behindert. ikh bin be·*hin*·dert
I need assistance.	Ich brauche Hilfe. ikh *brow*·khe *hil*·fe
Are guide dogs permitted?	Sind Blindenhunde erlaubt? zint *blin*·den·hun·de er·*lowpt*
Is there wheelchair access?	Gibt es eine Rollstuhlrampe? gipt es *ai*·ne *rol*·shtool·ram·pe
Are there parking spaces for people with a disability?	Gibt es Behinderten-parkplätze? geept es be·*hin*·der·ten·park·ple·tse
Are there rails in the bathroom?	Ist das Bad behindertengerecht? ist das baht be·*hin*·der·ten·ge·rekht
Are there toilets for people with a disability?	Gibt es Toiletten für Behinderte? gipt es to·a·*le*·ten für be·*hin*·der·te

How wide are the doors?	Wie breit sind die Türen? vee brait sind dee *tü*·ren
How many steps are there?	Wieviele Stufen sind es? vee·*fee*·le *shtoo*·fen sind es
Is there a lift?	Gibt es einen Aufzug? gipt es *ai*·nen owf·*tsook*
Is there somewhere I can sit down?	Kann ich mich hier irgendwo hinsetzen? kan ikh mikh heer ir·gent·*vaw* hin·ze·tsen
Could you help me cross this street safely?	Könnten Sie mich sicher über diese Straße bringen? *kern*·ten zee mikh *zi*·kher *ü*·ber *dee*·ze *shtrah*·se *bring*·en
Could you call me a taxi for the disabled?	Könnten Sie mir ein Taxi für Behinderte rufen? *kern*·ten zee meer ain *tak*·si für be·*hin*·der·te *roo*·fen
crutches	Krücke f pl *krü*·ke
guide dog	Blindenhund m *blin*·den·hunt
walking frame	Gehwagen m *gay*·vah·gen
walking stick	Gehstock m *gay*·shtok
wheelchair	Rollstuhl m *rol*·shtool
wheelchair ramp	Rollstuhlrampe f *rol*·shtool·ram·pe
wheelchair space	Rollstuhlplatz m *rol*·shtool·plats

Travel with Children

KEY PHRASES

Are children allowed?	Sind Kinder erlaubt?	zint *kin*·der er·*lowpl*
Is there a child discount?	Gibt es eine Kinderer·mäßigung?	gipt es *ai*·ne *kin*·der·er·may·si·gung
Is there a baby change room?	Gibt es einen Wickelraum?	gipt es *ai*·nen *vi*·kel·rowm

Is there a/an...?   Gibt es ...?
                          gipt es ...

baby change room	einen Wickelraum	*ai*·nen *vi*·kel·rowm
babysitter	einen Babysitter	*ai*·nen *bay*·bi·si·ter
child discount	eine Kinderermäßigung	*ai*·ne *kin*·der·er·may·si·gung
child-minding service	einen Babysitter-Service	*ai*·nen *bay*·bi·si·ter·*ser*·vis
children's menu	eine Kinderkarte	*ai*·ne *kin*·der·kar·te
family discount	eine Familienermäßigung	*ai*·ne fa·*mee*·li·en·er·may·si·gung
highchair	einen Kinderstuhl	*ai*·nen *kin*·der·shtool

Is there a park/ playground?	Gibt es einen Park/Spielplatz? gipt es *ai*·nen park/*shpeel*·plats
I need a ...	Ich brauche ... ikh *brow*·khe ...

baby seat	einen Babysitz	*ai*·nen *bay*·bi·zits
child seat	einen Kindersitz	*ai*·nen *kin*·der·zits
cot	ein Kinderbett	ain *kin*·der·bet
potty	ein Kinder-töpfchen	ain *kin*·der·terpf·khen
stroller	einen Kinderwagen	*ai*·nen *kin*·der·vah·gen

Do you sell ...?	Verkaufen Sie ...? fer·*kow*·fen zee ...

baby wipes	feuchte Tücher	*foykh*·te *tü*·kher
disposable nappies/diapers	Einweg-Windeln	*ain*·vek·vin·deln
milk formula	Muttermilch-ersatz	*mu*·ter·milkh·er·zats
painkillers for infants	Schmerzmittel für Kinder	*shmerts*·mi·tel für *kin*·der

Can I breastfeed here?	Kann ich meinem Kind hier die Brust geben? kan ikh *mai*·nem kint heer dee brust *gay*·ben
Are children allowed?	Sind Kinder erlaubt? zint *kin*·der er·*lowpt*
Is this suitable for (three)-year-old children?	Ist das für (drei) Jahre alte Kinder geeignet? ist das für (drai) *yah*·re *al*·te *kin*·der ge·*aig*·net

If your child is sick, see **health** (p152). For more on talking with children, see **meeting people** (p102).

Social

Meeting People

SOCIAL MEETING PEOPLE

KEY PHRASES

My name is ...	Mein Name ist ... pol Ich heiße ... inf	main *nah*·me ist ... ikh *hai*·se ...
I'm from ...	Ich komme aus ...	ikh *ko*·me ows ...
I work in ...	Ich arbeite ...	ikh *ar*·bai·te ...
I'm ... years old.	Ich bin ... Jahre alt.	ikh bin ... *yah*·re alt
And you?	Und Ihnen/dir? pol/inf	unt *ee*·nen/deer

Basics

Yes./No.	Ja./Nein. yah/nain
Please.	Bitte. *bi*·te
Thank you.	Danke. *dang*·ke
Thank you very much.	Vielen Dank. *fee*·len dangk
You're (very) welcome.	Bitte (sehr). *bi*·te (zair)
Excuse me./Sorry.	Entschuldigung. ent·*shul*·di·gung
Don't worry.	Macht nichts. makht nikhts

Greetings

Hello. (all of Germany)	Guten Tag. *goo·ten tahk*
Hello. (southern Germany)	Grüß Gott. *grüs got*
Hello. (Switzerland)	Grüezi. *grü·e·tsi*
Hello. (Austria)	Servus. *zer·vus*
Good morning.	Guten Morgen. *goo·ten mor·gen*
Good day/afternoon.	Guten Tag. *goo·ten tahk*
Good evening.	Guten Abend. *goo·ten ah·bent*
Hi.	Hallo. *ha·lo*
See you later.	Bis später. *bis shpay·ter*
Good night.	Gute Nacht. *goo·te nakht*
Goodbye.	Auf Wiedersehen. *owf vee·der·zay·en*
Bye.	Tschüss./Tschau. *chüs/chow*
Q How are you?	Wie geht es Ihnen/dir? pol/inf *vee gayt es ee·nen/deer*
A Fine. And you?	Danke, gut. Und Ihnen/dir? pol/inf *dang·ke goot unt ee·nen/deer*

LANGUAGE TIP — **Titles & Addressing People**

In the past *Fräulein froy*·lain was used to address all unmarried women regardless of age, but today the term is only used to address girls (and sometimes female waiters). All other women should be addressed using *Frau* frow. There's no equivalent of the English 'Ms' – use *Frau*. The equivalents of Sir and Madam, *Mein Herr* main her and *Meine Dame mai*·ne *dah*·me, are very old-fashioned.

If you want to include academic titles when addressing somebody, these are combined with *Herr* and *Frau*, eg *Frau Professor* frow pro·fe·sor or *Herr Doktor* her *dok*·tor.

Mr	Herr	her
Mrs	Frau	frow
Miss	Frau/Fräulein	frow/*froy*·lain

Q What's your name?	Wie ist Ihr Name? pol vee ist eer *nah*·me Wie heißt du? inf vee haist doo
A My name is ...	Mein Name ist ... pol main *nah*·me ist ... Ich heiße ... inf ikh *hai*·se ...
I'm pleased to meet you.	Angenehm. *an*·ge·naym
I'd like to introduce you to ...	Darf ich Ihnen/dir ... vorstellen? pol/inf darf ikh ee·nen/dir ... *fawr*·shte·len
✂ **This is ...**	Das ist ... das ist ...

This is my ...		Das ist mein/meine/mein ...
		m/f/n
		das ist main/*mai*·ne/main ...

child	Kind n	kint
colleague	Kollege m	ko·*lay*·ge
	Kollegin f	ko·*lay*·gin
friend	Freund(in) m/f	froynt/*froyn*·din
husband	Mann m	man
partner	Partner(in) m/f	*part*·ner/*part*·ne·rin
wife	Frau f	frow

Making Conversation

Do you live here?	Wohnen Sie hier? pol
	vaw·nen zee heer
	Wohnst du hier? inf
	vawnst doo heer
Where are you going?	Wohin fahren Sie? pol
	vaw·hin *fah*·ren zee
	Wohin fährst du? inf
	vaw·hin fairst doo
What are you doing?	Was machen Sie? pol
	vas *ma*·khen zee
	Was machst du? inf
	vas makhst doo
Nice day, isn't it?	Schönes Wetter heute!
	sher·nes *we*·ter *hoy*·te
Terrible weather today!	Furchtbares Wetter heute!
	furkht·bah·res *we*·ter *hoy*·te
🄠 Do you like it here?	Gefällt es Ihnen/dir hier? pol/inf
	ge·*felt* es *ee*·nen/deer heer
🄰 I love it here.	Mir gefällt es hier sehr gut.
	meer ge·*felt* es heer zair goot

SOCIAL MEETING PEOPLE

What do you think (about ...)?	Was denken Sie (über ...)? pol vas *deng*·ken zee (*ü*·ber ...) Was denkst du (über ...)? inf vas dengkst doo (*ü*·ber ...)
That's (beautiful), isn't it?	Ist das nicht (schön)? ist das nikht (shern)
Are you here on holiday?	Sind Sie hier im Urlaub? pol zint zee heer im *oor*·lowp Bist du hier im Urlaub? inf bist doo heer im *oor*·lowp
I'm here ...	Ich bin hier ... ikh bin heer ...

for a holiday	im Urlaub	im *oor*·lowp
on business	auf	owf
	Geschäfts-reise	ge·*shefts*·rai·ze
to study	zum	tsum
	Studieren	shtu·*dee*·ren
with my family	mit meiner	mit *mai*·ner
	Familie	fa·*mee*·li·e
with my partner	mit meinem	mit *mai*·nem
	Partner m	*part*·ner
	mit meiner	mit *mai*·ner
	Partnerin f	part·ne·rin

How long are you here for?	Für wie lange sind Sie hier? pol für vee *lang*·e zint zee heer Für wie lange bist du hier? inf für vee *lang*·e bist doo heer
I'm here for (four) days/weeks.	Ich bin für (vier) Tage/Wochen hier. ikh bin für (feer) *tah*·ge/*vo*·khen heer

Nationalities

Q Where are you from?	Woher kommen Sie? pol *vaw·hair ko·men zee* Woher kommst du? inf *vaw·hair komst doo*
A I'm from (Australia).	Ich komme aus (Australien) ikh *ko·me ows* (ows·*trah*·li·en)
A I'm from (the USA).	Ich komme aus (den USA). ikh *ko·me ows* (dayn oo·es·*ah*)
A I'm from (New Zealand).	Ich komme aus (Neuseeland). ikh *ko·me ows* (noy·*zay*·lant)

For more countries, see the **dictionary**.

> ### *Ist das nicht schön?*
> ist das nikht shern
> ***That's beautiful, isn't it?***

🔊 LISTEN FOR

Hi/Hey!	hai/hei	Hey!
Toll/Geil!/ Super!/Spitze!	tol/gail/*zoo*·per/ *shpi*·tse	Great!
Kein Problem.	kain pro·*blaym*	No problem.
Klar!	klahr	Sure.
Vielleicht.	fi·*laikht*	Maybe.
Auf keinen Fall!	owf *kai*·nen fal	No way!
Das ist OK.	das ist o·*kay*	It's OK.
Alles klar.	*a*·les klahr	I'm OK.
Das war nur ein Scherz!	das vahr noor ain sherts	Just joking!
Guck mal!	guk mahl	Look!
Hör mal!	her mahl	Listen!
Hör dir das an!	her deer das an	Listen to this!
Ich bin so weit.	ikh bin zaw vait	I'm ready.
Bist du so weit?	bist doo zaw vait	Are you ready?
Einen Augenblick.	*ai*·nen ow·gen·*blik*	Just a minute.

Age

🅠 **How old are you?**	Wie alt sind Sie? pol vee alt zint zee Wie alt bist du? inf vee alt bist doo
🅐 **I'm ... years old.**	Ich bin ... Jahre alt. ikh bin ... *yah*·re alt
Too old!	Zu alt! tsoo alt
I'm younger than I look.	Ich bin jünger als ich aussehe. ikh bin *yüng*·er als ikh *ows*·zay·e

Q How old is your daughter?	Wie alt ist Ihre/deine Tochter? pol/inf vee alt ist ee·re/dai·ne tokh·ter
Q How old is your son?	Wie alt ist Ihr/dein Sohn? pol/inf vee alt ist eer/dain zawn
A He's/She's ... years old.	Er/Sie ist ... Jahre alt. air/zee ist ... yah·re alt

For your age, see **numbers & amounts** (p30).

Occupations & Studies

Q What's your occupation?	Als was arbeiten Sie? pol als vas ar·bai·ten zee Als was arbeitest du? inf als vas ar·bai·test doo
A I'm a ...	Ich bin ein/eine ... m/f ikh bin ain/ain·e ...

farmer	Bauer m	bow·er
	Bäuerin f	boy·e·rin
student	Student m	shtu·dent
	Studentin f	shtu·den·tin
teacher	Lehrer m	lay·rer
	Lehrerin f	lay·re·rin
writer	Schriftsteller m	shrift·shte·ler
	Schriftstellerin f	shrift·shte·le·rin

I work in IT.	Ich arbeite in der IT-Branche. ikh ar·bai·te in dair ai·tee·brang·she
I work in sales and marketing.	Ich arbeite im Verkauf und Marketing. ikh ar·bai·te im fer·kowf unt mar·ke·ting

I'm retired.	Ich bin Rentner/Rentnerin. m/f ikh bin *rent*·ner/*rent*·ne·rin
I'm self-employed.	Ich bin selbstständig. ikh bin *zelpst*·shten·dikh
I'm unemployed.	Ich bin arbeitslos. ikh bin *ar*·baits·laws
🔲 What are you studying?	Was studieren Sie? pol vas shtu·*dee*·ren zee Was studierst du? inf vas shtu·*deerst* doo
🔲 I'm studying (engineering).	Ich studiere (Ingenieurwesen). ikh shtu·*dee*·re (in·zhe·*nyer*·vay·zen)

For more occupations and fields of study, see the **dictionary**.

Family

🔲 Do you have a ...?	Haben Sie einen/eine ...? m/f pol *hah*·ben zee *ai*·nen/*ai*·ne ... Hast du einen/eine ...? m/f inf hast doo *ai*·nen/*ai*·ne ...
🔲 I (don't) have a ...	Ich habe (k)einen/(k)eine ... m/f ikh *hah*·be (k)*ai*·nen/(k)*ai*·ne ...
🔲 Do you live with (your parents)?	Leben Sie bei (Ihren Eltern)? pol *lay*·ben zee bai (*ee*·ren el·tern) Lebst du bei (deinen Eltern)? inf laypst doo bai (*dai*·nen el·tern)
🔲 I live with my ...	Ich lebe bei meinem/meiner/ meinen ... m/f/pl ikh *lay*·be bai *mai*·nem/*mai*·ner/ *mai*·nen ...
This is my ...	Das ist mein/meine ... m/f das ist main/*mai*·ne ...

Q Are you married?	Sind Sie verheiratet? pol zint zee fer·*hai*·ra·tot Bist du verheiratet? inf bist doo fer·*hai*·ra·tet
A I'm married.	Ich bin verheiratet. ikh bin fer·*hai*·ra·tet
A I live with someone.	Ich lebe mit jemandem zusammen ikh *lay*·be mit *yay*·man·dem tsu·za·men
A I'm separated.	Ich bin getrennt. ikh bin ge·*trent*
A I'm single.	Ich bin ledig. ikh bin *lay*·dikh

Talking with Children

When's your birthday?	Wann hast du Geburtstag? van hast doo ge·*burts*·tahk
Do you go to school or kindergarten?	Gehst du in die Schule oder in den Kindergarten? gayst doo in dee *shoo*·le aw·dor in dayn *kin*·der·gar·ten
What grade are you in?	In welcher Klasse bist du? in *vel*·kher *kla*·se bist doo
Do you learn English?	Lernst du Englisch? lernst doo *eng*·lish
I come from very far away.	Ich komme von sehr weit her. ikh *ko*·me fon zair vait hair

Farewells

Tomorrow is my last day here.	Morgen ist mein letzter Tag hier. *mor*·gen ist main *lets*·ter tahk heer

Q What's your...?	Wie ist Ihre/deine ...? pol/inf
	vee ist *ee*·re/*dai*·ne ...
A Here's my ...	Hier ist meine ...
	heer ist *mai*·ne ...

address	Adresse	a·*dre*·se
email address	E-mail-Adresse	*ee*·mayl·a·dre·se
mobile number	Handynummer	*hen*·di·nu·mer
work number	Nummer bei der Arbeit	*nu*·mer bai dair *ar*·bait

For more on addresses, see **directions**, page 53.

Are you on Facebook?	Sind Sie auf Facebook? pol
	zint zee owf *fays*·buk
	Bist du auf Facebook? inf
	bist doo owf *fays*·buk
Keep in touch!	Melden Sie sich doch mal! pol
	mel·den zee zikh dokh mahl
	Melde dich mal! inf
	mel·de dikh mahl
It's been great meeting you.	Es war schön, Sie/dich kennen zu lernen. pol/inf
	es vahr shern zee/dikh *ke*·nen tsoo *ler*·nen

Well-Wishing

Bless you! (when sneezing)	Gesundheit!
	ge·*zunt*·hait
Bon voyage!	Gute Reise!
	goo·te *rai*·ze
Cheers!	Prost!
	prawst

LANGUAGE TIP

False Friends

Many German words look like English words but have a completely different meaning, so be careful! Here are a few examples:

blank
blank
shiny
(not 'blank', which is *leer* leer)

Chef
shef
boss
(not 'chef', which is *Koch* kokh)

komisch
kaw·mish
strange
(not 'comical', which is *lustig* lus·tikh)

Konfektion
kon·fekt·tsyawn
ready-made clothes
(not 'confectionary', which is *Konfekt* kon·fekt)

sensibel
zen·zee·bel
sensitive
(not 'sensible', which is *vernünftig* fer·nünf·tikh)

Tip
tip
advance information
(not 'tip', which is *Trinkgeld* trink·gelt)

Good luck!	Viel Glück! feel gluk
Happy birthday!	Herzlichen Glückwunsch zum Geburtstag! *herts*·li·khen *glük*·vunsh tsum ge·*burts*·tahk
What a pity!	Schade! *shah*·de
Congratulations!	Gratuliere! gra·too·*lee*·re

Interests

KEY PHRASES

What do you do in your spare time?	Was machen Sie in Ihrer Freizeit? pol	vas *ma*·khen zee in *ee*·rer *frai*·tsait
	Was machst du in deiner Freizeit? inf	vas makhst doo in *dai*·ner *frai*·tsait
Do you like ...?	Mögen Sie ...? pol	*mer*·gen zee ...
	Magst du ...? inf	mahkst doo ...
I (don't) like ...	Ich mag (keinen/ keine) ... m/f	ikh mahk (*kai*·nen/*kai*·ne) ...

Common Interests

Q What do you do in your spare time?	Was machen Sie in Ihrer Freizeit? pol vas *ma*·khen zee in *ee*·rer *frai*·tsait Was machst du in deiner Freizeit? inf vas makhst doo in *dai*·ner *frai*·tsait
Q Do you like ...?	Mögen Sie ...? pol *mer*·gen zee ... Magst du ...? inf mahkst doo ...
A I (don't) like art.	Ich mag (keine) Kunst. ikh mahk (*kai*·nen/*kai*·ne) kunst
A I (don't) like sport.	Ich mag (keinen) Sport. ikh mahk (*kai*·nen/*kai*·ne) shport

🅰 I like (cooking).	Ich (koche) gern.	
	ikh (ko·khe) gern	
🅰 I don't like (hiking).	Ich (wandere) nicht gern.	
	ikh (van·de·re) nikht gern	
And you?	Und Sie/du? pol/inf	
	unt zee/doo	

For more interests, see **sports** (p136) and the **dictionary**.

Music

Do you like to listen to music?	Hören Sie gern Musik? pol
	her·ren zee gern mu·zeek
	Hörst du gern Musik? inf
	horst doo gern mu·zeek
Do you like to dance?	Tanzen Sie gern? pol
	tan·tsen zee gern
	Tanzt du gern? inf
	tantst doo gern
Do you like to go to concerts?	Gehen Sie gern in Konzerte? pol
	gay·en zee gern in kon·tser·te
	Gehst du gern in Konzerte? inf
	gayst doo gern in kon·tser·te
Do you like to sing?	Singen Sie gern? pol
	zing·en zee gern
	Singst du gern? inf
	zingkst doo gern
Do you play an instrument?	Spielen Sie ein Instrument? pol
	shpee·len zee ain in·stru·ment
	Spielst du ein Instrument? inf
	shpeelst doo ain in·stru·ment

Which bands/ singers do you like?	Welche Bands/Sänger mögen Sie? pol *vel*·khe bents/*zeng*·er mer·gen zee Welche Bands/Sänger magst du? inf *vel*·khe bents/*zeng*·er mahkst doo
Which music do you like?	Welche Art von Musik mögen Sie? pol *vel*·khe art fon mu·*zeek* mer·gen zee Welche Art von Musik magst du? inf *vel*·khe art fon mu·*zeek* mahkst doo
classical music	klassische Musik f *kla*·si·she mu·*zeek*
electronic music	elektronische Musik f e·lek·*traw*·ni·she mu·*zeek*
metal	Metal m *me*·tel
pop	Popmusik f *pop*·mu·zeek
rock	Rockmusik f *rok*·mu·zeek
traditional music	traditionelle Musik f tra·di·tsyo·*ne*·le mu·*zeek*
world music	Weltmusik f *velt*·mu·zeek

Planning to go to a concert? See **buying tickets** (p40) and **going out** (p124).

Cinema & Theatre

I feel like going to a film/play.	Ich hätte Lust, ins Kino/Theater zu gehen.
	ikh *he*·te lust ins *kee*·no/te·*ah*·ter tsoo *gay*·en
What's showing at the cinema/theatre tonight?	Was gibt es heute im Kino/Theater?
	vas gipt es *hoy*·te im *kee*·no/te·*ah*·ter
Is it in English?	Ist es auf Englisch?
	ist es owf *eng*·lish
Is it dubbed?	Ist er synchronisiert?
	ist air zün·kro·nee·*zeert*
Does it have subtitles?	Hat es Untertitel?
	hat es *un*·ter·tee·tel
Have you seen ...?	Haben Sie ... gesehen? pol
	hah·ben zee ... ge·*zay*·en
	Hast du ... gesehen? inf
	hast doo ... ge·*zay*·en
🅠 **Who's in it?**	Wer spielt da mit?
	vair shpeelt dah mit
🅐 **It stars ...**	Es ist mit ...
	es ist mit ...
Are those seats taken?	Sind diese Plätze besetzt?
	zint *dee*·ze *ple*·tse be·*zetst*
🅠 **Did you like it?**	Hat es Ihnen/dir gefallen? pol/inf
	hat es *ee*·nen/deer ge·*fa*·len
🅐 **I thought it was excellent.**	Ich fand es ausgezeichnet.
	ikh fant es ows·ge·*tsaikh*·net
🅐 **I thought it was OK.**	Ich fand es okay.
	ikh fant es o·*kay*
I thought it was long.	Ich fand es lang.
	ikh fant es lang

SOCIAL INTERESTS

I (don't) like ...	Ich mag ... ikh mahk ...	
action movies	(keine) Actionfilme	(kai·ne) ek·shen·fil·me
animated films	(keine) Zeichen- trickfilme	(kai·ne) tsai·khen· trik·fil·me
comedies	(keine) Komödien	(kai·ne) ko·mer·di·en
documentaries	(keine) Dokumentar- filme	(kai·ne) do·ku·men·tahr· fil·me
drama	(keine) Schauspiele	(kai·ne) show·shpee·le
German cinema	(keine) deutsche(n) Filme	(kai·ne) doyt·she(n) fil·me
horror movies	(keine) Horrorfilme	(kai·ne) ho·ror·fil·me
sci-fi	(keinen) Sciencefiction	(kai·nen) sai·ens·fik·shen

Volunteering

I'd like to volunteer my skills.	Ich möchte meine Mitarbeit als Freiwilliger anbieten. ikh merkh·te mai·ne mit·ar·bait als frai·vi·li·ger an·bee·ten
Are there any volunteer programs available in the area?	Gibt es hier in der Region irgendwelche Freiwilligenprogramme? gipt es heer in dair re·gyawn ir·gent·vel·khe frai·vi·li·gen·pro·gra·me

Feelings & Opinions

KEY PHRASES

Are you ...?	Sind Sie ...? pol	zint zee ...
	Bist du ...? inf	bist doo ...
I'm (not) ...	Ich bin (nicht) ...	ikh bin (nikht) ...
What did you think of it?	Wie hat es Ihnen/ dir gefallen? pol/inf	vee hat es ee·nen/ deer ge·fa·len
It is/was ...	Es ist/war ...	es ist/vahr ...

Feelings

Q **Are you ...?**	Sind Sie ...? pol
	zint zee ...
	Bist du ...? inf
	bist doo ...
A **I'm (not) ...**	Ich bin (nicht) ...
	ikh bin (nikht) ...

annoyed	verärgert	fer·er·gert
disappointed	enttäuscht	en·*toysht*
happy	glücklich	*glük*·likh
sad	traurig	*trow*·rikh
tired	müde	*mü*·de

Q **Are you (hungry)?**	Haben Sie (Hunger)? pol
	hah·ben zee (*hung*·er)
	Hast du (Hunger)? inf
	hast doo (*hung*·er)
A **I'm not (thirsty).**	Ich habe kein (Durst).
	ikh *hah*·be kain (durst)

Q Are you (hot)?	Ist Ihnen/dir (heiß)? pol/inf ist *ee*·nen/deer (hais)
A I'm not (cold).	Mir ist nicht (kalt). meer ist nikht (kalt).
Q Are you worried?	Machen Sie sich Sorgen? pol *ma*·khen zee zikh *zor*·gen Machst du dir Sorgen? inf makhst doo deer *zor*·gen
A I'm (not) worried.	Ich mache mir (keine) Sorgen. ikh *ma*·khe meer (*kai*·ne) *zor*·gen
A I'm a little (sad).	Ich bin ein bisschen (traurig). ikh bin ain *bis*·khen (*trow*·rikh)
A I'm terribly (sorry).	Es tut mir furchtbar (Leid). es toot meer *furkht*·bahr (lait)
A I feel very (lucky).	Ich schätze mich sehr (glücklich). ikh *she*·tse mikh zair (*glük*·likh)

If you're not feeling well, see **health** (p152).

Opinions

Q Did you like it?	Hat es Ihnen/dir gefallen? pol/inf hat es *ee*·nen/deer ge·*fa*·len
Q What did you think of it?	Wie hat es Ihnen/dir gefallen? pol/inf vee hat es *ee*·nen/deer ge·*fa*·len
A It is/was ...	Es ist/war ... es ist/vahr ...

awful	schrecklich	*shrek*·likh
beautiful	schön	shern
boring	langweilig	*lang*·vai·likh
great	toll	tol
interesting	interessant	in·tre·*sant*
OK	okay	o·*kay*

Politics & Social Issues

Q Who do you vote for?	Wen wählen Sie? pol	
	vayn *vay*·len zee	
	Wen wählst du? inf	
	vayn vaylst doo	
A I support the labour party.	Ich unterstütze die Arbeiterpartei.	
	ikh un·ter·*shtü*·tse dee ar·bai·ter·par·tai	
A I support the ... party.	Ich unterstütze die ... Partei.	
	ikh un·ter·*shtü*·tse dee ... par·*lai*	

communist	kommunistische	ko·mu·*nis*·ti·she
conservative	konservative	*kon*·zer·va·tee·ve
democratic	demokratische	de·mo·*krah*·tish·e
green	grüne	*grün*·e
liberal	liberale	li·be·*rahl*·e
social	sozial·	zo·*tsyahl*·
democratic	demokratische	de·mo·*krah*·tish·e
socialist	sozialistische	zo·tsya·*lis*·tish·e

Did you hear about ...?	Haben Sie von ... gehört? pol
	hah·ben zee fon ... ge·*hert*
	Hast du von ... gehört? inf
	hast doo fon ... ge·*hert*
Are you in favour of ...?	Sind Sie für ...? pol
	zint zee für ...
	Bist du für ...? inf
	bist doo für ...
Are you against ... ?	Sind Sie gegen ...? pol
	zint zee *gay*·gen ...
	Bist du gegen ...? inf
	bist doo *gay*·gen ...

LANGUAGE TIP

German Idioms
If you'd like to underline your opinions with some colourful language and impress your new German-speaking acquaintances, try your hand at these sayings:

Das versteht sich von selbst.	das ver·*shtet* zikh fon zelbst That goes without saying.
Damit können Sie bei mir nicht landen.	da·mit *ker*·nen zee bai meer nikht *lan*·den That cuts no ice with me.
Danach kräht kein Hahn.	da·*nakh* krayt kain han Nobody cares two hoots about it.
Bleiben Sie sachlich!	*blai*·ben zee *zakh*·likh Stick to the facts!
Das führt zu nichts.	das fürt tsu nikhts That will get you nowhere.
Das können Sie uns nicht erzählen!	das *kern*·en zee uns nikht er·*tsay*·len Tell us another one!
das letzte Wort haben	das *lets*·te vort *hahb*·en to have the final say

Q Do you agree with it?	Sind Sie damit einverstanden? pol zint zee dah·*mit* ain·fer·shtan·den Bist du damit einverstanden? inf bist doo dah·*mit* ain·fer·shtan·den
A I (don't) agree with that.	Ich bin damit (nicht) einverstanden. ikh bin dah·*mit* (nikht) ain·fer·shtan·den

How do people feel about ...?	Was denken die Leute über ...? vas *deng*·ken dee *loy*·te *ü*·ber ...
economy	Wirtschaft f *virt*·shaft
environment	Umwelt f *um*·velt
health care	Gesundheitswesen n ge·*zunt*·hails·vay·zen
immigration	Einwanderung f *ain*·van·de·rung
war in ...	Krieg in ... m kreek in ...

The Environment

Where can I recycle this?	Wo kann ich das recyceln? vaw kan ikh das ri·*sai*·keln
Is there a ... problem here?	Gibt es hier ein Problem mit ...? gipt es heer ain pro·*blaym* mit ...
What should be done about ...?	Was sollte man gegen ... tun? vas *zol*·te man *gay*·gen ... toon
climate change	Klimawandel m *klee*·ma·wan·del
nuclear energy	Atomenergie f a·*tawm*·e·ner·gee
pollution	Umweltverschmutzung f *um*·velt·fer·shmu·tsung
sustainable energy	nachhaltige Energie f *nahkh*·hal·ti·ge ay·ner·gee
Is this a protected forest?	Ist das ein geschützter Wald? ist das ain ge·*shüts*·ter valt
Is this a protected species?	Ist das eine geschützte Art? ist das *ai*·ne ge·*shüts*·te art

Going Out

KEY PHRASES

What's on tonight?	Was ist heute Abend los?	vas ist *hoy*·te *ah*·bent laws
When shall we meet?	Wann sollen wir uns treffen?	van *zo*·len veer uns *tre*·fen
Where shall we meet?	Wo sollen wir uns treffen?	vaw *zo*·len veer uns *tre*·fen

Where to Go

What's there to do in the evenings?	Was kann man abends unternehmen? vas kan man *ah*·bents un·ter·*nay*·men
What's on today?	Was ist heute los? vas ist *hoy*·te laws
What's on tonight?	Was ist heute Abend los? vas ist *hoy*·te *ah*·bent laws
I feel like going out somewhere.	Ich hätte Lust, auszugehen. ikh *he*·te lust *ows*·tsu·*gay*·en
Where are the ...?	Wo sind die ...? vaw zint dee ...

clubs	Klubs	klups
gay venues	Schwulen- und Lesbenkneipen	*shvoo*·len unt *les*·ben·knai·pen
places to eat	Restaurants	res·to·*rangs*
pubs	Kneipen	*knai*·pen

Is there a local entertainment guide?	Gibt es einen Veranstaltung-skalender? gipt es *ai*·nen fer·*an*·shtal·tungks·ka·len·der
Is there a local gay guide?	Gibt es einen Führer für die Schwulen- und Lesbenszene? gipt es *ai*·nen *fü*·rer für dee *shvoo*·len unt *les*·bens·tsay·ne
I feel like going to a/the ...	Ich hätte Lust, ... zu gehen. ikh *he*·te lust ... tsoo *gay*·en

ballet	zum Ballett	tsum ba·*let*
bar/pub	in eine Kneipe	in *ai*·ne *knai* pe
cafe	in ein Café	in ain ka·*fay*
concert	in ein Konzert	in ain kon·*tsert*
movies	ins Kino	ins *kee*·no
nightclub	in einen Nachtklub	in *ai*·nen *nakht*·klup
opera	in die Oper	in dee *aw*·per
restaurant	in ein Restaurant	in ain res·to·*rang*
theatre	ins Theater	ins te·*ah*·ter

For more on bars, drinks and partying, see **eating out** (p172).

Invitations

What are you doing right now?	Was machst du jetzt gerade? vas makhst doo jetst ge·*rah*·de
What are you doing this evening?	Was machst du heute Abend? vas makhst doo *hoy*·te *ah*·bent
What are you doing this weekend?	Was machst du am Wochenende? vas makhst doo am *vo*·khen·en·de

Would you like to go (for a) ...?		Möchtest du ... gehen? *merkh*·test doo ... *gay*·en
coffee	einen Kaffee trinken	*ai*·nen *ka*·fay *tring*·ken
dancing	tanzen	*tan*·tsen
drink	etwas trinken	*et*·vas *tring*·ken
meal	essen	*e*·sen

Do you want to come to the ... concert with me?	Möchtest du mit mir zum ...-konzert gehen? *merkh*·test doo mit meer tsum ...·kon·*tsert gay*·en
We're having a party.	Wir machen eine Party. veer *ma*·khen *ai*·ne *par*·ti
Would you like to come?	Hättest du Lust zu kommen? *he*·test doo lust tsoo *ko*·men

Responding to Invitations

Sure!	Klar! klahr
Yes, I'd love to.	Ja, gerne. yah *ger*·ne
That's very kind of you.	Das ist sehr nett von dir/euch. **sg/pl** das ist zair net fon deer/oykh
Where shall we go?	Wo sollen wir hingehen? vaw *zo*·len veer *hin*·gay·en
No, I'm afraid I can't.	Nein, es tut mir Leid, aber ich kann nicht. nain es toot meer lait *ah*·ber ikh kan nikht
What about tomorrow?	Wie wäre es mit morgen? vee *vair*·re es mit *mor*·gen

Arranging to Meet

Q **When shall we meet?**	Wann sollen wir uns treffen? van *zo*·len veer uns *tre*·fen
A **Let's meet at (eight) o'clock.**	Wir treffen uns um (acht) Uhr. veer *tre*·fen uns um (akht) oor
Q **Where shall we meet?**	Wo sollen wir uns treffen? vaw *zo* len veer uns *tre*·fen
A **Let's meet at the entrance.**	Wir treffen uns am Eingang. veer *tre*·fen uns am *ain*·gang
I'll see you then.	Bis dann! bis dan
I'll pick you up.	Ich hole dich ab ikh *haw*·le dikh ap

SOCIAL

GO N3 OUT

Wo sollen wir uns treffen?
vaw *zo*·len veer uns *tre*·fen
Where shall we meet?

I'll be coming later. Where will you be?	Ich komme später. Wo wirst du sein?
	ikh *ko*·me *shpay*·ter vaw virst doo zain
If I'm not there by (nine), don't wait for me.	Wenn ich bis (neun) Uhr nicht da bin, warte nicht auf mich.
	ven ikh bis (noyn) oor nikht dah bin *var*·te nikht owf mikh
See you later/tomorrow.	Bis später/morgen.
	bis *shpay*·ter/*mor*·gen
I'm looking forward to it.	Ich freue mich darauf.
	ikh *froy*·e mikh da·*rowf*
Sorry I'm late.	Es tut mir Leid, dass ich zu spät komme.
	es toot meer lait das ikh tsoo shpayt *ko*·me
Never mind.	Macht nichts.
	makht nikhts

Drugs

I don't take drugs.	Ich nehme keine Drogen.
	ikh *nay*·me *kai*·ne *draw*·gen
I take ... occasionally.	Ich nehme ab und zu ...
	ikh *nay*·me ap unt tsoo ...
Do you want to have a smoke?	Wollen wir einen Joint rauchen?
	vo·len veer *ai*·nen dzhoynt *row*·khen
Do you have a light?	Haben Sie Feuer? pol
	hah·ben zee *foy*·er
	Hast du Feuer? inf
	hast doo *foy*·er

If the police are talking to you about drugs, see **police** (p150) for useful phrases.

Romance

KEY PHRASES

Would you like to do something tomorrow?	Hättest du Lust, morgen was zu unternehmen?	he·test doo lust mor·gen vas tsoo un·ter·nay·men
I love you.	Ich liebe dich.	ikh lee·be dikh
Leave me alone!	Lass mich zufrieden!	las mikh tsu free·den

Asking Someone Out

Q Would you like to do something tomorrow?	Hättest du Lust, morgen was zu unternehmen? he·test doo lust mor·gen vas tsoo un·ter·nay·men
A Yes, I'd love to.	Ja, gerne. yah ger·ne
A Sure, thanks.	Klar! Das wäre nett. klahr das vair·re net
A I'm busy.	Ich habe keine Zeit. ikh hah·be kai·ne tsait
Where would you like to go tonight?	Wo würdest du heute Abend gerne hingehen? vaw vür·dest doo hoy·te ah·bent ger·ne hin·gay·en
Where would you like to go on the weekend?	Wo würdest du am Wochenende gerne hingehen? vaw vür·dest doo am vo·khen·en·de ger·ne hin·gay·en

Pick-Up Lines

Haven't we met before?	Kennen wir uns nicht von irgendwoher? *ke*·nen veer uns nikht fon *ir*·gent·vo·*hair*
Would you like a drink?	Möchtest du etwas trinken? *merkh*·test doo *et*·vas *tring*·ken
Shall we get some fresh air?	Sollen wir ein bisschen an die frische Luft gehen? *zo*·len veer ain *bis*·khen an dee *fri*·she luft *gay*·en
You have a beautiful personality.	Du hast eine wundervolle Persönlichkeit. doo hast *ai*·ne *vun*·der·vo·ler per·*zern*·likh·kait
You have beautiful eyes.	Du hast schöne Augen. doo hast *sher*·ne *ow*·gen
You have a beautiful body.	Du hast einen schönen Körper. doo hast *ai*·nen *sher*·nen *ker*·per

Rejections

I'm here with my boyfriend.	Ich bin mit meinem Freund hier. ikh bin mit *mai*·nem froynt heer
I'm here with my girlfriend.	Ich bin mit meiner Freundin hier. ikh bin mit *mai*·ner *froyn*·din heer

> **LANGUAGE TIP**
>
> **M Before F**
> In this book, masculine forms appear before the feminine forms. If letters have been added to the masculine word to form the feminine word (often *-in*), these will appear in parentheses. Where the change involves more than the addition of *-in*, two words are given, separated by a slash. The neuter form – where applicable – is mentioned last. See also **gender** (p18) in the **grammar** chapter.

Excuse me, I have to go now.	Tut mir Leid, ich muss jetzt gehen.
	toot meer lait ikh mus yetst *gay*·en
No, thank you.	Nein, danke.
	nain *dang*·ke
I'd rather not.	Lieber nicht.
	lee·ber nikht
Perhaps some other time.	Vielleicht ein andermal.
	fi·*laikht* ain *an*·der·mahl
I'm not interested.	Ich bin nicht interessiert.
	ikh bin nikht in·tre·*seert*
Leave me alone!	Lass mich zufrieden!
	las mikh tsu·*free*·den

Getting Closer

I like you very much.	Ich mag dich sehr.
	ikh mahk dikh zair
I'm interested in you.	Ich interessiere mich für dich.
	ikh in·tre·*see*·re mikh für dikh
Do you like me too?	Magst du mich auch?
	mahkst doo mikh owkh

Will you take me home?	Kannst du mich nach Hause bringen? kanst doo mikh nahkh *how*·ze *bring*·en
Do you want to come inside for a while?	Möchtest du noch kurz mit reinkommen? *merkh*·test doo nokh kurts mit *rain*·ko·men
You're very nice.	Du bist sehr nett. doo bist zair net
You're great.	Du bist toll. doo bist tol
Can I stay over?	Kann ich hier übernachten? kan ikh heer ü·ber·*nakh*·ten
Can I see you again?	Kann ich dich wiedersehen? kan ikh dikh *vee*·der·zay·en

Sex

Kiss me.	Küss mich. küs mikh
I want to make love to you.	Ich möchte mit dir schlafen. ikh *merkh*·te mit deer *shlah*·fen
Let's go to bed!	Gehen wir ins Bett! *gay*·en veer ins bet
Touch me here.	Berühr mich hier! be·*rür* mikh heer
Q **Do you like this?**	Magst du das? mahkst doo das
A **I (don't) like that.**	Das mag ich (nicht). das mahk ikh (nikht)
Do you have (a condom)?	Hast du (ein Kondom)? hast doo (ain kon·*dawm*)

Let's use (a condom).	Lass uns (ein Kondom) benutzen.
	las uns (ain kon·*dawm*) be·*nu*·tsen
I won't do it without protection.	Ohne Kondom mache ich es nicht.
	aw·ne kon·*dawm ma*·khe ikh es nikht
Please (don't) stop!	Bitte hör (nicht) auf.
	bi·te her (nikht) owf
I think we should stop now.	Ich denke, wir sollten jetzt aufhören.
	ikh *deng*·ke veer *zol*·ten yetst *owf*·her·ren
Oh yeah!	Oh ja!
	aw yah
That's great.	Das ist geil.
	das ist gail
Easy tiger!	Sachte!
	zakh·te
That was amazing.	Das war fantastisch.
	das vahr fan·*tas*·tish

Love

I think we're good together.	Ich glaube, wir passen gut zueinander.
	ikh *glow*·be veer *pa*·sen goot tsu·ai·*nan*·der
I love you.	Ich liebe dich.
	ikh *lee*·be dikh
Will you go out with me?	Willst du mit mir gehen?
	vilst doo mit meer *gay*·en
Will you marry me?	Willst du mich heiraten?
	vilst doo mikh *hai*·ra·ten

Beliefs & Culture

KEY PHRASES

What's your religion?	Was ist Ihre/deine Religion? pol/inf	vas ist ee·re/ dai·ne re·li·gyawn
I'm (not) ...	Ich bin (kein/ keine) ... m/f	ikh bin (kain/ kai·ne) ...
I'm sorry, it's against my beliefs.	Es tut mir Leid, das ist gegen meine Anschauungen.	es toot meer lait das ist gay·gen mai·ne an·show·ung·en

Religion

Q What's your religion?
Was ist Ihre/deine Religion? pol/inf
vas ist ee·re/dai·ne re·li·gyawn

A I'm (not) ...
Ich bin (kein/keine) ... m/f
ikh bin (kain/kai·ne) ...

agnostic	Agnostiker(in) m/f	a·gnos·ti·ker/ a·gnos·ti·ke·rin
Buddhist	Buddhist(in) m/f	bu·dist/bu·dis·tin
Catholic	Katholik(in) m/f	ka·to·leek/ ka·to·lee·kin
Christian	Christ(in) m/f	krist/kris·tin
Hindu	Hindu m&f	hin·du
Jewish	Jude/Jüdin m/f	yoo·de/yü·din
Muslim	Moslem/Moslime m/f	mos·lem/ mos·lee·me

A I'm (not) religious.
Ich bin (nicht) religiös.
ikh bin (nikht) re·li·gyers

A I (don't) believe in God.	Ich glaube (nicht) an Gott.	ikh *glow*·be (nikht) an got
Where can I ...?	Wo kann ich ...?	vaw kan ikh ...

attend mass	eine Messe besuchen	*ai*·ne *me*·se be·*zoo*·khen
attend service	einen Gottesdienst besuchen	*ai*·nen go·tes·deenst be·*zoo*·khen
pray	beten	*bay*·ten
worship	meine Andacht verrichten	*mai*·ne *an*·dakht ter·*rikh*·ten

SOCIAL BELIEFS & CULTURE

Cultural Differences

Is this a local custom?	Ist das ein örtlicher Brauch? ist das ain *ert*·li·kher browkh
I'm not used to this.	Das ist ganz ungewohnt für mich. das ist gants un·ge·vawnt für mikh
I'll try it.	Ich versuche es. ikh fer·*zoo*·khe es
I'm sorry, I didn't mean to do/say anything wrong.	Es tut mir Leid, ich wollte nichts Falsches tun/sagen. es toot meer lait ikh *vol*·te nikhts *fal*·shes toon/*zah*·gen
I'm sorry, it's against my beliefs.	Es tut mir Leid, das ist gegen meine Anschauungen. es toot meer lait das ist *gay*·gen *mai*·ne *an*·show·ung·en

SOCIAL SPORTS

Sports

KEY PHRASES

What sport do you play?	Was für Sport treiben Sie? pol	vas für shport *trai*·ben zee
	Was für Sport treibst du? inf	vas für shport traipst doo
Who's your favourite team?	Was ist Ihre/deine Lieblings-mannschaft? pol/inf	vas ist *ee*·re/*dai*·ne *leep*·lingks·man·shaft
What's the score?	Wie steht es?	vee shtayt es

Sporting Interests

Q **What sport do you play?**	Was für Sport treiben Sie? pol
	vas für shport *trai*·ben zee
	Was für Sport treibst du? inf
	vas für shport traipst doo
A **I play ...**	Ich spiele ...
	ikh *shpee*·le ...
A **I follow ...**	Ich interessiere mich für ...
	ikh in·tre·*see*·re mikh für ...

basketball	Basketball	*bahs*·ket·bal
football (soccer)	Fußball	*foos*·bal
ice hockey	Eishockey	*ais*·ho·ki
tennis	Tennis	*te*·nis

For more sports, see the **dictionary**.

Q Do you like (sport)?	Mögen Sie (Sport)? pol *mer·gen zee* (shport) Magst du (Sport)? inf mahkst doo (shport)
A Yes, very much.	Ja, sehr. yah zair
A Not really.	Nicht besonders. nikht be·*zon*·ders
A I like watching it.	Ich sehe es mir gerne an. ikh *zay*·e es meer *ger*·ne an
Who's your favourite sportsperson?	Wer ist Ihr/dein Lieblingssportler? pol/inf vair ist eer/dain *leep*·lingks·shport·ler
Who's your favourite team?	Was ist Ihre/deine Lieblingsmannschaft? pol/inf vas ist *ee*·re/*dai*·ne *leep*·lingks·man·shaft
Can you play (football/ soccer)?	Spielen Sie (Fußball)? pol *shpee*·len zee (*foos*·bal) Spielst du (Fußball)? inf *shpeelst* doo (*foos*·bal)

Going to a Game

Would you like to go to a game?	Möchten Sie zu einem Spiel gehen? pol *merkh*·ten zee tsoo *ai*·nem shpeel *gay*·en Möchtest du zu einem Spiel gehen? inf merkh·test doo tsoo *ai*·nem shpeel *gay*·en

Who are you supporting?	Wen unterstützen Sie? pol vayn un·ter·*shtü*·tsen zee Wen unterstützt du? inf vayn un·ter·*shtütst* doo
Who's playing?	Wer spielt? vair speelt
Who's winning?	Wer gewinnt? vair ge·*vint*
What a ...!	Was für ...! vas für ...

goal	ein Tor	ain tawr
hit	ein Treffer	ain *tre*·fer
kick	ein Schuss	ain shus
pass	ein Pass	ain pas

What's the score?	Wie steht es? vee shtayt es
That was a bad/great game!	Das war ein schlechtes/tolles Spiel! das vahr ain *shlekh*·tes/*to*·les shpeel
What was the final score?	Was war das Endergebnis? vas vahr das *ent*·er·gayp·nis

Playing Sport

🔲 **Do you want to play?**	Möchten Sie mitspielen? pol *merkh*·ten zee *mit*·shpee·len Möchtest du mitspielen? inf *merkh*·test doo *mit*·shpee·len
🅰 **Yes, that'd be great.**	Ja, das wäre toll. yah das *vair*·re tol

I'm sorry, I can't.	Es tut mir Leid, ich kann nicht. es toot meer lait ikh kan nikht
I have an injury.	Ich habe eine Verletzung. ikh *hah*·be *ai*·ne fer·*le*·tsung
Can I join in?	Kann ich mitspielen? kan ikh *mit*·shpee·len
Your point.	Ihr/Dein Punkt. pol/inf eer/dain pungkt
My point.	Mein Punkt. main pungkt
Kick/Pass it to me!	Hierher! *heer*·hair
Thanks for the game.	Vielen Dank für das Spiel. *fee*·len dangk für das shpeel
Where's the nearest gym?	Wo ist das nächste Fitness-Studio? vaw ist das *naykhs*·te *fit*·nes shtoo·di·o
Where's the nearest swimming pool?	Wo ist das nächste Schwimmbad? vaw ist das *naykhs*·te *shvim*·baht
Where's the nearest tennis court?	Wo ist der nächste Tennisplatz? vaw ist dair *naykhs*·te *te*·nis·plats
Where's the best place to jog/run around here?	Wo kann man hier am besten joggen/laufen? vaw kan man heer am *bes*·ten *dzho*·gen/*low*·fen
Where are the change rooms?	Wo sind die Umkleideräume? vaw zint dee *um*·klai·de·roy·me

What's the charge per hour/day?	Wie viel kostet es pro Stunde/Tag?	vee feel *kos*·tet es praw *shtun*·de/tahk
What's the charge per game/visit?	Wie viel kostet es pro Spiel/Besuch?	vee feel *kos*·tet es praw shpeel/be·*zookh*
Can I hire a ...?	Kann ich ...?	kan ikh ...

ball	einen Ball leihen	*ai*·nen bal *lai*·en
bicycle	ein Fahrrad leihen	ain *fahr*·raht *lai*·en
court	einen Platz mieten	*ai*·nen plats *mee*·ten
racquet	einen Schläger leihen	*ai*·nen *shlay*·ger *lai*·en

Soccer/Football

Who plays for (Bayern München)?	Wer spielt für (Bayern München)?	vair shpeelt für (*bai*·ern *mün*·khen)
Which team is at the top of the league?	Welcher Verein steht an der Tabellenspitze?	*vel*·kher fer·*ain* shtayt an dair ta·*be*·len·shpi·tse
What a terrible team!	Was für eine furchtbare Mannschaft!	vas für *ai*·ne *furkht*·bah·re *man*·shaft
She's a great player.	Sie ist eine tolle Spielerin.	zee ist ain·e *to*·le *shpee*·ler·in

CULTURE TIP

König Fußball

The king of German amateur and professional sports is *König Fußball* ker·nikh *foos*·bal (king football). Football (or soccer, as it's known in the US and Australia) is played at thousands of amateur clubs known as *Fußballvereine foos*·bal·fe·rai·ne. Germans are passionate about the game and professional games draw around 25,000 fans. One of the longest words in the German language is also from the football sphere. Try getting your tongue around this: *Fußballweltmeisterschaftsqualifikationsspiel foos*·bal·*velt*·mais·ter·shafts·kva·li·fi·ka·*tsyawns*·shpeel (FIFA World Cup qualifying game).

He played brilliantly in the match against (Italy).	Im Spiel gegen (Italien) hat er fantastisch gespielt. im shpeel gay·gen (i·*tah*·li·en) hat air fan·*tas*·tish ge·*shpeelt*
She scored (three) goals.	Sie hat (drei) Tore geschossen. zee hat (drai) *taw*·re ge·*sho*·sen
corner	Ecke f *e*·ke
free kick	Freistoß m *frai*·shtaws
goalkeeper	Torhüter(in) m/f *tawr*·hü·ter/*tawr*·hü·te·rin
offside	Abseits n *ap*·zaits
penalty	Strafstoß m *shtrahf*·shtaws
3–1	drai tsoo ains 3:1 (drei zu eins)

Outdoors

KEY PHRASES

Do we need a guide?	Brauchen wir einen Führer?	*brow*·khen veer *ai*·nen *fü*·rer
I'm lost.	Ich habe mich verlaufen.	ikh *hah*·be mikh fer·*low*·fen
What's the weather like?	Wie ist das Wetter?	vee ist das *ve*·ter

Hiking

Where can I ...?		Wo kann ich ...? vaw kan ikh ...
buy supplies	Vorräte einkaufen	*fawr*·ray·te *ain*·kow·fen
find out about hiking trails	Informationen über Wanderwege bekommen	in·for·ma·*tsyaw*·nen *ü*·ber van·der·*vay*·ge be·*ko*·men
find someone who knows this area	jemanden finden, der die Gegend kennt	*yay*·man·den *fin*·den dair dee *gay*·gent kent
get a map	eine Karte bekommen	*ai*·ne *kar*·te be·*ko*·men
hire hiking gear	Wanderausrüstung leihen	van·der·ows·*rüs*·tung *lai*·en

CULTURE TIP

Pools & Spas

Aquatic pursuits are popular in Germany and it's hard to find a town that doesn't have a public *Schwimmbad shvim*·baht (swimming pool). Often there's a *Hallenbad ha*·len·baht (indoor pool) alongside the *Freibad frai*·baht (outdoor pool). Spas are popular too, with people seeking to cure a variety of conditions. The most famous spa town in Germany is called *Baden Baden bah*·den *bah*·den. This double-barrelled name represents both the name of the surrounding region and the German word for bathing.

Do we need to take food/water?	Müssen wir Essen/Wasser mitnehmen? *mü*·sen veer *e*·sen/*va*·ser *mit*·nay·men
How long is the trail?	Wie lang ist der Weg? vee lang ist dair vayk
How high is the climb?	Wie hoch führt die Klettertour hinauf? vee hawkh fürt dee *kle*·ter·toor hi·*nowf*
Do we need a guide?	Brauchen wir einen Führer? *brow*·khen veer *ai*·nen *fü*·rer
Are there guided treks?	Gibt es geführte Wanderungen? gipt es ge·*für*·te *van*·de·rung·en
Is it safe?	Ist es ungefährlich? ist es *un*·ge·*fair*·likh
Is there a hut there?	Gibt es dort eine Hütte? gipt es dort *ai*·ne *hü*·te
When does it get dark?	Wann wird es dunkel? van virt es *dung*·kel
Is the track (well-) marked?	Ist der Weg (gut) markiert? ist dair vayk (goot) mar·*keert*

Is the track open/ scenic?	Ist der Weg offen/schön? ist dair vayk o·fen/shern
Which is the easiest route?	Welches ist die einfachste Route? vel·khes ist dee ain·fakhs·te roo·te
Which is the most interesting route?	Welches ist die interessanteste Route? vel·khes ist dee in·te·re·san·tes·te roo·te
Where's the nearest village?	Wo ist das nächste Dorf? vaw ist das naykhs·te dorf
Where have you come from?	Wo kommen Sie gerade her? pol vaw ko·men zee ge·rah·de hair Wo kommst du gerade her? inf vaw komst doo ge·rah·de hair
How long did it take?	Wie lange hat das gedauert? vee lang·e hat das ge·dow·ert
Does this path go to ...?	Führt dieser Weg nach ...? fürt dee·zer vayk nahkh ...
Can we go through here?	Können wir hier durchgehen? ker·nen veer heer durkh·gay·en
Is the water OK to drink?	Kann man das Wasser trinken? kan man das va·ser tring·ken
I'm lost.	Ich habe mich verlaufen. ikh hah·be mikh fer·low·fen

At the Beach

Where's the best/ nearest beach?	Wo ist der beste/nächste Strand? vaw ist dair bes·te/naykhs·te shtrant
Do we have to pay?	Müssen wir bezahlen? mü·sen veer be·tsah·len

🔍 LOOK FOR

Schwimmen verboten!	shvi·men fer·*baw*·ten	No Swimming!
Sturmwarnung!	shturm *var*·nunk	Storm Warning!

Is it safe to dive/swim here?	Kann man hier gefahrlos tauchen/schwimmen? kan man heer ge·*fahr*·laws *tow*·khen/*shvi*·men
What time is high/ low tide?	Wann ist Flut/Ebbe? van ist floot/*e*·be
How much for a chair/ umbrella?	Was kostet ein Stuhl/Schirm? vas *kos*·tet ain shtool/shirm

Weather

Q What's the weather like?	Wie ist das Wetter? vee ist das *ve*·ter
A It's ...	Es ist ... es ist ...

cloudy	wolkig	*vol*·kikh
cold	kalt	kalt
freezing	eiskalt	*ais*·kalt
hot	heiß	hais
raining	regnerisch	*rayg*·ne·rish
sunny	sonnig	*zo*·nikh
warm	warm	varm
windy	windig	*vin*·dikh

It's snowing.	Es schneit.
	es shnait
What's the weather forecast?	Wie ist der Wetterbericht?
	vee ist dair *ve*·ter·be·rikht
Will it be ... tomorrow?	Wird es morgen ... sein?
	virt es *mor*·gen ... zain
Will it be snowing tomorrow?	Wird es morgen schneien?
	virt es *mor*·gen *shnai*·en
Where can I buy an umbrella?	Wo kann ich einen Regenschirm kaufen?
	vaw kan ikh *ai*·nen *ray*·gen·shirm *kow*·fen

Flora & Fauna

| **What ... is that?** | Wie heißt ...? |
| | vee haist ... |

animal	dieses Tier	*dee*·zes teer
bird	dieser Vogel	*dee*·zer *faw*·gel
flower	diese Blume	*dee*·ze *bloo*·me
plant	diese Pflanze	*dee*·ze *pflan*·tse
tree	dieser Baum	*dee*·zer bowm

Is it common?	Ist es weit verbreitet?
	ist es vait fer·*brai*·tet
Is it dangerous?	Ist es gefährlich?
	ist es ge·*fair*·likh
Is it protected?	Ist es geschützt?
	ist es ge·*shütst*
Can you eat it?	Kann man es essen?
	kan man es *e*·sen

For geographical and agricultural terms and names of animals and plants, see the **dictionary**.

Safe Travel

Emergencies

KEY PHRASES

Help!	Hilfe!	*hil*·fe
There's been an accident.	Es gab einen Unfall.	es gahp *ai*·nen *un*·fal
It's an emergency!	Es ist ein Notfall!	es ist ain *nawt*·fal

Help!	Hilfe! *hil*·fe
Stop!	Halt! halt
Go away!	Gehen Sie weg! *gay*·en zee vek
Thief!	Dieb! deeb
Fire!	Feuer! *foy*·er
Watch out!	Vorsicht! for·*zikht*
It's an emergency!	Es ist ein Notfall! es ist ain *nawt*·fal
There's been an accident.	Es gab einen Unfall. es gahp *ai*·nen *un*·fal
Do you have a first-aid kit?	Haben Sie einen Erste-Hilfe-Kasten? *hah*·ben zee *ai*·nen ayr·ste·*hil*·fe·ka·sten

 LOOK FOR

Polizei	po·li·*tsai*	Police
Polizeirevier	po·li·*tsai*·re·veer	Police Station
Unfallstation	un·fal·sta·*tsyawn*	Casualty

Call the police!	Rufen Sie die Polizei! *roo*·fen zee dee po·li·*tsai*
Call a doctor!	Rufen Sie einen Arzt! *roo*·fen zee *ai*·nen artst
Call an ambulance!	Rufen Sie einen Krankenwagen! *roo*·fen zee *ai*·nen *krang*·ken·vah·gen
Could you please help me/us?	Könnten Sie mir/uns bitte helfen? *kern*·ten zee meer/uns *bi*·te *hel*·fen
Where are the toilets?	Wo ist die Toilette? vo ist dee to·*a*·le·te
I have to use the telephone.	Ich muss das Telefon benutzen. ikh mus das te·le·*fawn* be·*nu*·tsen
I'm lost.	Ich habe mich verirrt. ikh *hah*·be mikh fer·*irt*

Police

KEY PHRASES

Where's the police station?	Wo ist das Polizeirevier?	vaw ist das po·li·*tsai*·re·veer
I want to contact my embassy.	Ich möchte mich mit meiner Botschaft in Verbindung setzen.	ikh *merkh*·te mikh mit *mai*·ner *bawt*·shaft in fer·*bin*·dung *ze*·tsen
My handbag was stolen.	Man hat mir meine Handtasche gestohlen.	man hat meer *mai*·ne *hant*·ta·she ge·*shtaw*·len

Where's the police station?	Wo ist das Polizeirevier? vaw ist das po·li·*tsai*·re·veer
I want to report an offence.	Ich möchte eine Straftat melden. ikh *merkh*·te *ai*·ne *shtrahf*·taht *mel*·den
I've been raped.	Ich bin vergewaltigt worden. ikh bin fer·ge·*val*·tikht *vor*·den
He has been assaulted.	Er ist angegriffen worden. air ist *an*·ge·gri·fen *vor*·den
She has been robbed.	Sie ist bestohlen worden. zee ist be·*shtaw*·len *vor*·den
It was him/her.	Es war er/sie. es vahr air/zee
My ... was/were stolen.	Man hat mir ... gestohlen. man hat meer ... ge·*shtaw*·len

I've lost my...	Ich habe ... verloren.	ikh *hah*·be ... fer·*law*·ren

bags	meine Reisetaschen	*mai*·ne *rai*·ze·ta·shen
handbag	meine Handtasche	*mai*·ne *hant*·ta·she
money	mein Geld	main gelt
passport	meinen Pass	*mai*·nen pas
purse	mein Portemonnaie	main port·mo·*nay*
wallet	meine Brieftasche	*mai*·ne *breef*·ta·she

What am I accused of?	Wessen werde ich beschuldigt? *ve*·sen *ver*·de ikh be·*shul*·dikht
I didn't do it.	Das habe ich nicht getan. das *hah*·be ikh nikht ge·*tahn*
Can I call someone?	Kann ich jemanden anrufen? kan ikh *yay*·man·den *an*·roo·ten
Can I call a lawyer?	Kann ich einen Rechtsanwalt anrufen? kan ikh *ai*·nen *rekhts*·an·valt *an*·roo·fen
I want to contact (my consulate/my embassy).	Ich möchte mich mit (meinem Konsulat/meiner Botschaft) in Verbindung setzen. ikh *merkh*·te mikh mit (*mai*·nem kon·zu·*laht*/*mai*·ner *bawt*·shaft) in fer·*bin*·dung ze·tsen
I have a prescription for this drug.	Ich habe ein Rezept für dieses Medikament. ikh *hah*·be ain re·*tsept* für *dee*·zes me·di·ka·*ment*

Health

KEY PHRASES

Where's the nearest hospital?	Wo ist das nächste Krankenhaus?	vaw ist das *naykhs*·te *krang*·ken·hows
I'm sick.	Ich bin krank.	ikh bin krangk
I need a doctor.	Ich brauche einen Arzt.	ikh *brow*·khe *ai*·nen artst
I'm allergic to ...	Ich bin allergisch gegen ...	ikh bin a·*lair*·gish *gay*·gen ...

Doctor

Where's the nearest ...?	Wo ist der/die/das nächste ...? m/f/n vaw ist dair/dee/das *naykhs*·te ...

chemist	Apotheke f	a·po·*tay*·ke
dentist	Zahnarzt m	*tsahn*·artst
doctor	Arzt m	artst
hospital	Krankenhaus n	*krang*·ken·hows
optometrist	Augenoptiker m	*ow*·gen·op·ti·ker

I need a doctor (who speaks English).	Ich brauche einen Arzt (der Englisch spricht). ikh *brow*·khe *ai*·nen artst (dair *eng*·lish shprikht)

Could I see a female doctor?	Könnte ich von einer Ärztin behandelt werden? *kern·te ikh fon ai·ner erts·tin be·han·delt ver·den*
Is there a (night) chemist nearby?	Gibt es in der Nähe eine (Nacht)Apotheke? *gipt es in dair nay·e ai·ne (nakht·)a·po·tay·ke*
I don't want a blood transfusion.	Ich möchte keine Bluttransfusion. *ikh merkh·te kai·ne bloot·trans·fu·zyawn*
Please use a new syringe.	Bitte benutzen Sie eine neue Spritze. *bi·te be·nu·tsen zee ai·ne noy·e shpri·tse*
I have my own syringe.	Ich habe meine eigene Spritze. *ikh hah·be mai·ne ai·ge·ne shpri·tse*
I've been vaccinated for ...	Ich bin gegen ... geimpft worden. *ikh bin gay·gen ... ge·impft vor·den*
He/She has been vaccinated for ...	Er/Sie ist gegen ... geimpft worden. *air/zee ist gay·gen ... ge·impft vor·den*

fever	Fieber	*fee·ber*
hepatitis A/B/C	Hepatitis A/B/C	*he·pa·tee·tis ah/bay/tsay*
tetanus	Tätanus	*tay·ta·nus*
typhoid	Typhus	*tü·fus*

I've run out of my medication.	Ich habe keine Medikamente mehr. ikh *hah*·be *kai*·ne me·di·ka·*men*·te mair
My prescription is ...	Mein Rezept ist ... main re·*tsept* ist ...

Symptoms & Conditions

I'm sick.	Ich bin krank. ikh bin krangk
My friend is sick.	Mein Freund/Meine Freundin ist krank. m/f main froynt/*mai*·ne *froyn*·din ist krangk
It hurts here.	Es tut hier weh. es toot heer *vay*
I've been vomiting.	Ich habe mich übergeben. ikh *hah*·be mikh *ü*·ber·*gay*·ben
I can't sleep.	Ich kann nicht schlafen. ikh kan nikht *shlah*·fen
I feel dizzy.	Mir ist schwindelig. meer ist *shvin*·de·likh
I feel hot and cold.	Mir ist abwechselnd heiß und kalt. meer ist *ap*·vek·selnt hais unt kalt
I feel nauseous.	Mir ist übel. meer ist *ü*·bel
I feel shivery.	Mich fröstelt. mikh *frers*·telt
I feel weak.	Ich fühle mich schwach. ikh *fü*·le mikh shvakh
I feel anxious.	Ich habe Ängste. ikh *hah*·be *engs*·te

🔊 LISTEN FOR

Was fehlt Ihnen?	vas faylt *ee*·nen What's the problem?
Wo tut es weh?	vaw toot es vay Where does it hurt?
Seit wann haben Sie diese Beschwerden?	zait van *hah*·ben zee *dee*·ze be·*shver*·den How long have you been like this?
Hatten Sie das schon einmal?	*ha*·ten zee das shawn *ain*·mahl Have you had this before?
Nehmen Sie irgendwelche Medikamente?	*nay*·men zee *ir*·gent·vel·khe me·di·ka·*men*·te Are you on medication?
Sind Sie gegen bestimmte Stoffe allergisch?	zint zee *gay*·gen be·*shtim*·te *shto*·fe a·*lair*·gish Are you allergic to anything?
Trinken Sie?	*tring*·ken zee Do you drink?
Rauchen Sie?	*row*·khen zee Do you smoke?
Nehmen Sie Drogen?	*nay*·men zee *draw*·gen Do you take drugs?
Hatten Sie ungeschützten Geschlechtsverkehr?	*ha*·ten zee *un*·ge·shüts·ten ge·*shlekhts*·fer·kair Have you had unprotected sex?

I feel depressed.	Ich bin deprimiert. ikh bin de·pri·*meert*
I feel better/worse.	Ich fühle mich besser/schlechter. ikh *fü*·le mikh *be*·ser/*shlekh*·ter

I have (a) ...	Ich habe ...	
	ikh *hah*·be ...	

diarrhoea	Durchfall	*durkh*·fal
fever	Fieber	*fee*·ber
headache	Kopfschmerzen	*kopf*·shmer·tsen
pain	Schmerzen	*shmer*·tsen

I have an infection.	Ich habe eine Infektion.
	ikh *hah*·be *ai*·ne in·fek·*tsyawn*

I have a rash.	Ich habe einen Ausschlag.
	ikh *hah*·be *ai*·nen *ows*·shlahk

I've recently had ...	Ich hatte vor kurzem ...
	ikh *ha*·te fawr *kur*·tsem ...

I'm on medication for ...	Ich nehme Medikamente gegen ...
	ikh *nay*·me me·di·ka·*men*·te *gay*·gen ...

For more symptoms and conditions, see the **dictionary**.

Women's Health

(I think) I'm pregnant.	(Ich glaube,) Ich bin schwanger.
	(ikh *glow*·be) ikh bin *shvang*·er

I'm on the Pill.	Ich nehme die Pille.
	ikh *nay*·me dee *pi*·le

I haven't had my period for ... weeks.	Ich habe seit ... Wochen meine Periode nicht gehabt.
	ikh *hah*·be zait ... *vo*·khen *mai*·ne pe·ri·*aw*·de nikht ge·*hahpt*

I have period pain.	Ich habe Regelschmerzen.
	ikh *hah*·be *ray*·gel·shmer·tsen

 **LISTEN FOR**

Benutzen Sie Verhütungsmittel?	be·*nu*·tsen zee fer·*hü*·tungks·mi·tel	Are you using contraception?
Haben Sie Ihre Periode?	*hah*·ben zee ee·re pe·ri·*aw*·de	Arc you menstruating?
Wann hatten Sie Ihre letzte Periode?	van *ha*·ten zee ee·re *lets*·te pe·ri·*aw*·de	When did you last have your period?
Sie sind schwanger.	zee zint *shvang*·er	You're pregnant.

pregnancy test	Schwangerschafts·test m *shvang*·er·shafts·test
the morning-after pill	die Pille danach f dee *pi*·le da·*nahkh*
contraception	Verhütungsmittel n fer·*hü*·tungks·mi·tel

Allergies

I have a skin allergy.	Ich habe eine Hautallergie. ikh *hah*·be ai·ne *howt*·a·ler·gee
I'm allergic to ...	Ich bin allergisch gegen ... ikh bin a·*lair*·gish *gay*·gen ...

antibiotics	Antibiotika	an·ti·bi·*aw*·ti·ka
anti-inflammatories	entzündungs-hemmende Mittel	en·*tsün*·dungks·he·men·de *mi*·tel
aspirin	Aspirin	as·pi·*reen*
bees	Bienen	*bee*·nen
codeine	Kodein	ko·de·*een*
penicillin	Penizillin	pe·ni·tsi·*leen*
pollen	Pollen	*po*·len

antihistamines	Antihistamine n pl *an·ti·his·ta·mee·ne*
inhaler	Inhalator m *in·ha·lah·tor*
injection	Injektion f *in·yek·tsyawn*
sulphur-based drugs	schwefel-basierte Arzneimittel n pl *shvay·fel·ba·zeer·te* *arts·nai·mi·tel*

For food-related allergies, see **special diets & allergies** (p185).

Parts of the Body

My ... hurts.	Mir tut der/die/das ... weh. m/f/n *meer toot dair/dee/das ...* *vay*
I can't move my ...	Ich kann meinen/meine/mein ... nicht bewegen. m/f/n *ikh kan mai·nen/mai·ne/main ...* *nikht be·vay·gen*
I have a cramp in my ...	Ich habe einen Krampf in meinem/meiner/meinem ... m/f/n *ikh hah·be ai·nen krampf in* *mai·nem/mai·ner/mai·nem ...*
My ... is swollen.	Mein/Meine/Mein ... ist geschwollen. m/f/n *main/mai·ne/main ... ist* *ge·shvo·len*

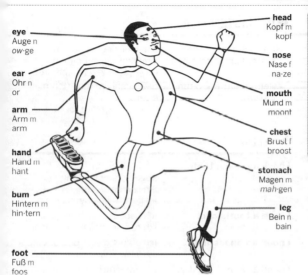

eye
Auge n
ow·ge

ear
Ohr n
or

arm
Arm m
arm

hand
Hand m
hant

bum
Hintern m
hin·tern

foot
Fuß m
foos

head
Kopf m
kopf

nose
Nase f
na·ze

mouth
Mund m
moont

chest
Brust f
broost

stomach
Magen m
mah·gen

leg
Bein n
bain

Chemist

I need something for ...	Ich brauche etwas gegen ... ikh *brow*·khe et·vas *gay*·gen ...
Do I need a prescription for ...?	Brauche ich für ... ein Rezept? *brow*·khe ikh für ... ain re·*tsept*
How many times a day?	Wie oft am Tag? vee oft am tahk
Will it make me drowsy?	Macht es müde? makht es *mü*·de

For pharmaceutical items, see the **dictionary**.

🔊 LISTEN FOR

Haben Sie das schon einmal eingenommen?	*hah*·ben zee das shawn *ain*·mahl *ain*·ge·no·men Have you taken this before?
Zweimal am Tag (zum Essen).	*tsvai*·mahl am tahk (tsum e·sen) Twice a day (with food).

Dentist

I have a broken tooth.	Ich habe einen abgebrochenen Zahn. ikh *hah*·be *ai*·nen *ap*·ge·bro·khe·nen tsahn
I have a toothache.	Ich habe Zahnschmerzen. ikh *hah*·be *tsahn*·shmer·tsen
I need an anaesthetic.	Ich brauche eine Betäubung. ikh *brow*·khe *ai*·ne be·*toy*·bung
I need a filling.	Ich brauche eine Füllung. ikh *brow*·khe *ai*·ne *fü*·lung
I've lost a filling.	Ich habe eine Füllung verloren. ikh *hah*·be ai·ne *fü*·lung fer·*law*·ren
My dentures are broken.	Mein Gebiss ist zerbrochen. main ge·*bis* ist tser·*bro*·khen
I don't want it extracted.	Ich will ihn nicht ziehen lassen. ikh vil een nikht *tsee*·en *la*·sen
My gums hurt.	Das Zahnfleisch tut mir weh. das *tsahn*·flaish toot meer vay

Food

Eating Out

KEY PHRASES

Can you recommend a restaurant?	Können Sie ein Restaurant empfehlen? pol	ker·nen zee ain res·to·*rang* emp·*fay*·len
	Kannst du ein Restaurant empfehlen? inf	kanst doo ain res·to·*rang* emp·*fay*·len
I'd like a table for (two), please.	Ich hätte gern einen Tisch für (zwei) Personen, bitte.	ikh *he*·te gern *ai*·nen tish für (tsvai) per·*zaw*·nen *bi*·te
Can I see the menu, please?	Kann ich die Speisekarte sehen, bitte?	kan ikh dee *shpai*·ze·*kar*·te *zay*·en *bi*·te
I'd like ...	Ich möchte ...	ikh *merkh*·te ...
Please bring the bill.	Bitte bringen Sie die Rechnung.	*bi*·te *bring*·en zee dee *rekh*·nung

Basics

breakfast	Frühstück n *frü*·shtük
lunch	Mittagessen n *mi*·tahk·e·sen
dinner	Abendessen n *ah*·bent·e·sen
snack	Snack m snek

eat/drink	essen/trinken *e·sen/tring·ken*
daily special	Gericht n des Tages *ge·rikht des tah·ges*
set menu	Menü n *may·nü*
I'd like ...	Ich möchte ... *ikh merkh·te ...*
Enjoy your meal!	Guten Appetit! *goo·ten a·pay·teet*
I'm starving!	Ich bin am Verhungern! *ikh bin am fer·hung·ern*

Finding a Place to Eat

Can you recommend a bar/pub?	Können Sie eine Kneipe empfehlen? *ker·nen zee ai·ne knai·pe emp·fay·len*
Can you recommend a coffee bar?	Kannst du eine Espressobar empfehlen? inf *kanst doo ai·ne es·pre·so·bahr emp·fay·len*

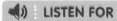 **LISTEN FOR**

Es tut mir Leid, wir haben geschlossen.	es toot meer lait veer hah·ben ge·shlo·sen Sorry, we're closed.
Wir haben keinen Tisch frei.	veer hah·ben kai·nen tish frai We have no free tables.
Wir sind voll ausgebucht.	veer zint fol ows·ge·bookht We're fully booked.
Wo möchten Sie sitzen?	vaw merkh·ten zee zi·tsen Where would you like to sit?

FOOD EATING OUT

Can you recommend a restaurant?	Kannst du ein Restaurant empfehlen? inf kanst doo ain res·to·*rang* emp·*fay*·len
Where would you go for a cheap meal?	Wo kann man hingehen, um etwas Billiges zu essen? vaw kan man *hin*·gay·en um *et*·vas *bi*·li·ges tsoo *e*·sen
Where would you go for local specialities?	Wo kann man hingehen, um örtliche Spezialitäten zu essen? vaw kan man *hin*·gay·en um *ert*·li·khe shpe·tsya·li·*tay*·ten tsoo *e*·sen
Are you still serving food?	Gibt es noch etwas zu essen? gipt es nokh *et*·vas tsoo *e*·sen
How long is the wait?	Wie lange muss man warten? vee *lang*·e mus man *var*·ten

At the Restaurant

I'd like to reserve a table for (two) people.	Ich möchte einen Tisch für (zwei) Personen reservieren. ikh *merkh*·te *ai*·nen tish für (tsvai) per·*zaw*·nen re·zer·*vee*·ren
I'd like to reserve a table for (eight) o'clock.	Ich möchte einen Tisch für (acht) Uhr reservieren. ikh *merkh*·te *ai*·nen tish für (akht) oor re·zer·*vee*·ren
I'd like a table for (two), please.	Ich hätte gern einen Tisch für (zwei) Personen, bitte. ikh *he*·te gern *ai*·nen tish für (tsvai) per·*zaw*·nen *bi*·te

✂ **For two, please.** Für zwei, bitte. für tsvai *bi*·te

🔊 LISTEN FOR

Was darf ich Ihnen bringen?	vas darf ikh *ee*·nen *bring*·en What can I get for you?
Ich empfehle Ihnen ...	ikh emp·*fay*·le *ee*·nen ... I suggest the ...
Mögen Sie ...?	*mer*·gen zee ... Do you like ...?
Wie möchten Sie das zubereitet haben?	vee *merkh*·ten zee das *tsoo*·be·rai·tet *hah*·ben How would you like that cooked?
Bitte!	*bi*·te Here you go!

I'd like the nonsmoking section, please.	Ich hätte gern einen Nichtrauchertisch, bitte. ikh *he*·te gern *ai*·nen *nikht*·row·kher·tish *bi*·te
I'd like the smoking section, please.	Ich hätte gern einen Rauchertisch, bitte. ikh *he*·te gern *ai*·nen *row*·kher·tish *bi*·te
Do you have a menu in English?	Haben Sie eine englische Speisekarte? *hah*·ben zee *ai*·ne *eng*·li·she *shpai*·ze·kar·te
Do you have children's meals?	Haben Sie Kinderteller? *hah*·ben zee *kin*·der·te·ler
I'd like the drink list, please.	Ich hätte gern die Getränkekarte, bitte. ikh *he*·te gern dee ge·*treng*·ke·kar·te *bi*·te

🔍 LOOK FOR

Beilagen	*bai*·lah·gen	Side Dishes
Hauptgerichte	*howpt*·ge·rikh·te	Main Courses
Nachspeisen	*nahkh*·shpai·zen	Desserts
Salate	za·*lah*·te	Salads
Suppen	*zu*·pen	Soups
Vorspeisen	*fawr*·shpai·zen	Appetisers

I'd like the menu, please.	Ich hätte gern die Speisekarte, bitte.
	ikh *he*·te gern dee *shpai*·ze·kar·te *bi*·te

✂ **Menu, please.** | Die Karte, bitte. | dee *kar*·te *bi*·te

What would you recommend?	Was empfehlen Sie?
	vas emp·*fay*·len zee
I'll have what they're having.	Ich nehme das gleiche wie sie.
	ikh *nay*·me das *glai*·khe vee zee
I'd like a local speciality.	Ich möchte etwas Typisches aus der Region.
	ikh *merkh*·te et·vas *tü*·pi·shes ows dair re·*gyawn*
Can you tell me which traditional foods I should try?	Können Sie mir sagen, welche traditionellen Speisen ich probieren sollte?
	ker·nen zee meer *zah*·gen *vel*·khe tra·di·tsyo·*ne*·len *shpai*·zen ikh pro·*bee*·ren *zol*·te
What's in that dish?	Was ist in diesem Gericht?
	vas ist in *dee*·zem ge·*rikht*

Eating Out

Can I see the menu, please?

Kann ich die Speisekarte sehen, bitte?
kan ikh dee *shpai·ze·kar·te* zay·en *bi·*te

What would you recommend for ...?

Was würden Sie als ... empfehlen?
vas *vür·*den zee als ... emp·*fay·*len

 the main meal
Hauptgericht
*howpt·*ge·rikht

 dessert
Dessert
de·*sairt*

 drinks
Getränk
ge·*trengk*

Can you bring me some ..., please?

Bitte bringen Sie ...
*bi·*te *bring·*en zee ...

I'd like the bill, please.

Ich hätte gern die Rechnung, bitte.
ikh *he·*te gern dee *rekh·*nung *bi·*te

Does it take long to prepare?	Dauert das lange? dow·ert das lang·e
Are these complimentary?	Sind die gratis? zint dee grah·tis
We're just having drinks.	Wir möchten nur etwas trinken. veer merkh·ten noor et·vas tring·ken

| ✂ Just drinks. | Nur Getränke. | noor ge·treng·ke |

Requests

| I'd like it ... | Ich hätte es gern ... ikh he·te es gern ... |
| I don't want it ... | Ich möchte es nicht ... ikh merkh·te es nikht ... |

boiled	gekocht	ge·kokht
broiled	gegrillt	ge·grilt
deep-fried	frittiert	fri·teert
fried	gebraten	ge·brah·ten
grilled	gegrillt	ge·grilt
mashed	püriert	pü·reert
medium	halb durch	halp durkh
rare	englisch	eng·lish
re-heated	aufgewärmt	owf·ge·vermt
steamed	gedämpft	ge·dempft
well-done	gut durchgebraten	goot durkh· ge·brah·ten
with the dressing on the side	mit dem Dressing daneben	mit daym dre·sing da·nay·ben
without ...	ohne ...	aw·ne ...

FOOD EATING OUT

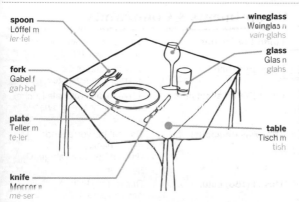

spoon
Löffel m
ler·fel

wineglass
Weinglas n
vain·glahs

glass
Glas n
glahs

fork
Gabel f
gah·bel

plate
Teller m
te·ler

table
Tisch m
tish

knife
Messer n
me·ser

Please bring a cloth.	Bitte bringen Sie eine Tischdecke. *bi·te bring·en zee ai·ne tish·de·ke*
Please bring a (wine) glass.	Bitte bringen Sie ein (Wein) Glas. *bi·te bring·en zee ain (vain·) glahs*
Is there any ...?	Gibt es ...? *gipt es ...*

chilli sauce	Chilisauce	*chi·li·zaw·se*
ketchup	Ketchup	*ket·chap*
pepper	Pfeffer	*pfe·fer*
salt	Salz	zalts
vinegar	Essig	*e·sikh*

For other specific requests, see **vegetarian & special meals** (p184).

Compliments & Complaints

I didn't order this.	Das habe ich nicht bestellt.
	das *hah*·be ikh nikht be·*shtelt*
I love this dish.	Ich mag dieses Gericht.
	ikh mahk *dee*·zes ge·*rikht*
I love the local cuisine.	Ich mag die regionale Küche.
	ikh mahk dee re·gyo·*nah*·le *kü*·khe
That was delicious!	Das hat hervorragend geschmeckt!
	das hat her·*fawr*·rah·gent ge·*shmekt*
This is (too) cold.	Das ist (zu) kalt.
	das ist (tsoo) kalt
This is spicy.	Das ist scharf.
	das ist sharf
This is superb.	Das ist exzellent.
	das ist ek·se·*lent*
My compliments to the chef.	Mein Kompliment an den Koch.
	main kom·pli·*ment* an dayn kokh
I'm full.	Ich bin satt.
	ikh bin zat

Paying the Bill

Please bring the bill.	Bitte bringen Sie die Rechnung.
	bi·te *bring*·en zee dee *rekh*·nung

✄	**Bill, please.**	Die Rechnung, bitte.	dee *rekh*·nung *bi*·te

FOOD

EATING OUT

 LOOK FOR

One of Germany's favourite and most famous foods is the not-so-humble *Wurst* (sausage). There are over 1500 types. Some of the more common:

Blutwurst f	*bloot·*vurst	blood sausage
Bockwurst f	*bok·*vurst	pork sausage
Bratwurst f	*braht·*vurst	fried pork sausage
Bregenwurst f	*bray·gen·*vurst	brain sausage
Cervelatwurst f	*ser·ve·laht·*vurst	sausage of spicy pork and beef
Katenwurst f	*kah·ten·*vurst	country-style smoked sausage
Knackwurst f	*knak·*vurst	mildly garlic-flavoured sausage
Krakauer f	*krah·kow·*er	thick, paprika-spiced sausage of Polish origin
Landjäger m	*lant·yay·*ger	thin, long, hard spicy sausage
Leberwurst f	*lay·ber·*vurst	liver sausage
Regensburger m	*ray·gens·bur·*ger	highly spiced smoked sausage
Rotwurst f	*rawt·*vurst	black pudding
Thüringer f	*tü·ring·*er	long, thin spicy sausage
Wiener Würstchen n	*vee·*ner *vürst·*khen	frankfurter (small smoked sausage)
Weißwurst f	*vais·*vurst	veal sausage
Würstchen n	*vürst·*khen	small sausage
Zwiebelwurst f	*tsvee·bel·*vurst	liver and onion sausage

FOOD EATING OUT

Is service included in the bill?	Ist die Bedienung inbegriffen? ist dee be·*dee*·nung *in*·be·gri·fen

Nonalcoholic Drinks

(boiled) water	(heißes) Wasser n (*hai*·ses) *va*·ser
mineral water	Mineralwasser n mi·ne·*rahl*·va·ser
soft drink	Softdrink m *soft*·dringk
coffee	Kaffee m *ka*·fay
tea	Tee m tay
with (milk)	mit (Milch) mit (milkh)
without (sugar)	ohne (Zucker) *aw*·ne (*tsu*·ker)

Alcoholic Drinks

beer	Bier n beer
light beer	Leichtbier n *laikht*·beer
nonalcoholic beer	alkoholfreies Bier n al·ko·*hawl*·frai·es beer
pilsner/lager	Pils n pils

CULTURE TIP

Soft Drinks
In Germany, *Softdrink soft*·dringk (soft drink) only designates sweet fizzy drinks, such as lemonade or cola. Mineral water is known as *ein alkoholfreies Getränk* ain al·ko·*hawl*·frai·es ge·*trengk* (a nonalcoholic drink).

wheat beer		Weißbier n
		vais·beer
brandy		Weinbrand m
		vahn·brant
(French) champagne		Champagner m
		sham·pan·yer
cocktail		Cocktail m
		kok·tayl
sparkling wine		Sekt m
		zekt
a shot of (gin)		einen (Gin)
		ai·nen (dzhin)
a beer on tap		ein Bier vom Fass
		ain beer fom fas
a ... (of) beer		ein ... Bier
		ain ... beer

glass	Glas	glahs
large	großes	*graw*·ses
pint	halbes	*halb*·es
small	kleines	*klai*·nes

🔍 LOOK FOR

Alkoholfreies Bier n	al·ko·*hawl*·frai·es beer nonalcoholic beer
Alster(wasser) n	*als*·ter(·va·ser) mixture of pilsner and orange lemonade
Alt(bier) n	*alt*(·beer) amber-coloured speciality beer from Düsseldorf, with a strong taste of hops
Altbierbowle f	*alt*·beer·baw·le Altbier with strawberries or other fruit
Alt-Schuss n	alt·*shus* Altbier with a shot of syrup or Malzbier
Berliner Weiße f	ber·*lee*·ner *vai*·se slightly fizzy and cloudy, often served with a shot of raspberry (rot) or woodruff (grün) syrup
Bockbier n	*bok*·beer light or dark beer with a high alcohol content
Eisbock m	*ais*·bok Bockbier from which water has been extracted by freezing thus increasing its alcoholic potency
Export n	eks·*port* lager
Gose f	*gaw*·ze wheat beer from Leipzig
Hefeweizen n	*hay*·fe·vai·tsen cloudy wheat beer – comes in light (hell) or dark (dunkel) varieties

Helles n	*he·les*	lager (Bavaria)
Kölsch n	kerlsh	yellow-golden coloured beer from Cologne
Kräusen n	*kroy·zen*	unfiltered beer, gold-coloured or dark
Krefelder n	*kray·fel·der*	Altbier mixed with cola
Kristallweizen n	kris·tal·vai·tsen	clear light (hell) or dark (dunkel) wheat beer
Leichtbier n	*laikht·beer*	beer with half the alcohol content of normal beer
Maibock m	*mai·bok*	special Bockbier brewed in May
Malzbier n	*malts·beer*	nonalcoholic malt beer
Märzen n	*mer·tsen*	special Bavarian beer brewed at the end of winter
Pils/ Pils(e)ner n	pils/*pil·z(e·)ner*	pilsner, similar to lager
Radler n	*raht·ler*	mixture of pilsner or lager and sweet lemonade
Rauchbier n	*rowkh·beer*	smoky-flavoured beer from Bamberg
Schwarzbier n	*shvarts·beer*	stout (lit: black beer)
Weizenbier/ Weißbier n	*vai·tsen·beer*/*vais·beer*	wheat beer

| a bottle of ... wine | eine Flasche ...
ai·ne fla·she ... |
| a glass of ... wine | ein Glas ...
ain glahs ... |

dessert	Dessertwein	*de·sair·vain*
mulled	Glühwein	*glü·vain*
red	Rotwein	*rawt·vain*
rose	Rosé	*ro·zay*
sparkling	Sekt	*zekt*
white	Weißwein	*vais·vain*

In the Bar

Excuse me!	Entschuldigung! *ent·shul·di·gung*
I'm next.	Ich bin dran. *ikh bin dran*
Q What would you like?	Was möchten Sie? pol *vas merkh·ten zee* Was möchtest du? inf *vas merkh·test doo*
A I'll have ...	Ich hätte gern ... *ikh he·te gern ...*
A Same again, please.	Dasselbe nochmal, bitte. *das·zel·be nokh·mahl bi·te*
I don't drink alcohol.	Ich trinke keinen Alkohol. *ikh tring·ke kai·nen al·ko·hawl*
No thanks, I'm driving.	Nein danke, ich fahre. *nain dang·ke ikh fah·re*
No ice, thanks.	Kein Eis, bitte. *kain ais bi·te*

CULTURE TIP

Grape Varieties
Germany is famous for its wines. There are three basic wine categories – *trocken* tro·ken (dry), *halbtrocken* halp·tro·ken (medium-dry), and *lieblich* leep·likh (sweet).

I'll buy you a drink.	Ich gebe Ihnen/dir einen aus. pol/inf ikh *gay*·be *ee*·nen/deer *ai*·nen ows
It's my round.	Diese Runde geht auf mich. *dee*·ze *run*·de gayt owf mikh
Do you serve meals here?	Gibt es hier auch etwas zu essen? gipt es heer owkh *et*·vas tsoo e·sen

FOOD EATING OUT

Drinking Up

Cheers!	Prost! prawst
This is hitting the spot.	Das kommt jetzt echt gut. das komt yetst ekht goot
I'm feeling drunk.	Ich glaube, ich bin betrunken. ikh *glow*·be ikh bin be·*trung*·ken
I feel fantastic!	Ich fühle mich fantastisch! ikh *fü*·le mikh fan·*tas*·tish
I'm tired, I'd better go home.	Ich bin müde, ich sollte besser nach Hause gehen. ikh bin *mü*·de ikh *zol*·te *be*·ser nahkh *how*·ze *gay*·en

CULTURE TIP

Dining Etiquette

The main meal of the day in German-speaking countries is *das Mittagessen* das *mi*·tahk·e·sen or lunch.

It's good manners to say *Guten Appetit goo*·ten a·pay·*teet* or *Mahlzeit mahl*·tsait (Enjoy your meal) to your fellow diners. Observing German table etiquette is easy – it's enough to eat in a basically civilized manner. It's customary, however, to keep your hands on the table at all times.

If you've really enjoyed your meal, say *Das hat geschmeckt* das hat gesh·*mekt*. To get the attention of a waiter, call out *Herr Ober* her *aw*·ber (to a man) or *Fräulein froy*·lain (to a woman). To indicate that you want to pay your bill, say *Die Rechnung bitte!* dee *rekh*·nung *bi*·te.

Germans are fond of toasts. If they break out the drink, wait until everyone is served. Then raise your glasses in unison, look your fellow toasters in the eye and give a hearty *Prost!* prawst or *Zum Wohl!* tsum vawl.

I think I've had one too many.	Ich glaube, ich habe ein bisschen zu viel getrunken. ikh *glow*·be ikh *hah*·be ain *bis*·khen tsoo feel ge·*trung*·ken
Can you call a taxi for me?	Können Sie mir ein Taxi rufen? pol *ker*·nen zee meer ain *tak*·si *roo*·fen Kannst du mir ein Taxi rufen? inf kanst doo meer ain *tak*·si *roo*·fen

Self-Catering

KEY PHRASES

What's the local speciality?	Was ist eine örtliche Spezialität?	vas ist *ai*·ne *ert*·li·khe shpe·tsya·li·*tayt*
Where can I find the ... section?	Wo kann ich die ... finden?	vaw kan ikh dee ... *fin*·den
I'd like some ...	Ich möchte etwas ...	ikh *merkh*·te *et*·vas ...

Buying Food

Where can I find the ... section?	Wo kann ich die ... finden?	vaw kan ikh dee ... *fin*·den

dairy	Abteilung für Milchprodukte	ap·*tai*·lung für *milkh*·pro·duk·te
frozen goods	Abteilung für Tiefkühlprodukte	ap·*tai*·lung für *teef*·kul·pro·duk·te
fruit and vegetable	Obst- und Gemüseabteilung	*awpst*· unt ge·*mü*·ze·ap·tai·lung
meat	Fleischabteilung	*flaish*·ap·tai·lung

Where's the health-food section?	Wo ist die Nahrungsmittel- und Drogerie-Abteilung? vaw ist dee *nah*·rungs·mi·tel· unt draw·ge·*ree*·ap·tai·lung

FOOD

SELF-CATERING

🔊 LISTEN FOR

Kann ich Ihnen helfen?	kan ikh *ee*·nen *hel*·fen Can I help you?
Was möchten Sie?	vas *merkh*·ten zee? What would you like?
Das ist aus.	das ist ows There's none left.
Möchten Sie noch etwas?	*merkh*·ten zee nokh *et*·vas Would you like anything else?

What's the local speciality?	Was ist eine örtliche Spezialität? vas ist *ai*·ne *ert*·li·khe shpe·tsya·li·*tayt*
Do you sell locally produced food?	Verkaufen Sie örtlich produzierte Lebensmittel? fer·*kow*·fen zee *ert*·likh pro·du·*tseer*·te *lay*·bens·mi·tel
Do you sell organic produce?	Verkaufen Sie Bioprodukte? fer·*kow*·fen zee *bee*·o·pro·duk·te
What's that?	Was ist das? vas ist das
Can I taste it?	Kann ich das probieren? kan ikh das pro·*bee*·ren
How much is (a kilo of cheese)?	Was kostet (ein Kilo Käse)? vas *kos*·tet (ain *kee*·lo *kay*·ze)
Do you have anything cheaper?	Haben Sie etwas Billigeres? *hah*·ben zee *et*·vas *bi*·li·ge·res
Do you have other kinds?	Haben Sie andere Sorten? *hah*·ben zee *an*·de·re *zor*·ten

How much?	Wie viel?
	vee feel
I'd like ...	Ich möchte ...
	ikh *merkh*·te ...

(200) grams	(200) Gramm	(*tsvai*·hun·dert) gram
(two) kilos	(zwei) Kilo	(tsvai) *kee*·lo
(three) pieces	(drei) Stück	(drai) shtük
(six) slices	(sechs) Scheiben	(zeks) *shai*·ben
some ...	etwas ...	*et*·vas ...

For other useful amounts, see **numbers & amounts** (p30).

FOOD

SELF-CATERING

Was ist eine örtliche Spezialität?

vas ist *ai*·ne *ert*·li·khe shpe·tsya·li·*tayt*

What's the local speciality?

A piece.	Ein Stück.
	ain shtük
A slice.	Eine Scheibe.
	ai·ne shai·be
That one.	Dieses da.
	dee·zes dah
This.	Dieses.
	dee·zes
A bit more.	Ein bisschen mehr.
	ain bis·khen mair
Less.	Weniger.
	vay·ni·ger
Enough.	Genug.
	ge·nook
Can I have a bag, please?	Könnte ich bitte eine Tüte haben?
	kern·te ikh bi·te ai·ne tü·te hah·ben

For food items see the **menu decoder** (p187), and the **dictionary**.

Cooking

| Could I please borrow a ...? | Könnte ich bitte ... ausleihen? |
| | *kern·te ikh bi·te ... ows·lai·en* |

bottle opener	einen Flaschenöffner	*ai·nen fla·shen·erf·ner*
chopping board	ein Schneidebrett	*ain shnai·de·bret*
frying pan	eine Bratpfanne	*ai·ne braht·pfa·ne*
knife	ein Messer	*ain me·ser*
saucepan	einen Kochtopf	*ai·nen kokh·topf*

LANGUAGE TIP

Tongue Twisters
If you're feeling comfortable with the language and want to impress the locals, try these tongue twisters:

Blaukraut bleibt Blaukraut und Brautkleid bleibt Brautkleid.
blow·krowt blaipt *blow*·krowt unt *browt*·klait blaipt *browt*·klait
Red cabbage remains red cabbage and a wedding dress remains a wedding dress.

Der Potsdamer Postkutscher putzt den Potsdamer Postkutschkasten.
dair *pots*·dah·mer *post*·ku·cher putst dayn *pots*·dah·mer *post*·kuch·kah·sten
The Potsdam mailcoach driver cleans the Potsdam mailcoach postboxes.

Der Dachdecker deckt dein Dach, drum dank dem Dachdecker, der dein Dach deckt.
dair *dakh*·de·ker dekt dain dakh drum dank daym *dakh*·de·ker dair dain dakh dekt
The roofer roofs your roof, for that thank the roofer, who roofs your roof.

cooked	gekocht ge·*kokht*
dried	getrocknet ge·*trok*·net
fresh	frisch frish
frozen	eingefroren *ain*·ge·fraw·ren
raw	roh raw
smoked	geräuchert ge·*roy*·khert

For more cooking terminology, see the **dictionary**.

Vegetarian & Special Meals

KEY PHRASES

Do you have vegetarian food?	Haben Sie vegetarisches Essen?	*hah*·ben zee ve·ge·*tah*·ri·shes *e*·sen
Could you prepare a meal without ...?	Können Sie ein Gericht ohne ... zubereiten?	*ker*·nen zee ain ge·*rikht aw*·ne ... *tsoo*·be·rai·ten
I'm allergic to ...	Ich bin allergisch gegen ...	ikh bin a·*lair*·gish *gay*·gen ...

Special Diets & Allergies

Is there a (vegetarian) restaurant near here?	Gibt es ein (vegetarisches) Restaurant hier in der Nähe? gipt es ain vege·*tar*·ish·shes res·to·*rang* heer in dair *nay*·e
Do you have halal food?	Haben Sie Halal Essen? *hah*·ben zee ha·*lal*·e·sen
Do you have kosher food?	Haben Sie koscheres Essen? *hah*·ben zee *kaw*·she·res *e*·sen
Do you have vegetarian food?	Haben Sie vegetarisches Essen? *hah*·ben zee ve·ge·*tah*·ri·shes *e*·sen
I'm vegan.	Ich bin Veganer(in). m/f ikh bin ve·*gah*·ner/ ve·*gah*·ne·rin

I'm vegetarian.	Ich bin Vegetarier(in). m/f
	ikh bin ve·ge·*tah*·ri·er/
	ve·ge·*tah*·ri·e·rin

I'm on a special diet.	Ich bin auf einer Spezialdiät.
	ikh bin owf *ai*·ner
	shpe·*tsyahl*·di·et

I'm allergic to ...	Ich bin allergisch gegen ...
	ikh bin a·*lair*·gish *gay*·gen ...

dairy produce	Milchprodukte	*milkh*·pro·duk·te
eggs	Eier	*ai*·er
fish	Fisch	fish
gelatin	Gelatine	zhe·la·*tee*·ne
gluten	Gluten	*gloo*·ten
honey	Honig	*haw*·nikh
MSG	Natriumglutamat	*nah*·tri·um·glu·ta·maht
nuts	Nüsse	*nü*·se
seafood	Meeresfrüchte	*mair*·res·frükh·te
shellfish	Schaltiere	*shahl*·tee·re

I don't eat ...	Ich esse kein ...
	ikh e·se kain ...

Ordering

Is it cooked with butter?	Ist es mit Butter zubereitet?
	ist es mit *bu*·ter
	tsoo·be·rai·tet

Is it cooked with eggs?	Ist es mit Eiern zubereitet?
	ist es mit *ai*·ern
	tsoo·be·rai·tet

FOOD | VEGETARIAN & SPECIAL MEALS

🔊 LISTEN FOR

Da ist überall (Fleisch) drin. dah ist ü·ber·*al* (flaish) drin
It all has (meat) in it.

Ich frage mal in der Küche. ikh *frah*·ge mahl in dair *kü*·khe
I'll check with the chef.

Können Sie ... essen? *ker*·nen zee ... *e*·sen
Can you eat ...?

Is it cooked in meat stock?	Ist es in Fleischbrühe zubereitet?	ist es in *flaish*·brü·e *tsoo*·be·rai·tet
Does this dish have ... in it?	Enthält dieses Gericht ...?	ent·*helt* dee·zes ge·*rikht* ...
Could you prepare a meal without ...?	Können Sie ein Gericht ohne ... zubereiten?	*ker*·nen zee ain ge·*rikht* aw·ne ... *tsoo*·be·rai·ten
Is this ...?	Ist das ...?	ist das ...

free of animal produce	ohne tierische Produkte	*aw*·ne *tee*·ri·she pro·*duk*·te
free-range	von freilaufenden Tieren	fon *frai*·low·fen·den *tee*·ren
genetically modified	genmanipuliert	*gayn*·ma·ni·pu·leert
gluten-free	glutenfrei	*gloo*·ten·frai
low in sugar	zuckerarm	*tsu*·ker·arm
low-fat	fettarm	*fet*·arm
organic	organisch	or·*gah*·nish
salt-free	ohne Salz	*aw*·ne zalts

Menu
~ DECODER ~
kulinarisches wörterverzeichnis

This miniguide to German cuisine is designed to help you navigate menus. German nouns, and adjectives affected by gender, have their gender indicated by ⓘ, ⓜ or ⓝ. If it's a plural noun, you'll also see pl.

~ A ~

Aachener Printen pl *ah·khe·ner prin·ten* cakes with chocolate, nuts, fruit peel, honey & spices
Aal ⓜ *ahl* eel
—suppe ⓘ *ahl·zu·pe* eel soup
geräucherter Aal ⓜ *ge·roy·kher·ter ahl* smoked eel
Alpzirler ⓜ *alp·tsir·ler* cow's milk cheese from Austria
Apfel ⓜ *ap·fel* apple
—strudel ⓜ *ap·fel·shtroo·del* apple strudel
Apfelsine ⓘ *ap·fel·zee·ne* orange
Aprikose ⓘ *a·pri·kaw·ze* apricot
—nmarmelade ⓘ *a·pri·kaw·zen·mar·me·lah·de* apricot jam
Artischocke ⓘ *ar·ti·sho·ke* artichoke
Auflauf ⓜ *owf·lowf* souffle • casserole
Auster ⓘ *ows·ter* oyster

~ B ~

Bäckerofen ⓜ *be·ker·aw·fen* 'baker's oven' – pork & lamb bake (Saarland)
Backhähnchen ⓝ *bak·hayn·khen* fried chicken
Backobst ⓝ *bak·awpst* dried fruit
Backpflaume ⓘ *bak·pflow·me* prune
Banane ⓘ *ba·nah·ne* banana
Barsch ⓜ *barsh* perch
Bauern
—brot ⓝ *bow·ern·brawt* 'farmer's bread' – rye or wholemeal bread
—frühstück ⓝ *bow·ern·frü·shtük* 'farmer's breakfast' – scrambled eggs, bacon, cooked diced potatoes, onions & tomatoes
—schmaus ⓜ *bow·ern·shmows* 'farmer's feast' – sauerkraut garnished with bacon, smoked pork, sausages & dumpling or potatoes
—suppe ⓘ *bow·ern·zu·pe* 'farmer's soup' – made of cabbage & sausage
Bayrisch Kraut ⓝ *bai·rish krowt* shredded cabbage cooked with sliced apples, wine & sugar
Beefsteak ⓝ *beef·stayk* hamburger patty
Berliner ⓜ *ber·lee·ner* jam doughnut
Beuschel ⓝ *boy·shel* heart, liver & kidney of a calf or lamb in a slightly sour sauce
Bienenstich ⓜ *bee·nen·shtikh* cake, baked on a tray with a coating of almonds & sugar

C

MENU DECODER

Birne ① *bir*·ne pear
Bischofsbrot ⑩ *bi*·shofs·brawt fruit & nut cake
Blaubeere ① *blow*·bair·re bilberry • blueberry
Blaukraut ⑩ *blow*·krowt red cabbage
Blumenkohl ⑩ *bloo*·men·kawl cauliflower
Blutwurst ① *bloot*·vurst blood sausage
Bockwurst ① *bok*·vurst pork sausage
Bohnen ① pl *baw*·nen beans
Brat
—huhn ⑩ *braht*·hoon roast chicken
—kartoffeln ① pl *braht*·kar·to·feln fried potatoes
—wurst ① *braht*·vurst fried pork sausage
Bregenwurst ① *bray*·gen·vurst brain sausage, found mainly in Lower Saxony & Western Saxony-Anhalt
Brezel ① *bray*·tsel pretzel
Brokkoli ⑩ pl *bro*·ko·li broccoli
Brombeere ① *brom*·bair·re blackberry
Brot ⑩ brawt bread
belegtes Brot ⑩ be·*layk*·tes brawt open sandwich
Brötchen ⑩ *brert*·khen roll
Brühwürfel ⑩ *brü*·vür·fel stock cube
Bulette ① bu·*le*·te meatball (Berlin)
Butter ① *bu*·ter butter

~ C ~

Cervelatwurst ① ser·ve·*laht*·vurst spicy pork & beef sausage
Christstollen ⑩ *krist*·shto·len spiced loaf with candied peel, traditionally eaten at Christmas
Cremespeise ① *kraym*·shpai·ze mousse

~ D ~

Damenkäse ⑩ *dah*·men·kay·ze soft, buttery cheese
Dampfnudeln ① pl *dampf*·noo·deln hot yeast dumplings with vanilla sauce
Dattel ① *da*·tel date
Dorsch ⑩ dorsh cod
Dotterkäse ⑩ *do*·ter·kay·ze cheese made from skimmed milk & egg yolk

~ E ~

Ei ⑩ ai egg
Eierkuchen ⑩ *ai*·er·koo·khen pancake
Eierschwammerln ⑩ pl *ai*·er·shva·merln chanterelle mushrooms (Austria)
Eierspeispfandl ⑩ *ai*·er·shpais·pfandl special Viennese omelette (Austria)
Eintopf ⑩ *ain*·topf stew
Eis ⑩ ais ice cream
Eisbein ⑩ *ais*·bain pickled pork knuckles
Emmentaler ⑩ *e*·men·tah·ler Swiss Emmental, whole-milk hard cheese
Ennstaler ⑩ *ens*·tah·ler blue cheese produced from mixed milk
Ente ① *en*·te duck
Erbse ① *erp*·se pea
Erbsensuppe ① *erp*·sen·zu·pe pea soup
Erdäpfel ⑩ pl *ert*·ep·fel potatoes
—gulasch ⑩ *ert*·ep·fel·goo·lash spicy sausage & potato stew
—knödel ⑩ pl *ert*·ep·fel·kner·del potato & semolina dumplings
—nudeln ① pl *ert*·ep·fel·noo·deln boiled potato balls fried & tossed in fried breadcrumbs
Erdbeere ① *ert*·bair·re strawberry
Erdbeermarmelade ① *ert*·bair·mar·me·lah·de strawberry jam

Erdnuss ① *ert*·nus peanut
Essig ⓜ *e*·sikh vinegar

~ **F** ~

Falscher Hase ⓜ *fal*·sher *hah*·ze 'false hare' – baked mince meatloaf
Fasan ⓜ fa·*zahn* pheasant
Feige ① *fai*·ge fig
Filet ⓝ fi·*lay* fillet
Fisch ⓜ fish fish
Fladen ⓜ *flah*·den round, flat dough cake
Flädle ⓝ pl *flayt*·le thin strips of pancake, added to soup
Fledermaus ① *flay*·der·mows 'bat' – boiled beef in horseradish cream browned in the oven
Fleisch ⓝ flaish meat
—brühe ① flaish·bru·e bouillon
—pflanzerl ⓝ flaish·pflan·tserl meatballs, a Bavarian speciality
—sülze ① flaish·zül·tse aspic
Fondue ⓝ fon·*dü* melted cheese with wine served with bread for dipping
Forelle ① fo·re·le trout
— blau fo·re·le blow steamed trout with potatoes & vegetables
— Müllerin fo·re·le mü·le·rin trout fried in batter with almonds
Frankfurter Kranz ⓜ *frank*·fur·ter krants sponge cake with rum, butter, cream & cherries (from Frankfurt)
Frikadelle ① fri·ka·de·le meatball
Frischling ⓜ *frish*·ling young wild boar
Frucht ① frukht fruit
Frühlingssuppe ① frü·lings·zu·pe vegetable soup
Frühstücksspeck ⓜ frü·shtüks·shpek bacon

~ **G** ~

Gans ① gans goose
Garnele ① gar·*nay*·le shrimp • prawn

Gebäck ⓝ ge·*bek* pastries
Geflügel ⓝ ge·*flü*·gel poultry
gekocht ge·*kokht* boiled • cooked
gekochte Eier ⓝ pl ge·*kokh*·te ai·er boiled eggs
gekochter Schinken ⓜ ge·*kokh*·ter *shing*·ken cooked ham
Gemüse ⓝ ge·*mü*·ze vegetables
—suppe ① ge·*mü*·ze·zu·pe vegetable soup
geräuchert ge·*roy*·khert smoked
geräucherte Forelle ①
ge·*roy*·kher·te fo·re·le smoked trout
geräucherter Lachs ⓜ
ge·*roy*·kher·ter laks smoked salmon
geräucherter Schinken ⓜ
ge·*roy*·kher·ter *shing*·ken gammon
Geschnetzeltes ⓝ ge·*shne*·tsel·tes small slices of meat
Gitziprägel ⓝ *gi*·tsi·pray·gel baked rabbit in batter (Switzerland)
Graf Görz ⓜ grahf gerts Austrian soft cheese
Granat ⓜ gra·*naht* shrimp
Granatapfel ⓜ gra·*naht*·ap·fel pomegranate
Gratin ⓜ gra·*teng* a dish topped with cheese & baked in the oven
Graupensuppe ① grow·pen·zu·pe barley soup
Greyerzer ⓜ grai·er·tser Gruyère, a smooth, rich cheese
Grießklößchensuppe ①
grees·klers·khen·zu·pe soup with semolina dumplings
Gröstl ⓝ grerstl grated fried potatoes with meat (Tyrol)
grüner Salat ⓜ grü·ner za·*laht* green salad
Grünkohl ⓜ **mit Pinkel** grün·kawl mit *ping*·kel cabbage with sausages (Bremen)
Güggeli ⓝ *gü*·ge·lee spring chicken (Switzerland)
Gurke ① *gur*·ke cucumber • gherkin

H

~ H ~

Hack
—braten ⓜ *hak·brah·ten* meatloaf
—fleisch ⓝ *hak·flaish* minced meat
Haferbrei ⓜ *hah·fer·brai* porridge
Hähnchen ⓝ *hayn·khen* chicken
Hämchen ⓝ *hem·khen* pork or hock shank, served with sauerkraut & potatoes (Cologne)
Handkäs ⓜ **mit Musik** *hant·kays mit mu·zeek* spicy cheese, marinated in vinegar & white wine
Hartkäse ⓜ *hart·kay·ze* hard cheese
Hase ⓜ *hah·ze* hare
—nläufe ⓜ pl **in Jägerrahmsauce** *hah·zen·loy·fe in yay·ger·rahm·zaw·se* hare thigh in dark cream sauce of mushroom, shallots, white wine & parsley
—npfeffer ⓜ *hah·zen·pfe·fer* hare stew with mushrooms & onions
Haselnuß ⓕ *hah·zel·nus* hazelnut
Haxe ⓕ *hak·se* knuckle
Hecht ⓜ *hekht* pike
Heidelbeere ⓕ *hai·del·bair·re* bilberry • blueberry
Heidelbeermarmelade ⓕ *hai·del·bair·mar·me·lah·de* blueberry/bilberry jam
Heilbutt ⓜ *hail·but* halibut
Hering ⓜ *hay·ring* herring
—sschmaus ⓜ *hay·rinkgs·shmows* herring in creamy sauce
—ssalat ⓜ *hay·rinkgs·za·laht* salad with herring & beetroot
Himbeere ⓕ *him·bair·re* raspberry
Himmel und Erde *hi·mel unt er·de* 'Heaven & Earth' – mashed potatoes & apple sauce, sometimes served with slices of black pudding
Hirsch ⓜ *hirsh* male deer
Holsteiner Schnitzel ⓝ *hol·shtai·ner shni·tsel* veal schnitzel with fried egg, accompanied by seafood

Honig ⓜ *haw·nikh* honey
Hörnchen ⓝ *hern·khen* croissant
Hühnerbrust ⓕ *hü·ner·brust* chicken breast
Hühnersuppe ⓕ *hü·ner·zu·pe* chicken soup
Hummer ⓜ *hu·mer* lobster
Husarenfleisch ⓝ *hu·zah·ren·flaish* braised beef, veal & pork fillets with sweet peppers, onions & sour cream
Hutzelbrot ⓝ *hu·tsel·brawt* bread made of prunes & other dried fruit

~ I ~

Ingwer ⓜ *ing·ver* ginger
italienischer Salat ⓜ *i·tal·yay·ni·sher za·laht* finely sliced veal, salami, anchovies, tomatoes, cucumber & celery in mayonnaise

~ J ~

Joghurt ⓜ *yaw·gurt* yoghurt

~ K ~

Kabeljau ⓜ *kah·bel·yow* cod
Kaiserschmarren ⓜ *kai·zer·shmar·ren* 'emperor's pancakes' – fluffy pancakes with raisins, served with fruit compote or chocolate sauce
Kaisersemmeln ⓕ pl *kai·zer·ze·meln* 'emperor's rolls' – Austrian bread rolls
Kalbfleisch ⓝ *kalp·flaish* veal
Kalbsnierenbraten ⓜ *kalps·nee·ren·brah·ten* roast veal stuffed with kidneys
Kaninchen ⓝ *ka·neen·khen* rabbit
Kapern ⓕ pl *kah·pern* capers
Karotte ⓕ *ka·ro·te* carrot
Karpfen ⓜ *karp·fen* carp
Kartoffel ⓕ *kar·to·fel* potato
—auflauf ⓜ *kar·to·fel·owf·lowf* potato casserole

—brei ⓜ kar·to·fel·brai mashed potatoes

—püree ⓜ kar·to·fel·pü·ray mashed potatoes

—salat ⓜ kar·to·fel·za·laht potato salad

Käse ⓜ kay·ze cheese

—fondue ⓜ kay·ze·fon·dü melted cheese flavoured with wine & kirsch, into which bread is dipped

Kasseler ⓘ kas·ler smoked pork

— Rippe mit Sauerkraut ⓕ kas·ler ri·pe mit zow·er·krowt smoked pork rib with sauerkraut

Katenwurst ⓕ kah·ten·vurst country-style smoked sausage

Katzenjammer ⓜ ka·tsen·ya·mer cold slices of beef in mayonnaise with cucumbers or gherkin

Keule ⓕ koy·le leg • haunch

Kieler Sprotten ⓕ pl kee·ler shpro·ten small smoked herring

Kirsche ⓕ kir·she cherry

Kirtagssuppe ⓕ kir·tahks·zu·pe soup with caraway seed, thickened with potato

Klöße ⓜ pl kler·se dumplings

Knackwurst ⓕ knak·vurst sausage lightly flavoured with garlic

Knoblauch ⓜ knawp·lowkh garlic

Knödel ⓜ kner·del dumpling

—beignets ⓜ pl kner·del·ben·yays fruit dumplings

Kohl ⓜ kawl cabbage

—rabi ⓕ kawl·rah·bi kohlrabi

—roulade ⓕ kawl·ru·lah·de cabbage leaves stuffed with minced meat

Kompott ⓜ kom·pot stewed fruit

Königinsuppe ⓕ ker·ni·gin·zu·pe creamy chicken soup with pieces of chicken breast

Königsberger Klopse ⓜ pl ker·niks·ber·ger klop·se meatballs in a sour cream & caper sauce

Königstorte ⓕ ker·niks·tor·te rum-flavoured fruit cake

Kopfsalat ⓜ kopf·za·laht lettuce

Kotelett ⓜ kot·let chop

Krabbe ⓕ kra·be crab

Krakauer ⓕ krah·kow·er thick, paprika-spiced sausage of Polish origin

Kraut ⓜ krowt cabbage

—salat ⓜ krowt·za·laht coleslaw

Kräuter ⓜ pl kroy·ter herbs

Krebs ⓜ krayps crab • crayfish

Kren ⓜ krayn horseradish (Bavaria & Austria)

Krokette ⓕ kro·ke·te croquette

Kuchen ⓜ koo·khen cake

Kümmel ⓜ kü·mel caraway (seeds)

Kürbis ⓜ kur·bis pumpkin

Kutteln ⓕ pl ku·teln tripe

L

Labskaus ⓜ laps·kows thick meat & potato stew

Lachs ⓜ laks salmon

Lamm ⓜ lam lamb

—fleisch ⓜ lam·flaish lamb

—keule ⓕ lam·koy·lo log of lamb

Landjäger ⓜ lant·yay·ger thin, long, hard, spicy sausage

Languste ⓕ lan·gus·te crayfish

Lappenpickert ⓜ la·pen·pi·kert pan-sized potato pancake usually served with jam or salted fish (Westphalia)

Lauch ⓜ lowkh leek

Leber ⓕ lay·ber liver

—käse ⓜ lay·ber·kay·ze seasoned meatloaf made of minced liver, pork & bacon

—knödel ⓜ lay·ber·kner·del liver dumpling

—knödelsuppe ⓕ lay·ber·kner·del·zu·pe hot broth with liver dumplings

—wurst ⓕ lay·ber·vurst liver sausage

Lebkuchen ⓜ layp·koo·khen gingerbread

Leckerli ⓝ *le·ker·lee* honey-flavoured ginger biscuit

Leipziger Allerlei ⓝ *laip·tsi·ger a·ler·lai* mixed vegetable stew (Leipzig)

Lende ⓕ *len·de* loin

Limburger ⓜ *lim·bur·ger* strong cheese flavoured with herbs

Linsen ⓝ pl *lin·zen* lentils

— mit Spätzle mit *shpets·le* lentil stew with noodles & sausages

—suppe ⓕ *lin·zen·zu·pe* lentil soup

Linzer Torte ⓕ *lin·tser tor·te* latticed tart with jam topping

Lorbeerblätter ⓝ pl *lor·bair·ble·ter* bay leaves

Lübecker Marzipan ⓝ *lü·be·ker mar·tsi·pahn* marzipan (Lübeck)

Lucullus-Eier ⓝ pl *lu·ku·lus·ai·er* poached, boiled or scrambled eggs with goose liver, truffle & other garnishes, served with a sauce

~ M ~

Mais ⓜ *mais* sweet corn

Majonnaise ⓕ *ma·yo·nay·ze* mayonnaise

Makrele ⓕ *ma·kray·le* mackerel

Mandarine ⓕ *man·da·ree·ne* mandarin • tangerine

Mandel ⓕ *man·del* almond

Marmelade ⓕ *mar·me·lah·de* jam

Matjes ⓜ *mat·yes* young herring

Maultasche ⓕ *mowl·ta·she* filled pasta (Swabia)

Meeresfrüchte ⓕ pl *mair·res·frükh·te* seafood

Meerrettich ⓜ *mair·re·tikh* horseradish

Mehl ⓝ *mayl* flour

Mett ⓝ *met* lean minced pork

Mettentchen ⓝ *met·ent·khen* beer stick

Milch ⓕ *milkh* milk

—rahmstrudel ⓜ *milkh·rahm·shtroo·del* strudel filled with egg custard & soft cheese

Mohnbrötchen ⓝ *mawn·brert·khen* bread roll with poppy seeds

Möhre ⓕ *mer·re* carrot

Muschel ⓕ *mu·shel* clam • mussel

Muskat ⓜ *mus·kaht* nutmeg

Müesli ⓝ *mü·es·li* muesli

Müsli ⓝ *müs·li* muesli

~ N ~

Nelken ⓕ pl *nel·ken* cloves

Niere ⓕ *nee·re* kidney

Nockerl ⓝ *no·kerl* small dumpling (Austria)

Nudeln ⓕ pl *noo·deln* noodles

Nudelauflauf ⓜ *noo·del·owf·lowf* pasta casserole

Nürnberger Lebkuchen ⓜ *nürn·ber·ger layp·koo·khen* cakes with chocolate, nuts, fruit peel, honey & spices

~ O ~

Obatzter ⓜ *aw·bats·ter* Bavarian soft cheese mousse

Obst ⓝ *awpst* fruit

—salat ⓜ *awpst·za·laht* fruit salad

Ochsenschwanz ⓜ *ok·sen·shvants* oxtail

—suppe ⓕ *ok·sen·shvants·zu·pe* oxtail soup

Öl ⓝ *erl* oil

Orangenmarmelade ⓕ *o·rahng·zhen·mar·me·lah·de* marmelade

~ P ~

Palatschinken ⓜ *pa·lat·shing·ken* pancake, usually filled with jam or cheese, sometimes served with a hot chocolate & nut topping

Pampelmuse ⓕ *pam·pel·moo·ze* grapefruit

Paprika ⓕ *pap·ri·kah* sweet pepper

Pastetchen ⓝ *pas·tayt·khen* filled puff-pastry case

Pastete ① pas·tay·te pastry • pie

Pellkartoffeln ① pl pel·kar·to·feln small jacket potatoes served in their skins, often served with quark

Petersilie ① pay·ter·zee·li·e parsley

Pfälzer Saumagen ⓜ pfel·tser zow·mah·gen stuffed stomach of pork

Pfannkuchen ⓜ pfan·koo·khen pancake

Pfeffer ⓜ pfe·fer pepper

Pfifferling ⓜ pfi·fer·ling chanterelle mushroom

Pfirsich ⓜ pfir·zikh peach

Pflaume ① pflow·me plum

Pilz ⓜ pilts mushroom

Pichelsteiner ⓜ pi·khel·shtai·ner meat & vegetable stew

Pökelfleisch ① pér·kel·flaish marinated meat

Pomeranzensoße ①
po·me·ran·tsen·zaw·se sauce made of bitter oranges, wine & brandy, usually served with duck

Pommes Frites pl pom frit French fries

Porree ⓜ por·ray leek

Preiselbeere ① prai·zel·bair·re cranberry

Printe ① prin·te honey-flavoured biscuit

Pumpernickel ⓜ pum·per·ni·kel very dark bread made with coarse wholemeal rye flour

Putenbrust ① poo·ten·brust turkey breast

Puter ⓜ poo·ter turkey

~ Q ~

Quargel ⓜ kvar·gel small, round, salty & slightly acidic cheese

Quark ⓜ kvark quark (curd cheese)

Quitte ① kvi·te quince

~ R ~

Radieschen ⓝ ra·dees·khen radish

Ragout ⓝ ra·goo stew

Rahm ⓜ rahm cream

Rebhuhn ⓝ rayp·hoon partridge

Regensburger ⓜ ray·gens·bur·ger highly spiced smoked sausage

Reh ⓝ ray venison

—pfeffer ⓜ ray·pfe·fer jugged venison, fried & braised in its marinade, served with sour cream

—rücken ⓜ ray·rü·ken saddle of venison

Reibekuchen ⓜ rai·be·koo·khen potato cake

Reis ⓜ rais rice

Remouladensauce ①
re·mu·lah·den·zaw·se mayonnaise sauce with mustard, anchovies, capers, gherkins, tarragon & chervil

Rettich ⓜ re·tikh radish

Rhabarber ⓜ ra·bar·ber rhubarb

Rheinischer Sauerbraten ⓜ
mit Kartoffelklößen rai·ni·sher zow·er·brah·ten mit kar·to·tel·kler·sen roasted marinated meat, slightly sour, often served with potato dumpling

Rindfleisch ⓝ rint·flaish beef

Rippenspeer ⓜ ri·pen·shpair spare ribs

Rogen ⓜ raw·gen roe

Roggenbrot ⓝ ro·gen·brawt rye bread

Rohkost ① raw·kost uncooked vegetables • vegetarian food

Rollmops ⓜ rol·mops pickled herring fillet rolled around chopped onions or gherkins

Rosenkohl ⓜ raw·zen·kawl Brussels sprouts

Rosinen ① pl ro·zee·nen raisins

Rosmarin ⓜ raws·ma·reen rosemary

Rost

—braten ⓜ *rost·brah·ten* roast

—brätl ⓝ *rost·braytl* grilled meat

—hähnchen ⓝ *rost·hayn·khen* roast chicken

Rösti pl *rers·tee* grated, fried potatoes (Switzerland)

rot *rawt* red

—e Beete ⓕ *raw·te bay·te* beetroot

—e Grütze ⓕ *raw·te grü·tse* fruit pudding of cooked & sweetened berries, thickened & put in moulds

—e Johannisbeere ⓕ *raw·te yo·ha·nis·bair·re* redcurrant

—kohl ⓜ *rawt·kawl* red cabbage

—e Rüben ⓕ pl *raw·te rü·ben* beetroot

—wurst ⓕ *rawt·vurst* black pudding

Roulade ⓕ *ru·lah·de* collared beef – thin slices of beef stuffed with onion, bacon and dill pickles then rolled & braised

Rührreier ⓝ pl *rür·ai·er* scrambled eggs

Russische Eier ⓝ pl *ru·si·she ai·er* 'Russian eggs' – eggs with mayonnaise

~ **S** ~

Sahne ⓕ *zah·ne* cream

Salat ⓜ *za·laht* salad

Salbei ⓜ *zal·bai* sage

Salz ⓝ *zalts* salt

Salzburger Nockerln ⓝ pl *zalts·bur·ger no·kerln* Austrian dessert of sweet dumplings poached in milk & served with warm vanilla sauce

Salzkartoffeln ⓕ pl *zalts·kar·to·feln* boiled potatoes

Sauerbraten ⓜ *zow·er·brah·ten* marinated roasted beef served with a sour cream sauce

Sauerkraut ⓝ *zow·er·krowt* pickled cabbage

Schafskäse ⓜ *shahfs·kay·ze* sheep's milk feta

Schellfisch ⓜ *shel·fish* haddock

Schinken ⓜ *shing·ken* ham

Schlachtplatte ⓕ *shlakht·pla·te* selection of pork & sausage

Schmalzbrot ⓝ *shmalts·brawt* slice of bread with dripping

Schmorbraten ⓜ *shmawr·brah·ten* beef pot roast

Schnitte ⓕ *shni·te* slice of bread • small square piece of cake

Schnittlauch ⓜ *shnit·lowkh* chives

Schnitzel ⓝ *shni·tsel* pork, veal or chicken breast pounded flat, covered in breadcrumbs & pan-fried

Scholle ⓕ *sho·le* plaice

schwarze Johannisbeere ⓕ *shvar·tse yo·ha·nis·bair·re* blackcurrant

Schwarzwälder Kirschtorte ⓕ *shvarts·vel·der kirsh·tor·te* Black Forest cake (chocolate layer cake filled with cream & cherries)

Schwein ⓝ *shvain* pork

—ebraten ⓜ *shvai·ne·brah·ten* roast pork

—efleisch ⓝ *shvai·ne·flaish* pork

—shaxe ⓕ *shvains·hak·se* crispy leg of pork served with dumplings

Seezunge ⓕ *zay·tsung·e* sole

Seidfleisch ⓝ *zait·flaish* boiled meat

Sekt ⓜ *zekt* German champagne

Selchfleisch ⓝ *zelkh·flaish* smoked pork

Sellerie ⓕ *ze·le·ree* celery

Semmel ⓕ *ze·mel* bread roll (Austria & Bavaria)

—knödel ⓜ pl *ze·mel·kner·del* dumplings made of dry rolls dunked in milk (Bavaria)

Senf ⓜ *zenf* mustard

Sonnenblumenkerne ⓜ pl *zo·nen·bloo·men·ker·ne* sunflower seeds

Soße ⓕ *zaw·se* sauce • gravy

spanische Soße ① *shpah·ni·she zaw·se* brown sauce with herbs

Spanferkel ⓜ *shpahn·fer·kel* suckling pig

Spargel ⓜ *shpar·gel* asparagus

Spätzle pl *shpets·le* thick noodles

Speck ⓜ *shpek* bacon

Spekulatius ⓜ *shpe·ku·lah·tsi·us* almond biscuits

Spiegelei ① *shpee·gel·ai* fried egg

Spinat ⓜ *shpi·naht* spinach

Sprossenkohl ⓜ *shpro·sen·kawl* Brussels sprouts

Sprotten ① pl *shpro·ten* sprats (small herring-like fish)

Steckrübe ① *shtek·rü·be* turnip

Steinbuscher ⓜ *shtain·bu·sher* semi-hard, creamy cheese with a strong, slightly bitter flavour

Steinbutt ⓜ *shtain·but* turbot (flatfish)

Stelze ① *shtel·tse* knuckle of pork

Sterz ⓜ *shterts* Austrian polenta

Stollen ⓜ *shto·len* spiced loaf with candied peel, traditionally eaten at Christmas

Strammer Max ⓜ *shtra·mer maks* sandwich with ham (or sausage or spiced minced pork), served with fried eggs & sometimes onions

Streichkäse ⓜ *shtraikh·kay·ze* any kind of soft cheese spread

Streuselkuchen ⓜ *shtroy·zel·koo·khen* coffee cake topped with a mixture of butter, sugar, flour & cinnamon

Strudel ⓜ *shtroo·del* loaf-shaped pastry filled with something sweet or savoury

Suppe ① *zu·pe* soup

~ T ~

Tascherl ⓝ *ta·sherl* pastry turnover with meat, cheese or jam filling

Tatarenbrot ⓝ *ta·tah·ren·brawt* open sandwich topped with raw spiced minced beef

Teigwaren pl *taik·vah·ren* pasta

Thunfisch ⓜ *toon·fish* tuna

Thüringer ① *tü·ring·er* long, thin, spiced sausage

Thymian ⓜ *tü·mi·ahn* thyme

Toast ⓜ *tawst* toast

Tomate ① *to·mah·te* tomato

—nketchup ⓜ *to·mah·ten·ket·chap* tomato sauce

—nsuppe ① *to·mah·ten·zu·pe* tomato soup

Topfen ⓜ *top·fen* curd cheese (Austria)

Törtchen ⓝ *tert·khen* small tart or cake

Torte ① *tor·te* layer cake

Truthahn ⓜ *troot·hahn* turkey

Tunke ① *tung·ke* sauce • gravy

~ V ~

Vollkornbrot ⓝ *fol·korn·brawt* wholemeal bread

Voressen ⓝ *fawr·e·sen* meat stew

~ W ~

Wachtel ① *vakh·tel* quail

Walnuss ① *val·nus* walnut

Wecke ① *ve·ke* bread roll (Austria & southern Germany)

Weichkäse ⓜ *vaikh·kay·ze* soft cheese

Weinbergschnecken ① pl *vain·berk·shne·ken* snails

Weinkraut ⓝ *vain·krowt* white cabbage, braised with apples & simmered in wine

Weintraube ① *vain·trow·be* grape

Weißbrot ⓝ *vais·brawt* white bread

Weißwurst ① *vais·vurst* veal sausage, found mainly in southern Germany

Westfälischer Schinken ⓜ *vest·fay·li·sher shing·ken* variety of cured & smoked ham

Z

Wiener *vee*·ner in the Viennese style
— Würstchen ⓝ *vee*·ner *vürst*·khen frankfurter (sausage)
— Schnitzel ⓝ *vee*·ner *shni*·tsel crumbed veal
Wiezenbrot ⓝ *vai*·tsen·brawt wheat bread
Wild ⓝ *vilt* game
—braten ⓜ *vilt*·brah·ten roast venison
—ente ⓕ *vilt*·en·te wild duck
—schwein ⓝ *vilt*·shvain wild boar
Wilstermarschkäse ⓜ *vils*·ter·marsh·kay·ze semi-hard cheese
Wurst ⓕ vurst sausage
Würstchen ⓝ *vürst*·khen small sausage
Wurstplatte ⓕ *vurst*·pla·te cold cuts

~ **Z** ~

Ziege ⓕ *tsee*·ge goat
Zimt ⓜ tsimt cinnamon

Zitrone ⓕ tsi·*traw*·ne lemon
Zucker ⓜ *tsu*·ker sugar
Zunge ⓕ *tsung*·e tongue
Züricher Geschnetzeltes ⓝ *tsü*·ri·kher ge·*shne*·tsel·tes sliced veal with mushrooms & onions cooked in a white wine & cream sauce
Zwetschge ⓕ *tsvetsh*·ge plum
—ndatschi ⓜ tsvetsh·gen·dat·shi damson plum tart
Zwieback ⓜ *tsvee*·bak rusk
Zwiebel ⓕ *tsvee*·bel onion
—fleisch ⓝ *tsvee*·bel·flaish beef sauteed with onion
—kuchen ⓜ *tsvee*·bel·koo·khen onion quiche, often served with *Federweißer* (new wine)
—suppe ⓕ *tsvee*·bel·zu·pe onion soup
—wurst ⓕ *tsvee*·bel·vurst liver & onion sausage
Zwischenrippenstück ⓝ *tsvi*·shen·ri·pen·shtük rib eye steak

Dictionary

ENGLISH *to* GERMAN

Englisch–Deutsch

Nouns in the dictionary, and adjectives affected by gender, have their gender indicated by ⓕ, ⓜ or ⓝ. If it's a plural noun, you'll also see pl. Where a word that could be either a noun or a verb has no gender indicated, it's a verb.

A

(to be) able können *ker·nen*
aboard an Bord *an bort*
abortion Abtreibung ⓕ *ap·trai·bung*
about über *ü·ber*
above über *ü·ber*
abroad im Ausland *im ows lant*
accident Unfall ⓜ *un·fal*
accommodation Unterkunft ⓕ *un·ter·kunft*
accountant Buchhalter(in) ⓜ/ⓕ *bookh·hal·ter/bookh·hal·te·rin*
across (from) gegenüber *gay·gen·ü·ber*
across (to) hinüber *hi·nü·ber*
activist Aktivist(in) ⓜ/ⓕ *ak·ti·vist/ak·ti·vis·tin*
actor Schauspieler(in) ⓜ/ⓕ *show·shpee·ler/show·shpee·le·rin*
acupuncture Akupunktur ⓕ *a·ku·pungk·toor*
adaptor Adapter ⓜ *a·dap·ter*
addicted abhängig *ap·heng·ikh*
address Adresse ⓕ *a·dre·se*
administration Verwaltung ⓕ *fer·val·tung*
admire bewundern *be·vun·dern*

admission price Eintrittspreis ⓜ *ain·trits·prais*
admit (allow to enter) einlassen *ain·la·sen*
admit (accept as true) zugeben *tsoo·gay·ben*
adult Erwachsene ⓜ&ⓕ *er·vak·se·ne*
advertisement Anzeige ⓕ *an·tsai·ge*
advice Rat ⓜ *raht*
advise raten *rah·ten*
aerobics Aerobics pl *e·ro·biks*
aerogram Aerogramm ⓝ *air·ro·gram*
aeroplane Flugzeug ⓝ *flook·tsoyk*
(to be) afraid Angst (haben) angkst *(hah·ben)*
Africa Afrika ⓝ *a·fri·kah*
after nach *nahkh*
(this) afternoon (heute) Nachmittag ⓜ *(hoy·te) nahkh·mi·tahk*
aftershave Aftershave ⓝ *ahf·ter·shayf*
again wieder *vee·der*
against gegen *gay·gen*
age Alter ⓝ *al·ter*
(three days) ago vor (drei Tagen) *fawr (drai tah·gen)*
agree zustimmen *tsoo·shti·men*

agriculture Landwirtschaft ⓕ
lant·virt·shaft
ahead vor uns fawr uns
AIDS AIDS ⓜ aydz
air Luft ⓕ luft
airmail Luftpost ⓕ *luft*·post
air pollution Luftverschmutzung ⓕ
luft·fer·shmu·tsung
air-conditioned mit Klimaanlage ⓕ
mit *klee*·ma·an·lah·ge
airline Fluglinie ⓕ *flook*·lee·ni·e
airplane Flugzeug ⓝ *flook*·tsoyk
airport Flughafen ⓜ
flook·hah·fen
airport tax Flughafengebühr ⓕ
flook·hah·fen·ge·bür
airsickness Luftkrankheit ⓕ
luft·krangk·hait
aisle Gang ⓜ gang
aisle seat Platz am Gang ⓜ plats
am gang
alarm clock Wecker ⓜ *ve*·ker
alcohol Alkohol ⓜ *al*·ko·hawl
alcoholic Alkoholiker(in) ⓜ/ⓕ
al·ko·*haw*·li·ker/al·ko·*haw*·li·ke·rin
alcoholic alkoholisch
al·ko·*haw*·lish
all alle *a*·le
allergy Allergie ⓕ a·lair·*gee*
allow erlauben er·*low*·ben
almond Mandel ⓕ *man*·del
almost fast fast
alone allein a·*lain*
already schon shawn
also auch owkh
altar Altar ⓜ al·*tahr*
altitude Höhe ⓕ *her*·e
always immer *i*·mer
amateur Amateur(in) ⓜ/ⓕ
a·ma·*ter*/a·ma·*ter*·rin
amazing erstaunlich er·*shtown*·likh
ambassador Botschafter(in) ⓜ/ⓕ
bawt·shaf·ter/*bawt*·shaf·te·rin
ambulance Krankenwagen ⓜ
krang·ken·vah·gen
among unter *un*·ter
amount Betrag ⓜ be·*trahk*

anaesthetic Betäubung ⓕ
be·*toy*·bung
anarchist Anarchist(in) ⓜ/ⓕ
a·nar·*khist*/a·nar·*khis*·tin
ancient alt alt
and und unt
angry wütend *vü*·tent
animal Tier ⓝ teer
ankle Knöchel ⓜ *kner*·khel
answer Antwort ⓕ *ant*·vort
answer antworten *ant*·vor·ten
ant Ameise ⓕ *ah*·mai·ze
antibiotics Antibiotika ⓝ pl
an·ti·bi·*aw*·ti·ka
antinuclear Anti-Atom- an·ti·a·*tawm*
antique Antiquität ⓕ an·ti·kvi·*tayt*
antiseptic Antiseptikum ⓝ
an·ti·*zep*·ti·kum
any irgendein ir·gent·*ain*
anything (irgend)etwas
(*ir*·gent·)et·vas
anywhere irgendwo ir·gent·*vaw*
apart from (besides) außer
ow·ser
apartment Wohnung ⓕ *vaw*·nung
appendix Blinddarm ⓜ *blint*·darm
apple Apfel ⓜ *ap*·fel
appointment Termin ⓜ ter·*meen*
apprentice Auszubildende ⓜ&ⓕ
ows·tsu·bil·den·de
approximately ungefähr un·ge·*fair*
apricot Aprikose ⓕ a·pri·*kaw*·ze
archaeological archäologisch
ar·khe·o·*law*·gish
architecture Architektur ⓕ
ar·khi·tek·*toor*
area code Vorwahl ⓕ *fawr*·vahl
argue streiten *shtrai*·ten
arm Arm ⓜ arm
aromatherapy Aromatheraphie ⓕ
a·*raw*·ma·tay·ra·pee
arrest Verhaftung ⓕ fer·*haf*·tung
arrivals Ankunft ⓕ *an*·kunft
arrive ankommen *an*·ko·men
art Kunst ⓕ kunst
art collection Kunstsammlung ⓕ
kunst·zam·lung

art gallery Kunstgalerie ①
kunst·ga·le·ree

artist Künstler(in) ⓜ/① *künst·ler/
künst·le·rin*

arts & crafts Kunstgewerbe ⓝ
kunst·ge·ver·be

as far as bis zu bis *tsoo*

ashtray Aschenbecher ⓜ
a·shen·be·kher

Asia Asien ⓝ *ah·zi·en*

ask a question eine Frage stellen
ai·ne fra·nge shte·len

ask (for something) um etwas
bitten um et·vas *bi·ten*

asleep schlafen *shlah·fen*

asparagus Spargel ⓜ *shpar·gel*

aspirin Kopfschmerztablette ①
kopf·shmerts·ta·ble·te

asthma Asthma ⓝ *ast·mah*

asylum seeker Asylant(in) ⓜ/①
a·zü·lant/a·zü·lan·tin

at in • an • auf • bei • zu in • an •
owf • bei • tsoo

athletics Leichtathletik ①
laikht·at·lay·tik

atmosphere Atmosphäre ①
at·mos·fair·re

attic Dachboden ⓜ
dakh·baw·den

aubergine Aubergine ①
aw·ber·zhee·ne

aunt Tante ① *tan·te*

Australia Australien ⓝ
ows·trah·li·en

Austria Österreich ⓝ *ers·ter·raikh*

author Autor(in) ⓜ/① *ow·tor/
ow·taw·rin*

automatic automatisch
ow·to·mah·tish

automatic teller machine (ATM)
Geldautomat ⓜ *gelt·ow·to·maht*

autumn Herbst ⓜ *herpst*

avalanche Lawine ① *la·vee·ne*

avenue Allee ① *a·lay*

avocado Avokado ①
a·vo·kah·do

axe Axt ① *akst*

B

baby Baby ⓝ *bay·bi*

baby food Babynahrung ①
bay·bi·nah·rung

baby powder Babypuder ⓝ
bay·bi·poo·der

babysitter Babysitter ⓜ *bay·bi·si·ter*

back (body) Rücken ⓜ *rü·ken*

back (return) zurück tsu·*rük*

backpack Rucksack ⓜ *ruk·zak*

bacon Frühstücksspeck ⓜ
frü·shtüks·shpek

bad schlecht *shlekht*

badger Dachs ⓜ *daks*

bag Tasche ① *ta·she*

baggage Gepäck ⓝ *ge·pek*

baggage allowance Freigepäck ⓝ
frai·ge·pek

baggage claim Gepäckausgabe ①
ge·pek·ows·gah·be

bait Köder ⓜ *ker·der*

bakery Bäckerei ① *be·ke·rai*

balance (account) Kontostand ⓜ
kon·to·shtant

balcony Balkon ⓜ *bal·kawn*

ball Ball ⓜ *bal*

ballet Ballett ⓝ *ba·let*

banana Banane ① *ba·nah·ne*

band (music) Band ① *bent*

bandage Verband ⓜ *fer·bant*

Band aids Pflaster ⓝ *pflas·ter*

bank Bank ① *bangk*

bank account Bankkonto ⓝ
bangk·kon·to

bankdraft Bankauszug ⓜ
bangk·ows·tsook

banknote Geldschein ⓜ *gelt·shain*

baptism Taufe ① *tow·fe*

bar Lokal ⓝ *lo·kahl*

baseball Baseball ⓜ *bays·bawl*

basket Korb ⓜ *korp*

bath Bad ⓝ *baht*

bath towel Badetuch ⓝ
bah·de·tookh

bathing suit Badeanzug ⓜ
bah·de·an·tsook

B

bathroom Badezimmer ⓝ *bah*·de·tsi·mer

battery Batterie ⓕ ba·te·*ree*

bay Bucht ⓕ bukht

be sein zain

beach Strand ⓜ shtrant

bean Bohne ⓕ *baw*·ne

bear Bär ⓜ bair

beautiful schön shern

beauty salon Schönheitssalon ⓜ *shern*·haits·za·long

because weil vail

because of wegen *vay*·gen

bed Bett ⓝ bet

bed & breakfast Pension ⓕ pahng·*zyawn*

bedding Bettzeug ⓝ *bet*·tsoyk

bedroom Schlafzimmer ⓝ *shlahf*·tsi·mer

bee Biene ⓕ *bee*·ne

beef Rindfleisch ⓝ *rint*·flaish

beer Bier ⓝ beer

beetroot rote Beete ⓕ *raw*·te *bay*·te

before vor fawr

beggar Bettler(in) ⓜ/ⓕ *bet*·ler/ *bet*·le·rin

begin beginnen be·*gi*·nen

behind hinter *hin*·ter

Belgium Belgien ⓝ *bel*·gi·en

below unter *un*·ter

belt Gürtel ⓜ *gür*·tel

beside neben *nay*·ben

best beste *bes*·te

bet Wette ⓕ *ve*·te

better besser *be*·ser

between zwischen *tsvi*·shen

bible Bibel ⓕ *bee*·bel

big groß graws

bike Fahrrad ⓕ *fahr*·raht

bike chain Fahrradkette ⓕ *fahr*·raht·ke·te

bike path Radweg ⓜ *raht*·vayk

bill (account) Rechnung ⓕ *rekh*·nung

bin (rubbish) Mülleimer ⓝ *mül*·ai·mer

binoculars Fernglas ⓝ *fern*·glahs

bird Vogel ⓜ *faw*·gel

birth certificate Geburtsurkunde ⓕ ge·*burts*·oor·kun·de

birthday Geburtstag ⓜ ge·*burts*·tahk

biscuit Keks ⓜ kayks

bite (dog) Biss ⓜ bis

bite (insect) Stich ⓜ shtikh

bitter bitter *bi*·ter

black schwarz shvarts

B&W (film) schwarzweiß shvarts·*vais*

blanket Decke ⓕ *de*·ke

bless segnen *zayg*·nen

blind blind blint

blister Blase ⓕ *blah*·ze

blocked blockiert blo·*keert*

blood Blut ⓝ bloot

blood group Blutgruppe ⓕ *bloot*·gru·pe

blood pressure Blutdruck ⓜ *bloot*·druk

blood test Bluttest ⓜ *bloot*·test

blue blau blow

boar Wildschwein ⓝ *vilt*·shvain

board Brett ⓝ bret

board (plane, ship) besteigen be·*shtai*·gen

boarding house Pension ⓕ pahng·*zyawn*

boarding pass Bordkarte ⓕ *bort*·kar·te

boat Boot ⓝ bawt

body Körper ⓜ *ker*·per

bone Knochen ⓜ *kno*·khen

book Buch ⓝ bookh

book (reserve) buchen *boo*·khen

booked out ausgebucht *ows*·ge·bookht

bookshop Buchhandlung ⓕ *bookh*·hand·lung

boot (trunk) Kofferraum ⓜ *ko*·fer·rowm

boot (footwear) Stiefel ⓜ *shtee*·fel

border Grenze ⓕ *gren*·tse

bored gelangweilt ge·*lang*·vailt

boring langweilig *lang*·vai·likh

borrow (aus)leihen *(ows·)lai·*en

boss Chef(in) ⓜ/ⓕ shef/*she·*fin

botanic garden Botanischer Garten
ⓜ bo·*tah*·ni·sher *gar*·ten

both beide *bai*·de

bottle Flasche ⓕ *fla·*she

bottle opener Flaschenöffner ⓜ
*fla·*shen·erf·ner

at the bottom unten *un·*ten

bouncer (doorman) Türsteher ⓜ
*tür·*shtay·er

bowl Schüssel ⓕ *shü·*sel

box Karton ⓜ kar·*tong*

boxer shorts Shorts pl shorts

boxing Boxen ⓝ *bok·*sen

boy Junge ⓜ *yung·*e

boyfriend Freund ⓜ froynt

bra BH ⓜ bay·*hah*

Braille Blindenschrift ⓕ
*blin·*den·shrift

brake fluid Bremsflüssigkeit ⓕ
*brems·*flü·sikh·kait

brakes Bremsen ⓕ pl *brem·*zen

brandy Weinbrand ⓜ *vain·*brant

brave mutig *moo·*tikh

bread Brot ⓝ brawt

bread roll Brötchen ⓝ *brert·*khen

break (zer)brechen *(tser·)bre·*khen

break down eine Panne haben *ai·*ne
*pa·*ne *hah·*ben

breakdown service Abschleppdienst ⓜ *ap·*shlep·deenst

breakfast Frühstück ⓝ *frü·*shtuk

breast Brust ⓕ brust

breathe atmen *aht·*men

brewery Brauerei ⓕ brow·e·*rai*

bribe bestechen be·*shte·*khen

bricklayer Maurer(in) ⓜ/ⓕ
*mow·*rer/*mow·*re·rin

bridge Brücke ⓕ *brü·*ke

bridle path Reitweg ⓜ *rait·*vayk

briefcase Aktentasche ⓕ
*ak·*ten·ta·she

brilliant brillant bril·*yant*

bring bringen *bring·*en

broccoli Brokkoli ⓜ pl *bro·*ko·li

brochure Broschüre ⓕ bro·*shü·*re

broken kaputt ka·*put*

bronchitis Bronchitis ⓕ
bron·*khee·*tis

brother Bruder ⓜ *broo·*der

brown braun brown

bruise Schramme ⓕ *shra·*me

Brussels sprouts Rosenkohl ⓜ
*raw·*zen·kawl

bucket Eimer ⓜ *ai·*mer

Buddhist Buddhist(in) ⓜ/ⓕ bu·*dist*/
bu·*dis·*tin

buffet Buffet ⓝ bü·*fay*

bug (animal) Insekt ⓝ in·*zekt*

build bauen *bow·*en

building Gebäude ⓝ ge·*boy·*de

bumbag Hüfttasche ⓕ *hüft·*ta·she

burn (ver)brennen *(fer·)bre·*nen

bus (city) Bus ⓜ bus

bus (intercity) Fernbus ⓜ
*fern·*bus

bus station Busbahnhof ⓜ
*bus·*bahn·hawf

bus stop Bushaltestelle ⓕ
*bus·*hal·te·shte·le

business Geschäft ⓝ ge·*sheft*

business class Business Class ⓕ
*bi·*zi·nes klahs

business person Geschäftsmann/
Geschäftsfrau ⓜ/ⓕ ge·*shefts·*man/
ge·*shefts·*frow

business trip Geschäftsreise ⓕ
ge·*shefts·*rai·ze

busker Straßenmusiker(in)
ⓜ/ⓕ *shtrah·*sen·moo·zi·ker/
*shtrah·*sen·moo·zi·ke·rin

busy (person) beschäftigt
be·*shef·*tikht

busy (phone) besetzt be·*zetst*

but aber *ah·*ber

butcher's shop Metzgerei ⓕ
mets·ge·*rai*

butter Butter ⓕ *bu·*ter

butterfly Schmetterling ⓜ
*shme·*ter·ling

button Knopf ⓜ knopf

buy kaufen *kow·*fen

C

cabbage Kohl ⓜ *kawl*
cable Kabel ⓝ *kah·bel*
cable car Seilbahn ⓕ *zail·bahn*
cafe Café ⓝ *ka·fay*
cake Kuchen ⓜ *koo·khen*
cake shop Konditorei ⓕ *kon·dee·to·rai*
calculator Taschenrechner ⓜ *ta·shen·rekh·ner*
calendar Kalender ⓜ *ka·len·der*
camera Kamera ⓕ *kah·me·ra*
camp zelten *tsel·ten*
camping ground Campingplatz ⓜ *kem·ping·plats*
camping stove Kocher ⓜ *ko·kher*
camp site Zeltplatz ⓜ *tselt·plats*
can (be able) können *ker·nen*
can (have permission) können *ker·nen*
can (tin) Dose ⓕ *daw·ze*
can opener Dosenöffner ⓜ *daw·zen·erf·ner*
Canada Kanada ⓝ *ka·na·dah*
canary Kanarienvogel ⓜ *ka·nah·ri·en·faw·gel*
cancel stornieren *shtor·nee·ren*
cancer Krebs ⓜ *krayps*
candle Kerze ⓕ *ker·tse*
candy Bonbon ⓜ *bong·bong*
cantaloupe Beutelmelone ⓕ *boy·tel·me·law·ne*
canteen Kantine ⓕ *kan·tee·ne*
cape (offshore) Kap ⓝ *kap*
capitalism Kapitalismus ⓜ *ka·pi·ta·lis·mus*
capsicum Paprika ⓕ *pap·ri·kah*
car Auto ⓝ *ow·to*
car hire Autoverleih ⓜ *ow·to·fer·lai*
car owner's title (document) Fahrzeugpapiere ⓝ pl *fahr·tsoyk·pa·pee·re*
car registration (PKW-)Zulassung ⓕ *(pay·kah·vay·)tsoo·la·sung*
caravan Wohnwagen ⓜ *vawn·vah·gen*

carburettor Vergaser ⓜ *fer·gah·zer*
cards Karten ⓕ pl *kar·ten*
care (for someone) sich kümmern um zikh *kü·mern um*
careful vorsichtig *fawr·zikh·tikh*
caring liebevoll *lee·be·fol*
carpark Parkplatz ⓜ *park·plats*
carpenter Schreiner(in) ⓜ/ⓕ *shrai·ner/shrai·ne·rin*
carriage (train) Wagen ⓜ *vah·gen*
carrot Mohrrübe ⓕ *mawr·rü·be*
carry tragen *trah·gen*
carton Karton ⓜ *kar·tong*
carton (milk) Tüte ⓕ *tü·te*
cash Bargeld ⓝ *bahr·gelt*
cash (a cheque) (einen Scheck) einlösen *(ai·nen shek) ain·ler·zen*
cash register Kasse ⓕ *ka·se*
cashew Cashewnuss ⓕ *kesh·yoo·nus*
cashier Kassierer(in) ⓜ/ⓕ *ka·see·rer/ka·see·re·rin*
casino Kasino ⓝ *ka·zee·no*
cassette Kassette ⓕ *ka·se·te*
castle Burg ⓕ *burk*
casual work Gelegenheitsarbeit ⓕ *ge·lay·gen·haits·ar·bait*
cat Katze ⓕ *ka·tse*
cathedral Dom ⓜ *dawm*
Catholic Katholik(in) ⓜ/ⓕ *ka·to·leek/ka·to·lee·kin*
cauliflower Blumenkohl ⓜ *bloo·men·kawl*
cave Höhle ⓕ *her·le*
caviar Kaviar ⓜ *kah·vi·ahr*
CD CD ⓕ *tsay·day*
celebration Feier ⓕ *fai·er*
cellar Keller ⓜ *ke·ler*
cemetery Friedhof ⓜ *freet·hawf*
cent Cent ⓜ *sent*
centigrade Celsius ⓝ *tsel·zi·us*
centimetre Zentimeter ⓜ *tsen·ti·may·ter*
central heating Zentralheizung ⓕ *tsen·trahl·hai·tsung*
centre Zentrum ⓝ *tsen·trum*

ceramic Keramik ① ke·*rah*·mik
cereal Frühstücksflocke ①
frü·shtüks·flo·ke
certificate Zertifikat ⑩ tser·ti·fi·*kaht*
chain Kette ① *ke*·te
chair Stuhl ⑩ shtool
chairlift (skiing) Sessellift ⑩
ze·se·lift
championships Meisterschaften ①
pl *mais*·ter·shaf·ten
chance Zufall ⑩ *tsoo*·tal
change (coins) Wechselgeld ⑩
vek·sel·gelt
change (money) wechseln *vek*·seln
change (trains) umsteigen
um·shtai·gen
changing room Umkleideraum ⑩
um·klai·de·rowm
chapel Kapelle ① ka·*pe*·le
charming charmant shar·*mant*
chat up anbaggern *an*·ba·gern
cheap billig *bi*·likh
cheat Betrüger(in) ⑩/① be·*trü*·ger/
be·*trü*·ge·rin
check (banking) Scheck ⑩ shek
check (bill) Rechnung ① *rekh*·nung
check prüfen *prü*·fen
check-in (desk) Abfertigungs-
chalter ⑩ *ap*·fer·ti·gungks·shal·ter
checkpoint Kontrollstelle ①
kon·*trol*·shte·le
cheese Käse ⑩ *kay*·ze
chef Koch/Köchin ⑩/① kokh/
ker·khin
chemist Apotheke ① a·po·*tay*·ke
cheque (banking) Scheck ⑩ shek
chess Schach ⑩ shakh
chest Brustkorb ⑩ *brust*·korp
chewing gum Kaugummi ⑩
kow·gu·mi
chicken Huhn ⑩ hoon
chicken breast Hühnerbrust ①
hü·ner·brust
chicken drumstick Hähnchenschenkel ⑩ *hayn*·khen·sheng·kel
chickpea Kichererbse ①
ki·kher·erp·se

child Kind ⑩ kint
child seat Kindersitz ⑩ *kin*·der·zits
childminding Kinderbetreuung ①
kin·der·be·troy·ung
children Kinder ⑩ pl *kin*·der
chiropractor Chiropraktiker ⑩
khee·ro·*prak*·ti·ker
chocolate Schokolade ①
sho·ko·*lah*·de
choose (aus)wählen (ows·)*vay*·len
christening Taufe ① *tow*·fe
Christian Christ(in) ⑩/① krist/
kris·tin
Christian name Vorname ⑩
fawr·nah·me
Christmas Weihnachten ⑩
vai·nakh·ten
Christmas Day (erster)
Weihnachtsfeiertag ⑩ (*ers*·ter)
vai·nakhts·fai·er·tahk
Christmas Eve Heiligabend ⑩
hai·likh·*ah*·bent
Christmas tree Weihnachtsbaum ⑩
vai·nakhts·bowm
church Kirche ① *kir*·khe
cider Apfelmost ⑩ *ap*·fel·most
cigar Zigarre ① tsi·*ga*·re
cigarette Zigarette ① tsi·ga·*re*·te
cigarette lighter Feuerzeug ⑩
foy·er·tsoyk
cinema Kino ⑩ *kee*·no
circus Zirkus ⑩ *tsir*·kus
citizenship Staatsbürgerschaft ①
shtahts·bür·ger·shaft
city Stadt ① shtat
city centre Innenstadt ① *i*·nen·shtat
civil rights Bürgerrechte ⑩ pl
bür·ger·rekh·te
civil servant Beamte/Beamtin ⑩/①
be·*am*·te/be·*am*·tin
class Klasse ① *kla*·se
classical klassisch *kla*·sish
clean sauber *zow*·ber
cleaning Reinigung ① *rai*·ni·gung
client Kunde/Kundin ⑩/① *kun*·de/
kun·din

cliff Klippe ⓕ *kli*·pe
climate Klima ⓝ *klee*·ma
climb klettern *kle*·tern
cloak Mantel ⓜ *man*·tel
cloakroom Garderobe ⓕ gar·*draw*·be
clock Uhr ⓕ oor
close (shut) schließen *shlee*·sen
close (nearby) nahe *nah*·e
closed geschlossen ge·*shlo*·sen
clothesline Wäscheleine ⓕ ve·she·lai·ne
clothing Kleidung ⓕ *klai*·dung
clothing store Bekleidungsgeschäft ⓝ be·*klai*·dungks·ge·sheft
cloud Wolke ⓕ *vol*·ke
cloudy wolkig *vol*·kikh
clove (spice) Gewürznelke ⓕ ge·*vürts*·nel·ke
clove (of garlic) Zehe ⓕ *tsay*·e
clutch (car) Kupplung ⓕ *kup*·lung
coach (bus) Bus ⓜ bus
coach (sport) Trainer(in) ⓜ/ⓕ *tray*·ner/*tray*·ne·rin
coast Küste ⓕ *küs*·te
coat Mantel ⓜ *man*·tel
cocaine Kokain ⓝ ko·ka·*een*
cockroach Kakerlake ⓕ *kah*·ker·lah·ke
cocoa Kakao ⓜ ka·*kow*
coffee Kaffee ⓜ *ka*·fay
coins Münzen ⓕ pl *mün*·tsen
cold kalt kalt
have a cold erkältet sein er·*kel*·tet zain
colleague Kollege/Kollegin ⓜ/ⓕ ko·*lay*·ge/ko·*lay*·gin
collect call R-Gespräch ⓝ *air*·ge·shpraykh
college College ⓝ ko·*lidzh*
colour Farbe ⓕ *far*·be
comb Kamm ⓜ kam
come kommen *ko*·men
comedy Komödie ⓕ ko·*mer*·di·e
comfortable bequem be·*kvaym*
communion Kommunion ⓕ ko·mun·*yawn*

companion Begleiter(in) ⓜ/ⓕ be·*glai*·ter/be·*glai*·te·rin
company Firma ⓕ *fir*·ma
compass Kompass ⓜ *kom*·pas
complain sich beschweren zikh be·*shvair*·ren
computer Computer ⓜ kom·*pyoo*·ter
computer game Computerspiel ⓝ kom·*pyoo*·ter·shpeel
concert Konzert ⓝ kon·*tsert*
concert hall Konzerthalle ⓕ kon·*tsert*·ha·le
conditioner Spülung ⓕ *shpü*·lung
condom Kondom ⓝ kon·*dawm*
conductor Schaffner(in) ⓜ/ⓕ *shaf*·ner/*shaf*·ne·rin
confession (religious) Beichte ⓕ *baikh*·te
confirm (a booking) bestätigen be·*shtay*·ti·gen
connection Verbindung ⓕ fer·*bin*·dung
conservative konservativ kon·zer·va·*teef*
constipation Verstopfung ⓕ fer·*shtop*·fung
consulate Konsulat ⓝ kon·zu·*laht*
contact lenses Kontaktlinsen ⓕ pl kon·*takt*·lin·zen
contraceptives Verhütungsmittel ⓝ fer·*hü*·tungks·mi·tel
contract Vertrag ⓜ fer·*trahk*
convenience store Kiosk ⓜ *kee*·osk
convent Kloster ⓝ *klaws*·ter
cook Koch/Köchin ⓜ/ⓕ kokh/*ker*·khin
cook kochen *ko*·khen
cookie Keks ⓜ kayks
corner Ecke ⓕ *e*·ke
cornflakes Cornflakes pl *korn*·flayks
corrupt korrupt ko·*rupt*
cost kosten *kos*·ten
cottage cheese Hüttenkäse ⓜ *hü*·ten·kay·ze
cotton Baumwolle ⓕ *bowm*·vo·le

cotton balls Watte-Pads pl
va·te·pedz
cough husten *hoos·ten*
cough medicine Hustensaft ⓜ
hoos·ten·zaft
count zählen *tsay·len*
counter (at bar) Theke ⓕ *tay·ke*
country Land ⓝ lant
countryside Land ⓝ lant
coupon Coupon ⓜ *ku·pong*
courgette Zucchini ⓕ *tsu·kee·ni*
court (legal) Gericht ⓝ *ge·rikht*
court (tennis) Platz ⓜ plats
couscous Couscous ⓜ *kus·kus*
cousin Cousin(e) ⓜ/ⓕ *ku·zen/*
ku·zee·ne
cover charge Eintrittsgeld ⓝ
ain·trits·gelt
cow Kuh ⓕ koo
cracker Cracker ⓜ *kre·ker*
crafts Handwerk ⓝ *hant·verk*
cramp Krampf ⓜ krampf
crash Zusammenstoß ⓜ
tsu·za·men·staws
crazy verrückt *fe·rükt*
cream Sahne ⓕ *zah·ne*
cream cheese Frischkäse ⓜ
frish·kay·ze
crèche Kinderkrippe ⓕ *kin·der·kri·pe*
credit card Kreditkarte ⓕ
kre·deet·kar·te
cricket Cricket ⓝ *kri·ket*
crop Feldfrucht ⓕ *felt·frukht*
cross (religious) Kreuz ⓝ kroyts
cross (angry) wütend *vü·tent*
crowded überfüllt *ü·ber·fült*
cuckoo clock Kuckucksuhr ⓕ
ku·kuks·oor
cucumber Gurke ⓕ *gur·ke*
cup Tasse ⓕ *ta·se*
cupboard Schrank ⓜ shrangk
currency Währung ⓕ *vair·rung*
currency exchange Geldwechsel ⓜ
gelt·vek·sel
current (electricity) Strom ⓜ
shtrawm

current affairs Aktuelles ⓝ
ak·tu·e·les
curry (powder) Curry(pulver) ⓝ
ker·ri(·pul·ver)
customs Zoll ⓜ tsol
cut schneiden *shnai·den*
cutlery Besteck ⓝ be·*shtek*
CV Lebenslauf ⓜ *lay·bens·lowf*
cycle radfahren *raht·fah·ren*
cycling Radsport ⓜ *raht·shport*
cyclist Radfahrer(in) ⓜ/ⓕ
raht·fah·rer/raht·fah·re·rin
cystitis Blasenentzündung ⓕ
blah·zen·en·tsün·dung

D

dad Papa ⓜ *pa·pa*
daily täglich *tayk·likh*
dairy products Milchprodukte ⓝ pl
milkh·pro·duk·te
damp feucht foykht
dance tanzen *tan·tsen*
dangerous gefährlich *ge·fair·likh*
dark dunkel *dung·kel*
date (a person) mit jemandem ausgehen *mit yay·man·dem ows·gay·en*
date (appointment) Verabredung
ⓕ *fer·ap·ray·dung*
date (day) Datum ⓝ *dah·tum*
date of birth Geburtsdatum ⓝ
ge·burts·dah·tum
daughter Tochter ⓕ *tokh·ter*
daughter-in-law Schwiegertochter
ⓕ *shvee·ger·tokh·ter*
dawn Dämmerung ⓕ *de·me·rung*
day Tag ⓜ tahk
day after tomorrow übermorgen
ü·ber·mor·gen
day before yesterday vorgestern
fawr·ges·tern
dead tot tawt
deaf taub towp
deal (cards) austeilen *ows·tai·len*
decide entscheiden
ent·shai·den
deep tief teef

D

deforestation Abholzung ⓕ
ap·hol·tsung

degree Grad ⓜ *graht*

delay Verspätung ⓕ *fer·shpay·tung*

delicatessen Feinkostgeschäft ⓝ
fain·kost·ge·sheft

delicious köstlich *kerst·likh*

deliver (aus)liefern *(ows·)lee·fern*

demand Forderung ⓕ *for·de·rung*

democracy Demokratie ⓕ
de·mo·kra·tee

demonstration Demonstration ⓕ
de·mons·tra·tsyawn

Denmark Dänemark ⓝ
dair·ne·mark

dental floss Zahnseide ⓕ
tsahn·zai·de

dentist Zahnarzt/Zahnärztin ⓜ/ⓕ
tsahn·artst/tsahn·erts·tin

deodorant Deo ⓝ *day·o*

depart (leave) abfahren *ap·fah·ren*

department store Warenhaus ⓝ
vah·ren·hows

departure Abfahrt ⓕ *ap·fahrt*

deposit Anzahlung ⓕ *an·tsah·lung*

descendant Nachkomme ⓜ
nahkh·ko·me

desert Wüste ⓕ *vüs·te*

design entwerfen *ent·ver·fen*

destination (Reise)Ziel ⓝ *(rai·ze·)·tseel*

detail Detail ⓝ *de·tai*

diabetes Diabetis ⓕ *di·a·bay·tis*

dial tone Wählton ⓜ *vayl·tawn*

diaper Windel ⓕ *vin·del*

diaphragm (body) Zwerchfell ⓝ
tsverkh·fel

diarrhoea Durchfall ⓜ *durkh·fal*

diary (for appointments)
Terminkalender ⓜ *ter·meen·ka·len·der*

diary (record of events) Tagebuch
ⓝ *tah·ge·bookh*

dice (die) Würfel ⓜ *vür·fel*

dictionary Wörterbuch ⓝ
ver·ter·bookh

die sterben *shter·ben*

diet Diät ⓕ *di·ayt*

different andere *an·de·re*

difficult schwierig *shvee·rikh*

dining car Speisewagen ⓜ
shpai·ze·vah·gen

dinner Abendessen ⓝ *ah·bent·e·sen*

direct direkt *di·rekt*

direct-dial Durchwahl ⓕ *durkh·vahl*

director Regisseur(in) ⓜ/ⓕ
re·zhi·ser/re·zhi·ser·rin

directory enquiries Telefonauskunft
ⓕ *te·le·fawn·ows·kunft*

dirty schmutzig *shmu·tsikh*

disabled behindert *be·hin·dert*

disco Disko(thek) ⓕ *dis·ko(·tayk)*

discount Rabatt ⓜ *ra·bat*

discrimination Diskriminierung ⓕ
dis·kri·mi·nee·rung

disease Krankheit ⓕ *krangk·hait*

disk (computer) Diskette ⓕ
dis·ke·te

diving Tauchen ⓝ *tow·khen*

dizzy schwindelig *shvin·de·likh*

do tun *toon*

doctor (medical) Arzt/Ärztin ⓜ/ⓕ
artst/erts·tin

doctor (title) Doktor(in) ⓜ/ⓕ
dok·tor/dok·taw·rin

documentary Dokumentation ⓕ
do·ku·men·ta·tsyawn

dog Hund ⓜ *hunt*

dole (unemployment benefit) Arbeitslosengeld ⓝ
ar·baits·law·zen·gelt

doll Puppe ⓕ *pu·pe*

dollar Dollar ⓜ *do·lahr*

door Tür ⓕ *tür*

dope (drugs) Dope ⓝ *dawp/dohp*

double doppelt *do·pelt*

double bed Doppelbett ⓝ *do·pel·bet*

down (nach) unten *(nahkh) un·ten*

downhill abwärts *ap·verts*

dozen Dutzend ⓝ *du·tsent*

drama Schauspiel ⓝ *show·shpeel*

dream träumen *troy·men*

dress Kleid ⓝ *klait*

dried fruit Trockenobst ⓝ
tro·ken·awpst

drink Getränk ⓝ ge·*trengk*
drink trinken *tring*·ken
drive fahren *fah*·ren
driving licence Führerschein ⓜ *fü*·rer·shain
drug Droge ⓕ *draw*·ge
drug addiction Drogenabhängigkeit ⓕ *draw*·gen·ap·heng·ikh·kait
drug dealer Drogenhändler ⓜ *draw*·gen·hen·dler
drunk betrunken be·*trung*·ken
dry (clothes) trocknen *trok*·nen
dry (wine) trocken *tro*·ken
dry-cleaner chemische Reinigung ⓕ *khay*·mi·she·*rai*·ni·gung
duck Ente ⓕ *en*·te
dummy (pacifier) Schnuller ⓜ *shnu*·ler
during während *vair*·rent
dusk Dämmerung ⓕ *de*·me·rung

E

each jeder/jede/jedes ⓜ/ⓕ/ⓝ *yay*·der/*yay*·de/*yay*·des
ear Ohr ⓝ awr
early früh frü
earn verdienen fer·*dee*·nen
earplugs Ohrenstöpsel ⓜ *aw*·ren·shterp·sel
earrings Ohrringe ⓜ pl *awr*·ring·e
Earth Erde ⓕ *er*·de
earthquake Erdbeben ⓝ *ert*·bay·ben
east Osten ⓜ *os*·ton
Easter Ostern ⓝ *aws*·tern
easy leicht laikht
eat essen *e*·sen
economy class Touristenklasse ⓕ tu·*ris*·ten·kla·se
eczema Ekzem ⓝ ek·*tsaym*
editor Herausgeber(in) ⓜ/ⓕ he·*rows*·gay·ber/he·*rows*·gay·be·rin
education Erziehung ⓕ er·*tsee*·ung
egg Ei ⓝ ai
eggplant Aubergine ⓕ aw·ber·*zhee*·ne
elections Wahlen ⓕ pl *vah*·len

electrical store Elektrogeschäft ⓝ e·*lek*·tro·ge·sheft
electrician Elektriker(in) ⓜ/ⓕ e·*lek*·tri·ker/e·*lek*·tri·ke·rin
electricity Elektrizität ⓕ e·lek·tri·tsi·*tayt*
elevator Lift ⓜ lift
embarrassed verlegen fer·*lay*·gen
embassy Botschaft ⓕ *bawt*·shaft
embroidery Stickerei ⓕ shti·ke·*rai*
emergency Notfall ⓜ *nawt*·fal
emotional emotional e·mo·tsyo·*nahl*
employee Angestellte ⓜ&ⓕ *an*·ge·shtel·te
employer Arbeitgeber ⓜ *ar*·bait·gay·ber
empty leer lair
end Ende ⓝ *en*·de
end beenden be·*en*·den
endangered (species) bedrohte (Art) ⓕ be·*draw*·te art
energy Energie ⓕ e·ner·*gee*
engagement (marriage) Verlobung ⓕ fer·*law*·bung
engine Motor ⓜ *maw*·tor/mo·*tawr*
engineer Ingenieur(in) ⓜ/ⓕ in·zhe·*nyer*/in·zhe·*nyer*·rin
engineering Ingenieurwesen ⓕ in·zhe·*nyer*·vay·zen
England England ⓝ *eng*·lant
English Englisch ⓝ *eng*·lish
enjoy (oneself) sich amüsieren zikh a·mü·*zee*·ren
enough genug ge·*nook*
enter eintreten *ain*·tray·ten
entertainment guide Veranstaltungskalender ⓜ fer·*an*·shtal·tungks·ka·len·der
envelope Briefumschlag ⓜ *breef*·um·shlahk
environment Umwelt ⓕ *um*·velt
epilepsy Epilepsie ⓕ e·pi·lep·*see*
equal opportunity Chancengleichheit ⓕ *shahng*·sen·glaikh·hait
equality Gleichheit ⓕ *glaikh*·hait
equipment Ausrüstung ⓕ *ows*·rüs·tung

F

escalator Rolltreppe ⓕ *rol*·tre·pe
euro Euro ⓜ *oy*·ro
Europe Europa ⓝ *oy*·raw·pa
euthanasia Euthanasie ⓕ
oy·ta·na·zee
evening Abend ⓜ *ah*·bent
every jeder/jede/jedes ⓜ/ⓕ/ⓝ
yay·der/*yay*·de/*yay*·des
every day alltäglich al·*tayk*·likh
everyone jeder *yay*·der
everything alles *a*·les
example Beispiel ⓝ *bai*·shpeel
for example zum Beispiel tsum
bai·shpeel
excellent ausgezeichnet
ows·ge·*tsaikh*·net
excess baggage Übergepäck ⓝ
ü·ber·ge·pek
exchange Umtausch ⓜ *um*·towsh
exchange wechseln *vek*·seln
exchange rate Wechselkurs ⓜ
vek·sel·kurs
excluded ausgeschlossen
ows·ge·*shlo*·sen
exhaust (car) Auspuff ⓜ *ows*·puf
exhibition Ausstellung ⓕ
ows·shte·lung
exit Ausgang ⓜ *ows*·gang
expensive teuer *toy*·er
experience Erfahrung ⓕ er·*fah*·rung
exploitation Ausbeutung ⓕ
ows·boy·tung
express Express- eks·*pres*·
express mail Expresspost ⓕ
eks·*pres*·post
extension (visa) Verlängerung ⓕ
fer·*leng*·e·rung
eye Auge ⓝ *ow*·ge
eye drops Augentropfen ⓜ pl
ow·gen·trop·fen

F

fabric Gewebe ⓝ ge·*vay*·be
face Gesicht ⓝ ge·*zikht*
face cloth Waschlappen ⓜ
vash·la·pen

factory Fabrik ⓕ fa·*breek*
factory worker Fabrik-arbeiter(in)
ⓜ/ⓕ fa·*breek*·ar·bai·ter/
fa·*breek*·ar·bai·te·rin
fair (trade) Messe ⓕ *me*·se
fall (autumn) Herbst ⓜ herpst
false falsch falsh
family Familie ⓕ fa·*mee*·li·e
family name Familienname ⓜ
fa·*mee*·li·en·nah·me
famous berühmt be·*rümt*
fan (sports) Fan ⓜ fen
fan (machine) Ventilator ⓜ
ven·ti·*lah*·tor
fanbelt Keilriemen ⓜ *kail*·ree·men
far weit vait
farm Bauernhof ⓜ *bow*·ern·hawf
farmer Bauer/Bäuerin ⓜ/ⓕ *bow*·er/
boy·e·rin
fast schnell shnel
fat dick dik
father Vater ⓜ *fah*·ter
father-in-law Schwiegervater ⓜ
shvee·ger·fah·ter
faucet Wasserhahn ⓜ *va*·ser·hahn
fault (someone's) Schuld ⓕ shult
faulty fehlerhaft *fay*·ler·haft
fax Fax ⓝ faks
feed füttern *fü*·tern
feel fühlen *fü*·len
feelings Gefühle ⓝ pl ge·*fü*·le
fence Zaun ⓜ tsown
fencing (sport) Fechten ⓝ *fekh*·ten
ferry Fähre ⓕ *fair*·re
festival Fest ⓝ fest
fever Fieber ⓝ *fee*·ber
few wenige *vay*·ni·ge
a few ein paar ain pahr
fiance/fiancee Verlobte ⓜ&ⓕ
fer·*lawp*·te
fiction Prosa ⓕ *praw*·za
field Feld ⓝ felt
fig Feige ⓕ *fai*·ge
fight Kampf ⓜ kampf
fill füllen *fü*·len
fillet Filet ⓝ fi·*lay*

film (cinema) Film ⓜ film
film (camera) Film ⓜ film
film speed Empfindlichkeit ①
emp·*fint*·likh·kait
filtered gefiltert ge·*fil*·tert
find finden *fin*·den
fine (payment) Geldbuße ①
gelt·boo·se
finger Finger ⓜ *fing*·er
finish beenden be·*en*·den
fire Feuer ⓝ *foy*·er
firewood Brennholz ⓝ *bren*·holts
first erste *ers*·te
first class erste Klasse ① *ers*·te
kla·se
first-aid kit Verbandskasten ⓜ
fer·*bants*·kas·ton
fish Fisch ⓜ fish
fish shop Fischgeschäft ⓝ
fish·ge·sheft
fishing Fischen ⓝ *fi*·shen
fishing rod Angel ① *ang*·el
flag Flagge ① *fla*·ge
flash Blitz ⓜ blits
flashlight Taschenlampe ①
ta·*shen*·lam·pe
flat flach flakh
flea Floh ⓜ flaw
flea-market Flohmarkt ⓜ *flaw*·markt
flight Flug ⓜ flook
flooding Überschwemmung ⑦
ü·ber·*shvem*·mung
floor Boden ⓜ *baw*·den
floor (storey) Stock ⓜ shtok
florist Blumenhändler ⓜ
bloo·men·hen·dler
flour Mehl ⓝ mayl
flower Blume ① *bloo*·me
fly Fliege ① *flee*·ge
fly fliegen *flee*·gen
foggy neblig *nay*·blikh
follow folgen *fol*·gen
food Essen ⓝ *e*·sen
food poisoning Lebensmittelvergiftung ① *lay*·bens·mi·tel·fer·*gif*·tung
foot Fuß ⓜ foos

football (soccer) Fußball ⓜ *foos*·bal
American football American
Football ⓜ e·*me*·ri·ken *fut*·bawl
Australian Rules Football
Australian Rules Football ⓜ
aws·*tray*·li·en roolz *fut*·bawl
footpath Gehweg ⓜ *gay*·vayk
for für für
foreign ausländisch *ows*·len·dish
forest Wald ⓜ valt
forever immer *i*·mer
forget vergessen fer·*ge*·sen
forgive verzeihen fer·*tsai*·en
fork Gabel ① *gah*·bel
formal formell for·*mel*
fortnight vierzehn Tage ⑦ pl
feer·*tsayn* *tah*·ge
foul Foul ⓝ fawl
fountain Brunnen ⓜ *bru*·nen
foyer Foyer ⓝ fo·a·*yay*
fragile zerbrechlich tser·*brekh*·likh
frame Rahmen ⓜ *rah*·men
franc Franc ⓜ frank
France Frankreich ⓝ *frangk*·raikh
free (gratis) gratis *grah*·tis
free (not bound) frei frai
freeze gefrieren ge·*free*·ren
fresh (not stale) frisch frish
Friday Freitag ⓜ *frai*·tahk
friend Freund(in) ⓜ/① *froynt*/
froyn·din
friendly freundlich *froynt*·likh
frog Frosch ⓜ frosh
from aus · von ows · fon
in front of vor fawr
frost Frost ⓜ frost
fruit Frucht ① frukht
fruit picking Obsternte ①
awpst·ern·te
fry braten *brah*·ten
frying pan Bratpfanne ①
braht·pfa·ne
fuel Brennstoff ⓜ *bren*·shtof
full voll fol
full-time Vollzeit ① *fol*·tsait
fun Spaß ⓜ shpahs
funeral Begräbnis ⓝ be·*grayp*·nis

funny lustig *lus*·tikh
furniture Möbel ⑩ pl *mer*·bel
fuse Sicherung ① *zi*·khe·rung
future Zukunft ① *tsoo*·kunft

G

game (sport) Spiel ⑩ shpeel
garage (car repair) Werkstatt ①
verk·shtat
garage (car shelter) Garage ①
ga·*rah*·zhe
garbage Abfall ⑩ *ap*·fal
garden Garten ⑩ *gar*·ten
garlic Knoblauch ⑩ *knawp*·lowkh
gas (cooking) Gas ⑩ gahs
gas (petrol) Benzin ⑩ ben·*tseen*
gas cartridge Gaskartusche ①
gahs·kar·tu·she
gas cylinder Gasflasche ①
gahs·fla·she
gastroenteritis Magen-Darm-
Katarrh ⑩ *mah*·gen·darm·ka·*tar*
gate Tor ⑩ tawr
gay schwul shvool
gears Gänge ⑩ pl *geng*·e
general allgemein al·ge·*main*
German Deutsch ⑩ doytsh
Germany Deutschland ⑩
doytsh·lant
gift Geschenk ⑩ ge·*shengk*
gig Auftritt ⑩ *owf*·trit
gin Gin ⑩ dzhin
ginger Ingwer ⑩ *ing*·ver
girl Mädchen ⑩ *mayt*·khen
girlfriend Freundin ① *froyn*·din
give geben *gay*·ben
glacier Gletscher ⑩ *glet*·sher
glandular fever Drüsenfieber ⑩
drü·zen·fee·ber
glass Glas ⑩ glahs
glasses (spectacles) Brille ① *bri*·le
glove Handschuh ⑩ *hant*·shoo
go (on foot) gehen *gay*·en
go (by vehicle) fahren *fah*·ren
go out with ausgehen mit
ows·gay·en mit

go shopping einkaufen gehen
ain·kow·fen gay·en
goal Tor ⑩ tawr
goalkeeper Torwart/Torhüterin
⑩/① *tawr*·vart/*tawr*·hü·te·rin
goat Ziege ① *tsee*·ge
god Gott ⑩ got
goggles (skiing) Skibrille ①
shee·bri·le
gold Gold ⑩ golt
golf ball Golfball ⑩ *golf*·bal
golf course Golfplatz ⑩ *golf*·plats
good gut goot
gorge Schlucht ① shlukht
government Regierung ①
re·*gee*·rung
gram Gramm ⑩ gram
grandchild Enkelkind ⑩ *eng*·kel·kint
grandfather Großvater • Opa ⑩
graws·fah·ter • *aw*·pa
grandmother Großmutter • Oma ①
graws·mu·ter • *aw*·ma
grandparents Großeltern ⑩ pl
graws·el·tern
grapefruit Pampelmuse ①
pam·pel·*moo*·ze
grapes Weintrauben ① pl
vain·trow·ben
graphic art grafische Kunst ①
grah·fi·she kunst
grass Gras ⑩ grahs
grave Grab ⑩ grahp
gray grau grow
great groß graws
green grün grün
greengrocer Lebensmittelhändler ⑩
lay·bens·mi·tel·hen·dler
grey grau grow
grocery store Lebensmittelladen ⑩
lay·bens·mi·tel·lah·den
groundnut Erdnuss ① *ert*·nus
grow wachsen *vak*·sen
guess raten *rah*·ten
guide (audio) Führer ⑩ *fü*·rer
guide (person) Führer ⑩ *fü*·rer
guide dog Blindenhund ⑩
blin·den·hunt

guidebook Reiseführer ⓜ
rai·ze·fü·rer
guided tour Führung ⓕ fü·rung
guilty schuldig shul·dikh
guitar Gitarre ⓕ gi·ta·re
gum (mouth) Zahnfleisch ⓝ
tsahn·flaish
gym Fitness-Studio ⓝ
fit·nes·shtoo·di·o
gymnastics Gymnastik ⓕ
güm·nas·tik
gynaecologist Gynäkologe/
Gynäkologin ⓜ/ⓕ gü·ne·ko·law·ge/
gü·ne·ko·law·gin

H

hair Haar ⓝ hahr
hairbrush Haarbürste ⓕ
hahr·bürs·te
hairdresser Friseur(in) ⓜ/ⓕ fri·zer/
fri·zer·rin
Halal Halal· ha·lal·
half Hälfte ⓕ helf·te
half a litre ein halber Liter ⓜ ain
hal·ber lee·ter
hallucinate halluzinieren
ha·lu·tsi·nee·ren
ham Schinken ⓦ shing·ken
hammer Hämmer ⓜ ha·mer
hammock Hängematte ⓕ
heng·e·ma·te
hamster Hamster ⓜ hams·ter
hand Hand ⓕ hant
handbag Handtasche ⓕ hant·ta·she
handicrafts Kunsthandwerk ⓝ
kunst·hant·verk
handlebar Lenker ⓜ leng·ker
handmade handgemacht
hant·ge·makht
handsome gutaussehend
goot·ows·zay·ent
hang-gliding Drachenfliegen ⓝ
dra·khen·flee·gen
happy glücklich glük·likh
harassment Belästigung ⓕ
be·les·ti·gung

harbour Hafen ⓜ hah·fen
hard (difficult) schwer shvair
hard (not soft) hart hart
hardware store Eisenwarengeschäft
ⓝ ai·zen·vah·ren·ge·sheft
hash Haschee ⓝ ha·shay
hat Hut ⓜ hoot
hate hassen ha·sen
have haben hah·ben
hay fever Heuschnupfen ⓜ
hoy·shnup·fen
he er air
head Kopf ⓜ kopf
headache Kopfschmerzen ⓜ pl
kopf·shmer·tsen
headlights Scheinwerfer ⓜ pl
shain·ver·fer
health Gesundheit ⓕ ge·zunt·hait
hear hören her·ren
hearing aid Hörgerät ⓝ her·ge·rayt
heart Herz ⓝ herts
heart condition Herzleiden ⓝ
herts·lai·den
heat Hitze ⓕ hi·tse
heater Heizgerät ⓝ haits·ge·rayt
heavy schwer shvair
hello hallo ha·lo
helmet Helm ⓜ holm
help helfen hel·fen
hepatitis Hepatitis ⓕ he·pa·tee·tis
her ihr eer
herbalist Naturheilkundige ⓜ&ⓕ
na·toor·hail·kun·di·ge
herbs Kräuter ⓝ pl kroy·ter
here hier heer
heroin Heroin ⓝ he·ro·een
herring Hering ⓝ hay·ring
high hoch hawkh
high school Sekundarschule ⓕ
ze·kun·dahr·shoo·le
hike wandern van·dern
hiking Wandern ⓝ van·dern
hiking boots Wanderstiefel ⓜ pl
van·der·shtee·fel
hiking route Wanderweg ⓜ
van·der·vayk
hill Hügel ⓜ hü·gel

I

Hindu Hindu ⓜ&ⓕ *hin*·du
hire mieten *mee*·ten
his sein zain
historical historisch his·*taw*·rish
hitchhike trampen *trem*·pen
HIV positive HIV-positiv
hah·ee·fow·*paw*·zi·teef
hockey Hockey ⓝ *ho*·ki
holiday Urlaub ⓜ *oor*·lowp
holidays Ferien pl *fair*·ri·en
holy heilig *hai*·likh
Holy Week Karwoche ⓕ *kahr*·vo·khe
home Heim ⓝ haim
(at) home zu Hause tsoo *how*·ze
(go) home nach Hause nahkh
how·ze
homeless obdachlos *op*·dakh·laws
homemaker Hausmann/Hausfrau
ⓜ/ⓕ *hows*·man/*hows*·frow
to be homesick Heimweh haben
haim·vay *hah*·ben
homeopathic medicine
homöopathisches Mittel ⓝ
haw·mer·o·*pah*·ti·shes *mi*·tel
homosexual homosexuell
haw·mo·zek·su·*el*
honest ehrlich *air*·likh
honey Honig ⓜ *haw*·nikh
honeymoon Flitterwochen ⓕ pl
fli·ter·vo·khen
horoscope Horoskop ⓝ ho·ros·*kawp*
horse Pferd ⓝ pfert
horse riding Reiten ⓝ *rai*·ten
horseradish Meerrettich ⓜ
mair·re·tikh
hospital Krankenhaus ⓝ
krang·ken·hows
hospitality Gastfreundschaft ⓕ
gast·froynt·shaft
hot heiß hais
hot water warmes Wasser ⓝ
var·mes *va*·ser
hotel Hotel ⓝ ho·*tel*
house Haus ⓝ hows
housework Hausarbeit ⓕ
hows·ar·bait
how wie vee

hug umarmen um·*ar*·men
huge riesig *ree*·sikh
human menschlich *mensh*·likh
human rights Menschenrechte ⓝ pl
men·shen·rekh·te
humanities Geisteswissenschaften
ⓕ pl *gais*·tes·vi·sen·shaf·ten
hundred hundert *hun*·dert
hungry hungrig *hung*·rikh
hunting Jagd ⓕ yahkt
in a hurry in Eile in *ai*·le
hurt verletzen fer·*le*·tsen
hurt (yourself) sich weh tun zikh
vay toon
husband Ehemann ⓜ *ay*·e·man
hut Hütte ⓕ *hü*·te

I

I ich ikh
ice Eis ⓝ ais
ice axe Eispickel ⓜ *ais*·pi·kel
ice cream Eiscreme ⓕ *ais*·kraym
ice cream parlour Eisdiele ⓕ
ais·dee·le
ice hockey Eishockey ⓝ *ais*·ho·ki
ice skating Eislaufen ⓝ *ais*·low·fen
idea Idee ⓕ i·*day*
identification Ausweis ⓜ ows·vais
identification card Personalausweis
ⓜ per·zo·*nahl*·ows·vais
idiot Idiot ⓜ i·di·*awt*
if wenn ven
ignition Zündung ⓕ *tsün*·dung
ill krank krangk
illegal illegal i·le·gahl
imagination Phantasie ⓕ fan·ta·*zee*
immediately sofort zo·*fort*
immigration Immigration ⓕ
i·mi·gra·*tsyawn*
important wichtig *vikh*·tikh
impossible unmöglich un·*merk*·likh
in in in
in front of vor fawr
included inbegriffen *in*·be·gri·fen
income tax Einkommensteuer ⓕ
ain·ko·men·shtoy·er

India Indien ⓝ *in*·di·en
indicator Blinker ⓜ *bling*·ker
indigestion Magenverstimmung ⓕ *mah*·gen·fer·shti·mung
industry Industrie ⓕ in·dus·*tree*
inequality Ungleichheit ⓕ *un*·glaikh·hait
infection Entzündung ⓕ en·*tsün*·dung
inflammation Entzündung ⓕ en·*tsün*·dung
influenza Grippe ⓕ *gri*·pe
information Auskunft ⓕ *ows*·kunft
ingredient Zutat ⓕ *tsoo*·taht
inject injizieren in·yi·*tsee*·ren
injection (car) Einspritzung ⓕ *ain*·shpri·tsung
injection (medical) Injektion ⓕ in·yek·*tsyawn*
injury Verletzung ⓕ fer·*le*·tsung
in-line skating Rollschuhfahren ⓝ *rol*·shoo·fah·ren
innocent unschuldig *un*·shul·dikh
insect repellent Insektenschutzmittel ⓝ in·*zek*·ten·shuts·mi·tel
inside innen *i*·nen
instead of (an)statt (an·)*shtat*
instructor Lehrer(in) ⓜ/ⓕ *lair*·rer/*lair*·re·rin
insurance Versicherung ⓕ fer·*zi*·khe·rung
interesting interessant in·tre·*sant*
intermission Pause ⓕ *pow*·ze
international international in·ter·na·tsyo·*nahl*
internet Internet ⓝ *in*·ter·net
internet cafe Internetcafé ⓝ *in*·ter·net·ka·fay
interpreter Dolmetscher(in) ⓜ/ⓕ *dol*·met·sher/*dol*·met·she·rin
interview Interview ⓝ *in*·ter·vyoo
invite einladen *ain*·lah·den
Ireland Irland ⓝ *ir*·lant
iron (clothes) bügeln *bü*·geln
island Insel ⓕ *in*·zel
IT Informationstechnologie ⓕ in·for·ma·*tsyawns*·tekh·no·lo·gee

Italy Italien ⓝ ee·*tah*·li·en
itch Juckreiz ⓜ *yuk*·raits
itemised einzeln aufgeführt *ain*·tseln *owf*·ge·fürt
itinerary Reiseroute ⓕ *rai*·ze·roo·te

J

jacket Jacke ⓕ *ya*·ke
jail Gefängnis ⓝ ge·*feng*·nis
jam Marmelade ⓕ mar·me·*lah*·de
Japan Japan ⓝ *yah*·pahn
jar Glas ⓝ glahs
jaw Kiefer ⓜ *kee*·fer
jealous eifersüchtig *ai*·fer·zükh·tikh
jeans Jeans ⓕ pl dzheens
jeep Jeep ⓜ dzheep
jet lag Jetlag ⓜ *dzhet*·lag
jewellery Schmuck ⓜ shmuk
Jewish jüdisch *yü*·dish
job Arbeitsstelle ⓕ *ar*·baits·shte·le
jockey Jockey ⓜ *dzho*·ki
jogging Joggen ⓝ *dzho*·gen
joke Witz ⓜ vits
journalist Journalist(in) ⓜ/ⓕ zhur·na·*list*/zhur·na·*lis*·tin
journey Reise ⓕ *rai*·ze
judge Richter(in) ⓜ/ⓕ *rikh*·ter/*rikh*·te·rin
juice Saft ⓜ zaft
jump springen *shpring*·en
jumper (sweater) Pullover ⓜ pu·*lawver*
jumper leads Überbrückungskabel ⓝ ü·ber·*brü*·kungks·kah·bel
justice Gerechtigkeit ⓕ ge·*rekh*·tikh·kait

K

ketchup Ketchup ⓜ *ket*·chap
kettle Kessel ⓜ *ke*·sel
key Schlüssel ⓜ *shlü*·sel
keyboard Tastatur ⓕ tas·ta·*toor*
kick treten *tray*·ten
kill töten *ter*·ten
kilogram Kilogramm ⓝ *kee*·lo·gram

L

kilometre Kilometer ⓜ ki·lo·*may*·ter
kind nett net
kindergarten Kindergarten ⓜ
kin·der·gar·ten
king König ⓜ *ker*·nikh
kiss Kuss ⓜ kus
kiss küssen *kü*·sen
kitchen Küche ⓕ *kü*·khe
kitten Kätzchen ⓝ *kets*·khen
kiwifruit Kiwifrucht ⓕ *kee*·vi·frukht
knapsack Rucksack ⓜ *ruk*·zak
knee Knie ⓝ knee
knife Messer ⓝ *me*·ser
know (a person) kennen *ke*·nen
know (something) wissen *vi*·sen
kosher koscher *kaw*·sher

L

labourer Arbeiter(in) ⓜ/ⓕ
ar·bai·ter/*ar*·bai·te·rin
lace Spitze ⓕ *shpi*·tse
lager Lager ⓝ *lah*·ger
lake See ⓜ zay
lamb Lamm ⓝ lam
land Land ⓝ lant
landlady Vermieterin ⓕ
fer·*mee*·te·rin
landlord Vermieter ⓜ fer·*mee*·ter
language Sprache ⓕ *shprah*·khe
laptop Laptop ⓜ *lep*·top
lard Schmalz ⓝ shmalts
large groß graws
last (week) letzte (Woche) *lets*·te
(*vo*·khe)
late spät shpayt
laugh lachen *la*·khen
laundrette Wäscherei ⓕ ve·she·*rai*
laundry (room) Waschküche ⓕ
vash·kü·khe
law (subject) Jura ⓝ *yoo*·ra
law (rules) Gesetz ⓝ ge·*zets*
lawyer Rechtsanwalt/Rechtsanwältin ⓜ/ⓕ *rekhts*·an·valt/
rekhts·an·vel·tin
laxatives Abführmittel ⓝ
ap·*für*·mi·tel

lazy faul fowl
leader Anführer ⓜ *an*·fü·rer
leaf Blatt ⓝ blat
learn lernen *ler*·nen
lease Mietvertrag ⓜ *meet*·fer·trahk
leather Leder ⓝ *lay*·der
leave (depart) abfahren *ap*·fah·ren
lecturer Dozent(in) ⓜ/ⓕ do·*tsent*/
do·*tsen*·tin
leek Lauch ⓜ lowkh
left (direction) links lingks
left luggage Gepäckaufbewahrung
ⓕ ge·*pek*·owf·be·vah·rung
left-wing links(gerichtet)
lingks(·ge·rikh·tet)
leg (body) Bein ⓝ bain
legal legal le·*gahl*
legislation Gesetzgebung ⓕ
ge·*zets*·gay·bung
legume Hülsenfrucht ⓕ
hül·zen·frukht
lemon Zitrone ⓕ tsi·*traw*·ne
lemonade Limonade ⓕ
li·mo·*nah*·de
lens (camera) Objektiv ⓝ
op·yek·*teef*
Lent Fastenzeit ⓕ *fas*·ten·tsait
lentil Linse ⓕ *lin*·ze
lesbian Lesbierin ⓕ *les*·bi·e·rin
less weniger *vay*·ni·ger
letter Brief ⓜ breef
lettuce Kopfsalat ⓜ *kopf*·za·laht
liar Lügner(in) ⓜ/ⓕ *lüg*·ner/
lüg·ne·rin
library Bibliothek ⓕ bi·bli·o·*tayk*
lice Läuse ⓕ pl *loy*·ze
license plate number Autokennzeichen ⓝ *ow*·to·ken·tsai·khen
lie (not stand) liegen *lee*·gen
life Leben ⓝ *lay*·ben
lifejacket Schwimmweste ⓕ
shvim·ves·te
lift (elevator) Lift ⓜ lift
light (weight) Licht ⓝ likht
light hell hel
light bulb Glühbirne ⓕ *glü*·bir·ne

light meter Belichtungsmesser ⓜ
be·*likh*·tungks·me·ser
lighter (cigarette) Feuerzeug ⓝ
foy·er·tsoyk
lightning Blitz ⓜ blits
lights (on car) Scheinwerfer ⓜ pl
shain·ver·fer
like mögen *mer*·gen
lime Limone ⓕ li·*maw*·ne
line Linie ⓕ *lee*·ni·e
linen (bed) Bettwäsche ⓕ
bet·ve·she
linen (fabric) Leinen ⓝ *lai*·nen
lip balm Lippenbalsam ⓜ
li·pen·bal·zahm
lips Lippen ⓕ pl *li*·pen
lipstick Lippenstift ⓜ *li*·pen·shtift
liquor store Getränkehandel ⓝ
ge·*treng*·ke·han·del
listen hören *her*·ren
little klein klain
little (not much) wenig *vay*·nikh
a little ein bisschen ain *bis*·khen
live leben *lay*·ben
live (reside) wohnen *vaw*·nen
liver Leber ⓕ *lay*·ber
lizard Echse ⓕ *ek*·se
local örtlich *ert*·likh
lock Schloss ⓝ shlos
locked abgeschlossen *ap*·ge·shlo·sen
lollies Süßigkeiten ⓕ pl
zü·sikh·kai·ten
lonely einsam *ain*·zahm
long lang lang
long-sleeved langärmelig
lang·er·me·likh
look (an)sehen (*an*·)*zay*·en
look after sich kümmern um zikh
kü·mern um
look for suchen nach *zoo*·khen
nahkh
lookout Aussichtspunkt ⓜ
ows·zikhts·pungkt
loose change Kleingeld ⓝ
klain·gelt
lose verlieren fer·*lee*·ren
lost verloren fer·*law*·ren

lost property office Fundbüro ⓝ
funt·bü·raw
a lot (of) viel feel
loud laut lowt
love lieben *lee*·ben
lover Liebhaber(in) ⓜ/ⓕ
leep·hah·ber/*leep*·hah·be·rin
low niedrig *nee*·drikh
lubricant Schmiermittel ⓝ
shmeer·mi·tel
luck Glück ⓝ glük
lucky glücklich *glük*·likh
luggage Gepäck ⓝ ge·*pek*
luggage lockers Schließfächer ⓝ pl
shlees·fe·kher
luggage tag Adressanhänger ⓜ
a·*dres*·an·heng·er
lump (health) Knoten ⓜ *knaw*·ten
lunch Mittagessen ⓝ *mi*·tahk·e·sen
lungs Lungen ⓕ pl *lung*·en
luxury luxuriös luk·su·ri·*ers*

M

machine Maschine ⓕ ma·*shee*·ne
made of (cotton) aus (Baumwolle)
ows (*bowm*·vo·le)
magazine Zeitschrift ⓕ *tsait*·shrift
magician Zauberer(in) ⓜ/ⓕ
tsow·be·rer/*tsow*·be·re·rin
mail Post ⓕ post
mailbox Briefkasten ⓜ
breef·kas·ten
main Haupt- *howpt*·
main square Hauptplatz ⓜ
howpt·plats
make machen *ma*·khen
make-up Schminke ⓕ *shming*·ke
mammogram Mammogramm ⓝ
ma·mo·*gram*
man Mann ⓜ man
man (human being) Mensch ⓜ
mensh
manager Manager(in) ⓜ/ⓕ
me·ne·dzher/*me*·ne·dzhe·rin
mandarin Mandarine ⓕ
man·da·*ree*·ne

M

mango Mango ⓝ *mang*·go
manual worker Arbeiter(in) ⓜ/ⓕ *ar*·bai·ter/*ar*·bai·te·rin
many viele *fee*·le
map Karte ⓕ *kar*·te
margarine Margarine ⓕ mar·ga·*ree*·ne
marijuana Marihuana ⓝ ma·ri·hu·*ah*·na
marital status Familienstand ⓜ fa·*mee*·li·en·shtant
market Markt ⓜ markt
market square Marktplatz ⓜ *markt*·plats
marmalade Orangenmarmelade ⓕ o·*rahng*·zhen·mar·me·lah·de
marriage Ehe ⓕ *ay*·e
marry heiraten *hai*·rah·ten
martial arts Kampfsport ⓜ *kampf*·shport
mass (Catholic) Messe ⓕ *me*·se
massage Massage ⓕ ma·*sah*·zhe
masseur Masseur ⓜ ma·*ser*
masseuse Masseurin ⓕ ma·*ser*·rin
mat Matte ⓕ *ma*·te
match (sport) Spiel ⓝ shpeel
matches Streichhölzer ⓝ pl *shtraikh*·herl·tser
material Material ⓝ ma·te·ri·*ahl*
mattress Matratze ⓕ ma·*tra*·tse
maybe vielleicht fi·*laikht*
mayonnaise Majonnaise ⓕ ma·yo·*nay*·ze
mayor Bürgermeister(in) ⓜ/ⓕ *bür*·ger·mais·ter/*bür*·ger·mais·te·rin
measles Masern pl *mah*·zern
meat Fleisch ⓝ flaish
mechanic Mechaniker(in) ⓜ/ⓕ me·*khah*·ni·ker/me·*khah*·ni·ke·rin
media Medien pl *may*·di·en
medicine Medizin ⓕ me·di·*tseen*
meditation Meditation ⓕ me·di·ta·*tsyawn*
meet treffen *tre*·fen
melon Melone ⓕ me·*law*·ne
member Mitglied ⓝ *mit*·gleet

member of parliament Abgeordnete ⓜ&ⓕ *ap*·ge·ord·ne·te
menstruation Menstruation ⓕ mens·tru·a·*tsyawn*
menu Speisekarte ⓕ *shpai*·ze·kar·te
message Mitteilung ⓕ *mi*·tai·lung
metal Metall ⓝ me·*tal*
metre Meter ⓜ *may*·ter
metro station U-Bahnhof ⓜ *oo*·bahn·hawf
microwave Mikrowelle ⓕ *mee*·kro·ve·le
Middle East Nahe Osten ⓜ *nah*·e os·ten
midnight Mitternacht ⓕ *mi*·ter·nakht
migraine Migräne ⓕ mi·*gray*·ne
military Militär ⓝ mi·li·*tair*
military service Wehrdienst ⓜ *vair*·deenst
milk Milch ⓕ milkh
millimetre Millimeter ⓜ mi·li·*may*·ter
million Million ⓕ mi·*lyawn*
mince Gehacktes ⓝ ge·*hak*·tes
mind (look after) aufpassen *owf*·pa·sen
mineral water Mineralwasser ⓝ mi·ne·*rahl*·va·ser
mints Pfefferminzbonbons ⓝ pl pfe·fer·*mints*·bong·bongs
minute Minute ⓕ mi·*noo*·te
mirror Spiegel ⓜ *shpee*·gel
miscarriage Fehlgeburt ⓕ *fayl*·ge·burt
miss (feel absence of) vermissen fer·*mi*·sen
miss (the bus) verpassen fer·*pa*·sen
mistake Fehler ⓜ *fay*·ler
mix mischen *mi*·shen
mobile phone Handy ⓝ *hen*·di
modem Modem ⓝ *maw*·dem
moisturiser Feuchtigkeitscreme ⓕ *foykh*·tikh·kaits·kraym
monastery Kloster ⓝ *klaws*·ter
Monday Montag ⓜ *mawn*·tahk
money Geld ⓝ gelt
month Monat ⓜ *maw*·nat

monument Denkmal ⓝ *dengk*·mahl

(full) moon (Voll) Mond ⓜ *(fol·)* mawnt

more mehr mair

morning (6am–10am) Morgen ⓜ *mor*·gen

morning (10am–12pm) Vormittag ⓜ *fawr*·mi·tahk

morning sickness (Schwangerschafts-)Erbrechen ⓝ (*shvang*·er·shafts·)*er bre*·khen

mosque Moschee ⓕ mo·*shay*

mosquito Stechmücke ⓕ *shtekh*·mü·ke

mosquito coil Moskitospirale ⓕ mos·*kee*·to·shpi·rah·le

mother Mutter ⓕ *mu*·ter

mother-in-law Schwiegermutter ⓕ *shvee*·ger·mu·ter

motorboat Motorboot ⓝ *maw*·tor·bawt

motorcycle Motorrad ⓝ *maw*·tor·raht

motorway (tollway) Autobahn ⓕ *ow*·to·bahn

mountain Berg ⓜ *herk*

mountain bike Mountainbike ⓝ *mown*·tén·baik

mountain hut Berghütte ⓕ *berk·hü*·te

mountain path Bergweg ⓜ *herk*·vayk

mountain range Gebirgszug ⓜ ge·*birks*·tsook

mountaineering Bergsteigen ⓝ *berk*·shtai·gen

mouse Maus ⓕ mows

mouth Mund ⓜ munt

movie Film ⓜ film

mud Schlamm ⓜ shlam

muesli Müsli ⓝ *müs*·li

muggy schwül shvül

mum Mama ⓕ *ma*·ma

muscle Muskel ⓜ *mus*·kel

museum Museum ⓝ mu·*zay*·um

mushroom Pilz ⓜ pilts

music Musik ⓕ mu·*zeek*

musician Musiker(in) ⓜ/ⓕ *moo*·zi·ker/moo·zi·ke·rin

Muslim Moslem/Moslime ⓜ/ⓕ *mos*·lem/mos·*lee*·me

mussel Muschel ⓕ *mu*·shel

mustard Senf ⓜ zenf

mute stumm shtum

my mein/meine/mein ⓜ/ⓕ/ⓝ main/*mai*·ne/main

N

nail clippers Nagelknipser ⓜ pl *nah*·gel·knip·ser

name Name ⓜ *nah*·me

nappy Windel ⓕ *vin*·del

nappy rash Windeldermatitis ⓕ *vin*·del·der·ma·tee·tis

national park Nationalpark ⓜ na·tsyo·*nahl*·park

nationality Staatsangehörigkeit ⓕ *shtahts*·an·ge·her·rikh·kait

nature Natur ⓕ na·*toor*

nature reserve Naturreservat ⓝ na·*toor*·re·zer·vaht

naturopathy Naturheilkunde ⓕ na·*toor*·hail·kun·de

nausea Übelkeit ⓕ *ü*·bel·kait

near nahe *nah*·e

nearby in der Nähe in dair *nay*·e

nearest nächste *naykhs*·te

necessary notwendig *nawt*·ven·dikh

necklace Halskette ⓕ *hals*·ke·te

need brauchen *brow*·khen

needle (sewing) Nadel ⓕ *nah*·del

needle (syringe) Nadel ⓕ *nah*·del

neither auch nicht owkh nikht

nephew Neffe ⓜ *ne*·fe

net Netz ⓝ nets

Netherlands Niederlande pl *nee*·der·lan·de

never nie nee

new neu noy

New Year's Day Neujahrstag ⓜ *noy*·yahrs·tahk

O

New Year's Eve Silvester ⓜ
zil·ves·ter

New Zealand Neuseeland ⓝ
noy·zay·lant

news Nachrichten ⓕ pl
nahkh·rikh·ten

newsagency Zeitungshändler ⓜ
tsai·tungks·hen·dler

newspaper Zeitung ⓕ tsai·tung

newsstand Zeitungskiosk ⓜ
tsai·tungks·kee·osk

next nächste naykhs·te

next to neben nay·ben

nice nett net

nickname Spitzname ⓜ
shpits·nah·me

niece Nichte ⓕ nikh·te

night Nacht ⓕ nakht

no nein nain

noisy laut lowt

none keine kai·ne

non-smoking Nichtraucher-
nikht·row·kher·

noodles Nudeln ⓕ pl noo·deln

noon Mittag ⓜ mi·tahk

north Norden ⓜ nor·den

nose Nase ⓕ nah·ze

not nicht nikht

notebook Notizbuch ⓝ
no·teets·bookh

nothing nichts nikhts

now jetzt yetst

nuclear energy Atomenergie ⓕ
a·tawm·e·ner·gee

nuclear testing Atomtest ⓜ
a·tawm·test

nuclear waste Atommüll ⓜ
a·tawm·mül

number (numeral) Zahl ⓕ tsahl

number (telephone) Nummer ⓕ
nu·mer

nun Nonne ⓕ no·ne

nurse Krankenpfleger/Kranken-
schwester ⓜ/ⓕ krang·ken·pflay·ger/
krang·ken·shves·ter

nut Nuss ⓕ nus

O

oats Hafer(flocken) ⓜ pl
hah·fer(·flo·ken)

obvious offensichtlich o·fen·zikht·likh

occupation Beruf ⓜ be·roof

ocean Ozean ⓜ aw·tse·ahn

off (food) schlecht shlekht

office Büro ⓝ bü·raw

office worker Büroangestellte ⓜ&ⓕ
bü·raw·an·ge·shtel·te

offside abseits ap·zaits

often oft oft

oil Öl ⓝ erl

OK okay o·kay

old alt alt

olive Olive ⓕ o·lee·ve

olive oil Olivenöl ⓝ o·lee·ven·erl

Olympic Games Olympische Spiele
ⓝ pl o·lüm·pi·she shpee·le

on auf owf

once einmal ain·mahl

one ein(s) ain(s)

onion Zwiebel ⓕ tsvee·bel

only nur noor

open offen o·fen

open (unlock) öffnen erf·nen

opening hours Öffnungszeiten ⓕ pl
erf·nungks·tsai·ten

opera Oper ⓕ aw·per

opera house Opernhaus ⓝ
aw·pern·hows

operation Operation ⓕ
o·pe·ra·tsyawn

operator Vermittlung ⓕ
fer·mit·lung

opinion Meinung ⓕ mai·nung

opposite gegenüber gay·gen·ü·ber

optician Optiker(in) ⓜ/ⓕ op·ti·ker/
op·ti·ke·rin

or oder aw·der

orange (fruit) Orange ⓕ
o·rahng·zhe

orange (colour) orange o·rahngzh

orange juice Orangensaft ⓜ
o·rahng·zhen·zaft

orchestra Orchester ⓝ or·kes·ter

order (restaurant) Bestellung ⓕ
be·*shte*·lung
order bestellen be·*shte*·len
ordinary normal nor·*mahl*
organ (church) Orgel ⓕ *or*·gel
organise organisieren
or·ga·ni·*zee*·ren
orgasm Orgasmus ⓜ or·*gas*·mus
original (not copied) Original·
o·ri·gi·*nahl*·
other andere *an*·de·re
our unser *un*·zer
out aus ows
outside draußen *drow*·sen
ovarian cyst Eierstockzyste ⓕ
ai·er·shtok·tsüs·te
oven Ofen ⓜ *aw*·fen
over über *ü*·ber
overcoat Mantel ⓜ *man*·tel
overdose Überdosis ⓕ *ü*·ber·daw·zis
overnight über Nacht *ü*·ber nakht
owe schulden *shul*·den
owner Besitzer(in) ⓜ/ⓕ be·*zi*·tser/
be·*zi*·tse·rin
oxygen Sauerstoff ⓜ *zow*·er·shtof
oyster Auster ⓕ *ows*·ter
ozone layer Ozonschicht ⓕ
o·*tsawn*·shikht

P

pacemaker (heart) Herzschrittmacher ⓜ *herts*·shrit·ma·her
pacifier (dummy) Schnuller ⓜ
shnu·ler
package Paket ⓝ pa·*kayt*
packet (general) Packung ⓕ
pa·kung
padlock Vorhängeschloss ⓜ
fawr·heng·e·shlos
page Seite ⓕ *zai*·te
pain Schmerz ⓜ shmerts
painful schmerzhaft *shmerts*·haft
painkillers Schmerzmittel ⓝ
shmerts·mi·tel
painter Maler(in) ⓜ/ⓕ *mah*·ler/
mah·le·rin

painting (the art) Malerei ⓕ
mah·le·*rai*
paints Farben ⓕ pl *far*·ben
pair (couple) Paar ⓝ pahr
palace Schloss ⓝ shlos
pan Pfanne ⓕ *pfa*·ne
pants (trousers) Hose ⓕ *haw*·ze
panty liner Slipeinlage ⓕ
slip·ain·lah·ge
pantyhose Strumpfhose ⓕ
shtrumpf·haw·ze
pap smear Abstrich ⓜ *ap*·shtrikh
paper Papier ⓝ pa·*peer*
paperback Taschenbuch ⓝ
ta·shen·bookh
paperwork Schreibarbeit ⓕ
shraip·ar·bait
parachuting Fallschirmspringen ⓝ
fal·shirm·shpring·en
paragliding Gleitschirmfliegen ⓝ
glait·shirm·flee·gen
paraplegic Querschnittsgelähmte
ⓜ&ⓕ *kvair*·shnits·ge·laym·te
parcel Paket ⓝ pa·*kayt*
parents Eltern ⓝ pl *el*·tern
park Park ⓜ park
park (car) Parkplatz ⓜ *park*·plats
parliament Parlament ⓝ
par·la·*ment*
parrot Papagei ⓜ pa·pa·*gai*
parsley Petersilie ⓕ pay·ter·*zee*·li·e
part Teil ⓝ tail
participate sich beteiligen zikh
be·*tai*·li·gen
part-time Teilzeit· ⓕ *tail*·tsait·
party (fiesta/ball) Fest ⓝ fest
party (politics) Partei ⓕ par·*tai*
pass Pass ⓜ pas
passenger (bus/taxi) Fahrgast ⓜ
fahr·gast
passenger (plane) Fluggast ⓜ
flook·gast
passenger (train) Reisende(r) ⓜ/ⓕ
rai·zen·de
passport (Reise)Pass ⓜ
(*rai*·ze·)pas

P

passport number Passnummer ⓕ
pas·nu·mer

past Vergangenheit ⓕ
fer·gang·en·hait

pasta Nudeln ⓕ pl noo·deln

path Pfad ⓜ pfaht

patio Terrasse ⓕ ter·ra·se

pay bezahlen be·tsah·len

pay phone Münztelefon ⓝ
münts·te·le·fawn

payment Zahlung ⓕ tsah·lung

pea Erbse ⓕ erp·se

peace Frieden ⓜ free·den

peach Pfirsich ⓜ pfir·zikh

peak Gipfel ⓜ gip·fel

peanuts Erdnüsse ⓕ pl ert·nü·se

pear Birne ⓕ bir·ne

pedal Pedal ⓝ pe·dahl

pedestrian Fußgänger(in) ⓜ/ⓕ
foos·geng·er/foos·geng·e·rin

pen (ballpoint) Kugelschreiber ⓜ
koo·gel·shrai·ber

pencil Bleistift ⓜ blai·shtift

penis Penis ⓜ pay·nis

penknife Taschenmesser ⓝ
ta·shen·me·ser

pensioner Rentner(in) ⓜ/ⓕ
rent·ner/rent·ne·rin

people Menschen ⓜ pl men·shen

pepper Pfeffer ⓜ pfe·fer

pepper (bell) Paprika ⓕ pap·ri·kah

per pro praw

percent Prozent ⓝ pro·tsent

performance Aufführung ⓕ
owf·fü·rung

perfume Parfüm ⓝ par·füm

period pain Menstruationsbeschwerden ⓕ pl
mens·tru·a·tsyawns·be·shver·den

permission Erlaubnis ⓕ er·lowp·nis

permit Genehmigung ⓕ
ge·nay·mi·gung

person Person ⓕ per·zawn

personal persönlich per·zern·likh

petition Petition ⓕ pe·ti·tsyawn

petrol Benzin ⓝ ben·tseen

petrol can Benzinkanister ⓜ
ben·tseen·ka·nis·ter

pharmacy Apotheke ⓕ a·po·tay·ke

phone book Telefonbuch ⓝ
te·le·fawn·bookh

phone box Telefonzelle ⓕ
te·le·fawn·tse·le

phonecard Telefonkarte ⓕ
te·le·fawn·kar·te

photo Foto ⓝ faw·to

photograph Fotografie ⓕ
fo·to·gra·fee

photograph fotografieren
fo·to·gra·fee·ren

photographer Fotograf(in) ⓜ/ⓕ
fo·to·grahf/fo·to·grah·fin

photography Fotografie ⓕ
fo·to·gra·fee

phrasebook Sprachführer ⓜ
shprahkh·fü·rer

physics Physik ⓕ fü·zeek

piano Klavier ⓝ kla·veer

pick pflücken pflü·ken

pick up aufheben owf·hay·ben

pickaxe Spitzhacke ⓕ shpits·ha·ke

picnic Picknick ⓝ pik·nik

pie Pastete ⓕ pas·tay·te

piece Stück ⓝ shtük

pig Schwein ⓝ shvain

pilgrimage Pilgerfahrt ⓕ
pil·ger·fahrt

pill Pille ⓕ pi·le

the Pill die Pille ⓕ dee pi·le

pillow Kissen ⓝ ki·sen

pillowcase Kissenbezug ⓜ
ki·sen·be·tsook

pineapple Ananas ⓕ a·na·nas

pink rosa raw·za

pipe Pfeife ⓕ pfai·fe

pistachio Pistazie ⓕ pis·tah·tsi·e

place Platz ⓜ plats

place of birth Geburtsort ⓜ
ge·burts·ort

plain Ebene ⓕ ay·be·ne

plane Flugzeug ⓝ flook·tsoyk

planet Planet ⓜ pla·nayt

plant Pflanze ① *pflan*·tse
plastic Plastik ⑩ *plas*·tik
plate Teller ⑩ *te*·ler
plateau Hochebene ①
hawkh·ay·be·ne
platform Bahnsteig ⑩ *bahn*·shtaik
play (theatre) Schauspiel ⑪
show·shpeel
play (game) spielen *shpee*·len
play (instrument) spielen *shpee*·len
please bitte *bi*·te
plenty viel *feel*
plug (bath) Stöpsel ⑩ *shterp*·sel
plug (electricity) Stecker ⑩
shte·ker
plum Pflaume ① *pflow*·me
plumber Installateur(in) ⑩/①
in·sta·la·*ter*/in·sta·la·*ter*(·rin)
pocket Tasche ① *ta*·she
poetry Dichtung ① *dikh*·tung
point Punkt ⑩ *pungkt*
point zeigen *tsai*·gen
poisonous giftig *gif*·tikh
poker (game) Poker ⑪ *paw*·ker
police Polizei ① po·li·*tsai*
police station Polizeirevier ⑩
po·li·*tsai*·re·veer
policy Politik ① po·li·*teek*
politician Politiker(in) ⑩/①
po·*lee*·ti·ker/po·*lee*·ti·ke·rin
politics Politik ① po·li·*teek*
pollen Pollen ⑩ *po*·len
polls Umfrage ① um·*frah*·ge
pollution Umweltverschmutzung ①
um·*velt*·fer·shmu·tsung
pony Pony ⑪ *po*·ni
pool (game) Billard ⑩ *bil*·yart
pool (swimming, indoors) Hallenbad ⑪ *ha*·len·baht
pool (swimming, outdoors) Freibad
⑪ *frai*·baht
poor arm *arm*
popular beliebt be·*leept*
pork Schweinefleisch ⑪
shvai·ne·flaish
port Hafen ⑩ *hah*·fen

possible möglich *merk*·likh
post office Postamt ⑪ *post*·amt
postage Porto ⑪ *por*·to
postcard Postkarte ① *post*·kar·te
postcode Postleitzahl ①
post·lai·tsahl
poste restante postlagernd
post·lah·gernt
poster Plakat ⑪ pla·*kaht*
pot (ceramics) Topf ⑩ *topf*
pot (dope) Gras ⑪ *grahs*
potato Kartoffel ① kar·*to*·fel
pottery Töpferwaren ① pl
terp·fer·vah·ren
pound (money & weight) Pfund
⑪ *pfunt*
poverty Armut ① *ar*·moot
power Kraft ⑩ *kraft*
practical praktisch *prak*·tish
prawn Garnele ① gar·*nay*·le
prayer Gebet ⑪ ge·*bayt*
prefer vorziehen *fawr*·tsee·en
pregnancy test kit Schwangerschaftstest ⑩ *shvang*·er·shafts·test
pregnant schwanger *shvang*·er
premenstrual tension
prämenstruelle Störung ①
pray·mens·tru·e·le *shter*·rung
prepare vorbereiten *fawr*·be·rai·ten
present (gift) Geschenk ⑪
ge·*shengk*
present (time) Gegenwart ①
gay·gen·vart
president Präsident(in) ⑩/①
pre·zi·*dent*/pre·zi·*den*·tin
pressure Druck ⑩ *druk*
pretty hübsch *hüpsh*
prevent verhindern fer·*hin*·dern
price Preis ⑩ *prais*
priest Priester ⑩ *prees*·ter
prime minister Premierminister(in)
⑩/① prem·*yay*·mi·nis·ter/
prem·*yay*·mi·nis·te·rin
**prime minister (in Germany
& Austria)** Bundeskanzler(in)
⑩/① *bun*·des·kants·ler/
bun·des·kants·le·rin

Q

print (artwork) Druck ⓜ druk
print (photography) Abzug ⓜ *ap*·tsook
prison Gefängnis ⓝ ge·*feng*·nis
prisoner Gefangene ⓜ&ⓕ ge·*fang*·e·ne
private privat pri·*vaht*
produce produzieren pro·du·*tsee*·ren
profession Beruf ⓜ be·*roof*
profit Gewinn ⓜ ge·*vin*
program Programm ⓝ pro·*gram*
projector Projektor ⓜ pro·*yek*·tor
promise versprechen fer·*shpre*·khen
proposal Vorschlag ⓜ *fawr*·shlahk
prostitute Prostituierte ⓕ pros·ti·tu·*eer*·te
protect beschützen be·*shü*·tsen
protected geschützte ge·*shüts*·te
protest Protest ⓜ pro·*test*
protest protestieren pro·tes·*tee*·ren
provisions Verpflegung ⓕ fer·*pflay*·gung
prune Backpflaume ⓕ *bak*·pflow·me
psychology Psychologie ⓕ psü·kho·lo·*gee*
pub Kneipe ⓕ *knai*·pe
public telephone öffentliches Telefon ⓝ *er*·fent·li·khes te·le·*fawn*
public toilet öffentliche Toilette ⓕ *er*·fent·li·khe to·a·le·te
pull ziehen *tsee*·en
pump (Luft)Pumpe ⓕ (*luft*·)*pum*·pe
pumpkin Kürbis ⓜ *kür*·bis
puncture Reifenpanne ⓕ *rai*·fen·pa·ne
punish bestrafen be·*shtrah*·fen
pure rein rain
purple lila *lee*·la
push schieben *shee*·ben
put (horizontal) legen *lay*·gen
put (vertical) stellen *shte*·len

Q

qualifications Qualifikationen ⓕ pl kva·li·fi·ka·*tsyaw*·nen
quality Qualität ⓕ kva·li·*tayt*

quarantine Quarantäne ⓕ ka·ran·*tay*·ne
quarrel Streit ⓜ shtrait
quarter Viertel ⓝ *feer*·tel
queen Königin ⓕ *ker*·ni·gin
question Frage ⓕ *frah*·ge
queue Schlange ⓕ *shlang*·e
quick schnell shnel
quiet ruhig *roo*·ikh
quit (job) kündigen *kün*·di·gen

R

rabbit Kaninchen ⓝ ka·*neen*·khen
race (sport) Rennen ⓝ *re*·nen
racetrack Rennbahn ⓕ *ren*·bahn
racing bike Rennrad ⓝ *ren*·raht
racism Rassismus ⓜ ra·*sis*·mus
racquet Schläger ⓜ *shlay*·ger
radiator Kühler ⓜ *kü*·ler
radio Radio ⓝ *rah*·di·o
radish Rettich ⓜ *re*·tikh
railway station Bahnhof ⓜ *bahn*·hawf
rain Regen ⓜ *ray*·gen
raincoat Regenmantel ⓜ *ray*·gen·man·tel
raisin Rosine ⓕ ro·*zee*·ne
rally Rallye ⓕ *re*·li
rape vergewaltigen fer·ge·*val*·ti·gen
rapids Stromschnellen ⓕ pl *shtrawm*·shne·len
rare selten *zel*·ten
rash Ausschlag ⓜ *ows*·shlahk
raspberry Himbeere ⓕ *him*·bair·re
rat Ratte ⓕ *ra*·te
rate of pay Lohn(satz) ⓜ *lawn*(·zats)
raw roh raw
razor Rasierer ⓜ ra·*zee*·rer
razor blades Rasierklingen ⓕ pl ra·*zeer*·kling·en
read lesen *lay*·zen
reading Lesung ⓕ *lay*·zung
ready fertig *fer*·tikh
real estate agent Makler(in) ⓜ/ⓕ *mahk*·ler/*mahk*·le·rin
realistic realistisch re·a·*lis*·tish

R

reason Grund ⓜ grunt
receipt Quittung ⓕ kvi·tung
receive erhalten er·hal·ten
recently vor kurzem fawr kur·tsem
recharge aufladen owf·lah·den
recommend empfehlen emp·fay·len
recording Aufnahme ⓕ owf·nah·me
recyclable wiederverwertbar vee·der·fer·vert·bahr
recycle recyceln ri·sai·keln
red rot rawt
referee Schiedsrichter(in) ⓜ/ⓕ sheets·rikh·ter/sheets·rikh·te·rin
reference (work) Zeugnis ⓝ tsoyk·nis
referendum Volksentscheid ⓜ folks·ent·shait
reflexology Fußreflexzonenmassage ⓕ foos·ray·fleks·tsaw·nen·ma·sah·zhe
refrigerator Kühlschrank ⓜ kül·shrangk
refugee Flüchtling ⓜ flükht·ling
refund Rückzahlung ⓕ rük·tsah·lung
refuse ablehnen ap·lay·nen
region Region ⓕ re·gyawn
registered mail Einschreiben ⓝ ain·shrai·ben
regulation Vorschrift ⓕ fawr·shrift
relation (family) Verwandte ⓜ&ⓕ fer·van·te
relationship Beziehung ⓕ be·tsee·ung
relax sich entspannen zikh ent·shpa·nen
relic (religious) Reliquie ⓕ re·lee·kvi·e
religion Religion ⓕ re·li·gyawn
religious religiös re·li·gyers
remote abgelegen ap·ge·lay·gen
remote control Fernbedienung ⓕ fern·be·dee·nung
rent mieten mee·ten
repair reparieren re·pa·ree·ren
repeat wiederholen vee·der·haw·len
republic Republik ⓕ re·pu·bleek
reservation Reservierung ⓕ re·zer·vee·rung

reserve reservieren re·zer·vee·ren
rest eine Pause machen ai·ne pow·ze ma·khen
restaurant Restaurant ⓝ res·to·rahng
resume (CV) Lebenslauf ⓜ lay·bens·lowf
retired pensioniert pahng·zyo·neert
return zurückkommen tsu·rük·ko·men
return (ticket) Rückfahrkarte ⓕ rük·fahr·kar·te
review (arts) Kritik ⓕ kri·teek
rhythm Rhythmus ⓜ rüt·mus
rice Reis ⓜ rais
rich (wealthy) reich raikh
ride Ritt ⓜ rit
ride (horse) reiten rai·ten
riding school Reitschule ⓕ rait·shoo·le
right (correct) richtig rikh·tikh
right (direction) rechts rekhts
right there gleich dort glaikh dort
right-wing rechts(gerichtet) rekhts(·ge·rikh·tet)
ring (on finger) Ring ⓜ ring
ring (of phone) klingeln kling·eln
rip-off Abzockerei ⓕ ap·tso·ke·rai
risk Risiko ⓝ ree·zi·ko
river Fluss ⓜ flus
road Straße ⓕ shtrah·se
road map Straßenkarte ⓕ shtrah·sen·kar·te
rob berauben be·row·ben
robbery Raub ⓜ rowp
rock Fels ⓜ fels
rock (music) Rockmusik ⓕ rok·mu·zeek
rock climbing Klettern ⓝ kle·tern
rock group Rockgruppe ⓕ rok·gru·pe
roll (bread) Brötchen ⓝ brert·khen
romantic romantisch ro·man·tish
roof Dach ⓝ dakh
room Zimmer ⓝ tsi·mer
rope Seil ⓝ zail
rouble Rubel ⓜ roo·bel

S

round rund runt
roundabout Kreisverkehr ⓜ *krais·fer·kair*
route Route ⓕ *roo·te*
rowing Rudern ⓝ *roo·dern*
rubbish Müll ⓜ *mül*
rug Teppich ⓜ *te·pikh*
rugby Rugby ⓝ *rag·bi*
ruins Ruinen ⓕ pl *ru·ee·nen*
rules Regeln ⓕ pl *ray·geln*
rum Rum ⓜ *rum*
run laufen *low·fen*
run out of ausgehen *ows·gay·en*

S

Sabbath Sabbat ⓜ *za·bat*
sad traurig *trow·rikh*
saddle Sattel ⓜ *za·tel*
safe Safe ⓜ *sayf*
safe sicher *zi·kher*
safe sex Safe Sex ⓜ *sayf seks*
safety Sicherheit ⓕ *zi·kher·hait*
sailing Segeln ⓝ *zay·geln*
saint Heilige ⓜ&ⓕ *hai·li·ge*
salad Salat ⓜ *za·laht*
salami Salami ⓕ *za·lah·mi*
salary Gehalt ⓝ *ge·halt*
sale (Sonder)Angebot ⓝ *(zon·der·)an·ge·bawt*
sales tax Umsatzsteuer ⓕ *um·zats·shtoy·er*
salmon Lachs ⓜ *laks*
salt Salz ⓝ *zalts*
same gleiche *glai·khe*
sand Sand ⓜ *zant*
sandals Sandalen ⓕ pl *zan·dah·len*
sanitary napkins Damenbinden ⓕ pl *dah·men·bin·den*
sardine Sardine ⓕ *zar·dee·ne*
Saturday Samstag ⓜ *zams·tahk*
sauce Sauce/Soße ⓕ *zaw·se*
sauna Sauna ⓕ *zow·na*
sausage Wurst ⓕ *vurst*
save (money) sparen *shpah·ren*
save (someone) retten *re·ten*
say sagen *zah·gen*

scarf Schal ⓜ *shahl*
scenery Landschaft ⓕ *lant·shaft*
school Schule ⓕ *shoo·le*
science Wissenschaft ⓕ *vi·sen·shaft*
scientist Wissenschaftler(in) ⓜ/ⓕ *vi·sen·shaft·ler/vi·sen·shaft·le·rin*
scissors Schere ⓕ *shair·re*
score ein Tor schießen *ain tawr shee·sen*
scoreboard Anzeigetafel ⓕ *an·tsai·ge·tah·fel*
Scotland Schottland ⓝ *shot·lant*
screen (TV/computer) Bildschirm ⓜ *bilt·shirm*
screwdriver Schraubenzieher ⓜ *shrow·ben·tsee·er*
script Drehbuch ⓝ *dray·bookh*
sculpture Skulptur ⓕ *skulp·toor*
sea Meer ⓝ *mair*
seagull Möwe ⓕ *mer·ve*
seasick seekrank *zay·krangk*
seaside Meeresküste ⓕ *mair·res·küs·te*
season Jahreszeit ⓕ *yah·res·tsait*
seat (car) Sitz ⓜ *zits*
seat (train/cinema) Platz ⓜ *plats*
seatbelt Sicherheitsgurt ⓜ *zi·kher·haits·gurt*
second Sekunde ⓕ *ze·kun·de*
second zweite *tsvai·te*
secondhand gebraucht *ge·browkht*
secondhand shop Secondhandgeschäft ⓝ *se·kend·hend·ge·sheft*
secret Geheimnis ⓝ *ge·haim·nis*
secretary Sekretär(in) ⓜ/ⓕ *ze·kre·tair(·rin)*
see sehen *zay·en*
self-employed selbstständig *zelpst·shten·dikh*
selfish egoistisch *e·go·is·tish*
self-service Selbstbedienung ⓕ *zelpst·be·dee·nung*
sell verkaufen *fer·kow·fen*
send senden *zen·den*
sensible vernünftig *fer·nünf·tikh*
sensual sinnlich *zin·likh*
separate getrennt *ge·trent*

serial Serien- *zair·ri·en·*
series Serie ① *zair·ri·e*
serious ernst *ernst*
service charge Bedienungszuschlag ⑩ *be·dee·nungks·tsoo·shlahk*
service station Tankstelle ①
tangk·shte·le
several einige *ai·ni·ge*
sew nähen *nay·en*
sex Sex ⑩ *seks*
sexism Sexismus ⑩ *sek·sis·mus*
sexy sexy *sek·si*
shade Schatten ⑩ *sha·ten*
shadow Schatten ⑩ *sha·ten*
shampoo Shampoo ⑩ *sham·poo*
shape Form ① *form*
share (with) teilen (mit) *tai·len (mit)*
shave rasieren *ra·zee·ren*
shaving cream Rasiercreme ①
ra·zeer·kraym
she sie *zee*
sheep Schaf ⑩ *shahf*
sheet (bed) Bettlaken ⑩ *bet·lah·ken*
shelf Regal ⑩ *re·gahl*
ship Schiff ⑩ *shif*
shirt Hemd ⑩ *hemt*
shoe shop Schuhgeschäft ⑩
shoo·ge·sheft
shoes Schuhe ⑩ pl *shoo·e*
shoot (gun) schießen *shee·sen*
shop Geschäft ⑩ *ge·sheft*
shopping centre Einkaufszentrum ⑩ *ain·kowfs·tsen·trum*
short kurz *kurts*
short (height) klein *klain*
shortage Knappheit ① *knap·hait*
shortcut Abkürzung ①
ap·kür·tsung
shorts Shorts pl *shorts*
short-sleeved kurzärmelig
kurts·er·me·likh
shoulder Schulter ① *shul·ter*
shout schreien *shrai·en*
show Show ① *shoh*
show zeigen *tsai·gen*
shower Dusche ① *doo·she*
shrine Schrein ⑩ *shrain*

shut (closed) geschlossen
ge·shlo·sen
shut (close) schließen *shlee·sen*
shy schüchtern *shükh·tern*
sick krank *krangk*
side Seite ① *zai·te*
sign Schild ⑩ *shilt*
signature Unterschrift ①
un·ter·shrift
signpost Wegweiser ⑩ *vayk·vai·zer*
silk Seide ① *zai·de*
silver silbern *zil·bern*
similar ähnlich *ayn·likh*
simple einfach *ain·fakh*
since (May) seit (Mai) *zait (mai)*
sing singen *zing·en*
Singapore Singapur ⑩ *zing·a·poor*
singer Sänger(in) ⑩/① *zeng·er/ zeng·e·rin*
single (person) Single ⑩ *singl*
single (unmarried) ledig *lay·dikh*
single room Einzelzimmer ⑩
ain·tsel·tsi·mer
singlet Unterhemd ⑩ *un·ter·hemt*
sister Schwester ① *shves·ter*
sit sitzen *zi·tsen*
situation Lage ① *lah·ge*
size Größe ① *grer·se*
skate eislaufen *ais·low·fen*
skateboarding Skateboarden ⑩
skayt·bor·den
ski skifahren *shee·fah·ren*
skiing Skifahren ⑩ *shee·fah·ren*
skimmed milk fettarme Milch ①
fet·ar·me milkh
skin Haut ① *howt*
skirt Rock ⑩ *rok*
sky Himmel ⑩ *hi·mel*
sleep schlafen *shlah·fen*
sleeping bag Schlafsack ⑩
shlahf·zak
sleeping car Schlafwagen ⑩
shlahf·vah·gen
sleeping pills Schlaftabletten ① pl
shlahf·ta·ble·ten
sleepy schläfrig *shlayf·rikh*
slide (film) Dia ⑩ *dee·a*

slippery glatt glat
slope Hang ⓜ hang
slow langsam *lang*·zahm
slowly langsam *lang*·zahm
small klein klain
smell Geruch ⓜ ge·*rookh*
smile lächeln *le*·kheln
smoke rauchen *row*·khen
snack Snack ⓜ snek
snail Schnecke ⓕ *shne*·ke
snake Schlange ⓕ *shlang*·e
snorkelling Schnorcheln ⓝ *shnor*·kheln
snow Schnee ⓜ shnay
snow pea Zuckererbse ⓕ *tsu*·ker·erp·se
snowboarding Snowboarden ⓝ *snoh*·bor·den
snowfield Schneefeld ⓝ *shnay*·felt
soap Seife ⓕ *zai*·fe
soap opera Seifenoper ⓕ *zai*·fen·aw·per
soccer Fußball ⓜ *foos*·bal
social welfare Wohlfahrt ⓕ *vawl*·fahrt
socialist sozialistisch zo·tsya·*lis*·tish
socks Socken ⓕ pl *zo*·ken
soft drink alkoholfreies Getränk ⓝ al·ko·*hawl*·frai·es ge·*trengk*
sold out ausverkauft *ows*·fer·kowft
solid fest fest
some einige *ai*·ni·ge
someone jemand *yay*·mant
something etwas *et*·vas
sometimes manchmal *mankh*·mahl
son Sohn ⓜ zawn
song Lied ⓝ leet
son-in-law Schwiegersohn ⓜ *shvee*·ger·zawn
soon bald balt
sore schmerzhaft *shmerts*·haft
sore throat Halsschmerzen ⓜ pl *hals*·shmer·tsen
soup Suppe ⓕ *zu*·pe
sour cream Schmand ⓜ shmant
south Süden ⓜ *zü*·den
souvenir Souvenir ⓝ zu·ve·*neer*

souvenir shop Souvenirladen ⓜ zu·ve·*neer*·lah·den
soy milk Sojamilch ⓕ *zaw*·ya·milkh
soy sauce Sojasauce ⓕ *zaw*·ya·zaw·se
space Raum ⓜ rowm
spade Spaten ⓜ *shpah*·ten
Spain Spanien ⓝ *shpah*·ni·en
spare tyre Reservereifen ⓜ re·*zer*·ve·rai·fen
speak sprechen *shpre*·khen
special speziell shpe·*tsyel*
specialist Spezialist(in) ⓜ/ⓕ shpe·tsya·*list*/shpe·tsya·*lis*·tin
speed Geschwindigkeit ⓕ ge·*shvin*·dikh·kait
speed limit Geschwindigkeitsbegrenzung ⓕ ge·*shvin*·dikh·kaits·be·gren·tsung
spicy würzig *vür*·tsikh
spider Spinne ⓕ *shpi*·ne
spinach Spinat ⓜ shpi·*naht*
spokes Speichen ⓕ pl *shpai*·khen
spoon Löffel ⓜ *ler*·fel
sport Sport ⓜ shport
sportsperson Sportler(in) ⓜ/ⓕ *shport*·ler/*shport*·le·rin
sprain Muskelzerrung ⓕ *mus*·kel·tser·rung
spring (coil) Feder ⓕ *fay*·der
spring (season) Frühling ⓜ *frü*·ling
square (town) Platz ⓜ plats
stadium Stadion ⓝ *shtah*·di·on
stage Stadium ⓝ *shtah*·di·um
stage (theatre) Bühne ⓕ *bü*·ne
stairway Treppe ⓕ *tre*·pe
stamp Briefmarke ⓕ *breef*·mar·ke
standby ticket Standby-Ticket ⓝ stend·*bai*·ti·ket
standing room Stehplatz ⓜ *shtay*·plats
star sign Sternzeichen ⓝ *shtern*·tsai·khen
star Stern ⓜ shtern
(four-)star (Vier-)Sterne- (*feer*·) *shter*·ne·

start Beginn ⓜ be·*gin*

start (sport) Start ⓜ shtart

start anfangen *an*·fang·en

state Staat ⓜ shtaht

station Bahnhof ⓜ *bahn*·hawf

stationer Schreibwarenhandlung ⓕ *shraip*·vah·ren·han·dlung

statue Statue ⓕ *shtah*·tu·e

stay (at a hotel) übernachten ü·ber·*nakh*·ten

stay (not leave) bleiben *blai*·ben

steak (beef) Steak ⓝ stayk

steal stehlen *shtay*·len

steep steil shtail

step (stairs) Stufe ⓕ *shtoo*·fe

stereo Stereoanlage ⓕ *shtair*·re·o·an·lah·ge

stingy geizig *gai*·tsikh

stock Vorrat ⓜ *fawr*·raht

stockings Strümpfe ⓜ pl *shtrump*·fe

stomach Magen ⓜ *mah*·gen

stomachache Magenschmerzen ⓜ pl *mah*·gen·shmer·tsen

stone Stein ⓜ shtain

stoned (drugged) stoned shtohnd

stop Halt ⓜ halt

stop anhalten *an*·hal·ten

storm Sturm ⓜ shturm

story Geschichte ⓕ ge·*shikh*·te

stove Herd ⓜ hert

straight gerade ge·*rah*·de

strange fremd fremt

stranger Fremde ⓜ&ⓕ *frem*·de

strawberry Erdbeere ⓕ *ert*·bair·re

stream Bach ⓜ bakh

street Straße ⓕ *shtrah*·se

street kids Straßenkinder ⓜ pl *shtrah*·sen·kin·der

on strike streiken *shtrai*·ken

string Schnur ⓕ shnoor

strong stark shtark

stubborn stur shtoor

student Student(in) ⓜ/ⓕ shtu·*dent*/shtu·*den*·tin

student card Studentenausweis ⓜ shtu·*den*·ten·ows·vais

studio Studio ⓝ *shtoo*·di·o

studio (art) Atelier ⓝ a·tel·*yay*

study studieren shtu·*dee*·ren

stupid dumm dum

style Stil ⓜ shteel

subtitles Untertitel ⓜ pl *un*·ter·tee·tel

suburb Vorort ⓜ *fawr*·ort

subway U-Bahn ⓕ *oo*·bahn

sugar Zucker ⓜ *tsu*·ker

suitcase Koffer ⓜ *ko*·fer

summer Sommer ⓜ *zo*·mer

sun Sonne ⓕ *zo*·ne

sunblock Sonnencreme ⓕ *zo*·nen·kraym

sunburn Sonnenbrand ⓜ *zo*·nen·brant

Sunday Sonntag ⓜ *zon*·tahk

sunglasses Sonnenbrille ⓕ *zo*·nen·bri·le

sunny sonnig *zo*·nikh

sunrise Sonnenaufgang ⓜ *zo*·nen·owf·gang

sunset Sonnenuntergang ⓜ *zo*·nen·un·ter·gang

supermarket Supermarkt ⓜ *zoo*·per·markt

superstition Aberglaube ⓜ *ah*·ber·glow·be

supporters Anhänger ⓜ pl *an*·heng·er

surf surfen ser·fen

surface mail normale Post ⓕ nor·*mah*·le post

surfboard Surfbrett ⓝ *serf*·bret

surname Nachname ⓜ *nahkh*·nah·me

surprise Überraschung ⓕ ü·ber·*ra*·shung

sweater Pullover ⓜ pu·*law*·ver

Sweden Schweden ⓝ *shvay*·den

sweet süß züs

swim schwimmen *shvi*·men

swimming pool Schwimmbad ⓝ *shvim*·baht

swimsuit Badeanzug ⓜ *bah*·de·an·tsook

T

Switzerland Schweiz ① shvaits
synagogue Synagoge ①
zü·na·*gaw*·ge
synthetic synthetisch zün·*tay*·tish
syringe Spritze ① *shpri*·tse

T

table Tisch ⓜ tish
table tennis Tischtennis ⓝ
tish·te·nis
tablecloth Tischdecke ① *tish*·de·ke
tail Schwanz ⓜ shvants
tailor Schneider(in) ⓜ/① *shnai*·der/
shnai·de·rin
take nehmen *nay*·men
take (to) bringen *bring*·en
take off Abflug ⓜ *ap*·flook
talk sprechen *shpre*·khen
tall groß graws
tampons Tampons ⓜ pl *tam*·pons
tanning lotion Bräunungsmilch ①
broy·nungks·milkh
tap Wasserhahn ⓜ *va*·ser·hahn
target Ziel ⓝ tseel
tasty schmackhaft *shmak*·haft
tax Steuer ① *shtoy*·er
taxi Taxi ⓝ *tak*·si
taxi stand Taxistand ⓜ *tak*·si·shtant
tea Tee ⓜ tay
teacher Lehrer(in) ⓜ/① *lair*·rer/
lair·re·rin
team Mannschaft ① *man*·shaft
teaspoon Teelöffel ⓜ *tay*·ler·fel
technique Technik ① *tekh*·nik
teeth Zähne ⓜ pl *tsay*·ne
telegram Telegramm ⓝ te·le·*gram*
telephone Telefon ⓝ te·le·*fawn*
telephone telefonieren
te·le·fo·*nee*·ren
telephone book Telefonbuch ⓝ
te·le·*fawn*·bookh
telephone centre Telefonzentrale ①
te·le·*fawn*·tsen·trah·le
telescope Teleskop ⓝ te·les·*kawp*
television Fernseher ⓜ *fern*·zay·er
tell erzählen er·*tsay*·len

temperature (fever) Fieber ⓝ
fee·ber
temperature (weather) Temperatur
① tem·pe·ra·*toor*
temple Tempel ⓜ *tem*·pel
ten zehn tsayn
tennis Tennis ⓝ *te*·nis
tennis court Tennisplatz ⓜ
te·nis·plats
tent Zelt ⓝ tselt
tent pegs Heringe ⓜ pl *hay*·ring·e
terminal (transport) Endstation ①
ent·shta·tsyawn
terrible schrecklich *shrek*·likh
test Test ⓜ test
thank danken *dang*·ken
theatre Theater ⓝ te·*ah*·ter
their ihr eer
there dort dort
thermos Thermosflasche ①
ter·mos·fla·she
they sie zee
thick dick dik
thief Dieb ⓜ deep
thin dünn dün
think denken *deng*·ken
third dritte *dri*·te
thirsty durstig *durs*·tikh
this (month) diesen (Monat)
dee·zen (*maw*·nat)
this (one) dieser/diese/dieses
ⓜ/①/ⓝ *dee*·zer/*dee*·ze/*dee*·zes
thousand tausend *tow*·zent
thread Faden ⓜ *fah*·den
throat Hals ⓜ hals
through durch durkh
thrush (condition) Mundfäule ①
munt·foy·le
thunder Donner ⓜ *do*·ner
Thursday Donnerstag ⓜ
do·ners·tahk
ticket (bus/metro/train) Fahrkarte
① *fahr*·kar·te
ticket (cinema/museum)
Eintrittskarte ① *ain*·trits·kar·te
ticket (plane) Flugticket ⓝ
flook·ti·ket

ticket collector Fahrkartenkontrolleur/in ⓜ/ⓕ *fahr·kar·ten·kon·tro·ler/ fahr·kar·ten·kon·tro·ler·rin*

ticket machine Fahrkartenautomat ⓜ *fahr·kar·ten·ow·to·maht*

ticket office Fahrkartenverkauf ⓜ *fahr·kar·ten·fer·kowf*

ticket office (theatre) Theaterkasse ⓕ *te·ah·ter·ka·se*

tides Gezeiten pl ge·*tsai*·ten

tight eng eng

time Zeit ⓕ tsait

time difference Zeitunterschied ⓜ *tsait·un·ter·sheet*

timetable Fahrplan ⓜ *fahr*·plahn

tin (can) Dose ⓕ *daw*·ze

tin opener Dosenöffner ⓜ *daw·zen·erf·ner*

tiny winzig *vin*·tsikh

tip (gratuity) Trinkgeld ⓝ *tringk*·gelt

tire ermüden er·*mü*·den

tired müde *mü*·de

tissues Papiertaschentücher ⓝ pl *pa·peer·ta·shen·tü·kher*

toast Toast ⓜ *lawst*

toaster Toaster ⓜ *taws*·ter

tobacco Tabak ⓜ ta·bak

tobacconist Tabakladen ⓜ *ta·bak·lah·den*

tobogganing Rodeln ⓝ *raw*·deln

today heute *hoy*·te

toe Zehe ⓕ *tsay*·e

tofu Tofu ⓜ *taw*·fu

together zusammen tsu·*za*·men

toilet Toilette ⓕ to·a·*le*·te

toilet paper Toilettenpapier ⓝ *to·a·le·ten·pa·peer*

tomato Tomate ⓕ to·*mah*·te

tomato sauce Tomatensauce ⓕ *to·mah·ten·zaw·se*

tomb Grab ⓝ grahp

tomorrow morgen *mor*·gen

tomorrow morning morgen früh *mor*·gen frü

tonight heute Abend *hoy*·te *ah*·bent

too (also) auch owkh

too (many) zu (viele) tsoo (*fee*·le)

tools Werkzeug ⓝ *verk*·tsoyk

tooth Zahn ⓜ tsahn

toothache Zahnschmerzen ⓜ pl *tsahn·shmer·tsen*

toothbrush Zahnbürste ⓕ *tsahn·bürs·te*

toothpaste Zahnpasta ⓕ *tsahn·pas·ta*

toothpick Zahnstocher ⓜ *tsahn·shto·kher*

torch (flashlight) Taschenlampe ⓕ *ta·shen·lam·pe*

touch berühren be·*rü*·ren

tour Tour ⓕ toor

tourist Tourist/in ⓜ/ⓕ tu·*rist/ tu·ris*·tin

tourist office Fremdenverkehrsbüro ⓝ *frem·den·fer·kairs·bü·raw*

towards auf ... zu owf ... tsoo

towel Handtuch ⓝ *hant*·tookh

tower Turm ⓜ turm

town Stadt ⓕ shtat

toxic waste Giftmüll ⓜ *gift*·mül

toy Spielzeug ⓝ *shpeel*·tsoyk

track (path) Weg ⓜ vayk

track (sports) Bahn ⓕ bahn

trade Handel ⓜ *han*·del

traffic Verkehr ⓜ fer·*kair*

traffic lights Ampel ⓕ *am*·pel

trail Pfad ⓜ pfaht

train Zug ⓜ tsook

train station Bahnhof ⓜ *bahn*·hawf

tram Straßenbahn ⓕ *shtrah·sen·bahn*

transit lounge Transitraum ⓜ *tran·zeet·rowm*

translate übersetzen ü·ber·*ze*·tsen

transport Transport ⓜ trans·*port*

travel reisen *rai*·zen

travel agency Reisebüro ⓝ *rai·ze·bü·raw*

travel sickness Reisekrankheit ⓕ *rai·ze·krangk·hait*

travellers cheque Reisescheck ⓜ *rai·ze·shek*

ENGLISH to GERMAN

T

U

tree Baum ⓜ bowm
trip Reise ⓕ *rai*·ze
trousers Hose ⓕ *haw*·ze
truck Lastwagen ⓜ *last*·vah·gen
true wahr vahr
trust trauen *trow*·en
try (attempt) versuchen fer·*zoo*·khen
T-shirt T-Shirt ⓝ *tee*·shert
tube (tyre) Schlauch ⓜ shlowkh
Tuesday Dienstag ⓜ *deens*·tahk
tuna Thunfisch ⓜ *toon*·fish
tune Melodie ⓕ me·lo·*dee*
turkey Truthahn ⓜ *troot*·hahn
turn abbiegen *ap*·bee·gen
TV (set) Fernseher ⓜ *fern*·zay·er
TV series Fernsehserie ⓕ *fern*·zay·zair·ri·e
tweezers Pinzette ⓕ pin·*tse*·te
twice zweimal *tsvai*·mahl
twin beds zwei Einzelbetten ⓝ pl tsvai *ain*·tsel·be·ten
twins Zwillinge ⓝ pl *tsvi*·ling·e
type Typ ⓜ tüp
typical typisch *tü*·pish
tyre Reifen ⓜ *rai*·fen

U

ultrasound Ultraschall ⓜ *ul*·tra·shal
umbrella Regenschirm ⓜ *ray*·gen·shirm
uncle Onkel ⓜ *ong*·kel
uncomfortable unbequem *un*·be·kvaym
under unter *un*·ter
underground U-Bahn ⓕ *oo*·bahn
understand verstehen fer·*shtay*·en
underwear Unterwäsche ⓕ *un*·ter·ve·she
unemployed arbeitslos *ar*·baits·laws
unemployment Arbeitslosigkeit ⓕ *ar*·baits·law·zikh·kait
unfair unfair *un*·fair
uniform Uniform ⓕ u·ni·*form*
universe Universum ⓝ u·ni·*vair*·zum

university Universität ⓕ u·ni·ver·zi·*tayt*
unleaded bleifrei *blai*·frai
unsafe nicht sicher nikht zi·kher
until (June) bis (Juni) bis (*yoo*·ni)
unusual ungewöhnlich *un*·ge·vern·likh
up nach oben nahkh *aw*·ben
uphill aufwärts *owf*·verts
upstairs oben *aw*·ben
urgent dringend *dring*·ent
USA USA ⓕ pl oo·es·*ah*
useful nützlich *nüts*·likh

V

vacant frei frai
vacation Ferien pl *fair*·i·en
vaccination Schutzimpfung ⓕ *shuts*·im·pfung
vagina Vagina ⓕ va·*gee*·na
validate (ticket) entwerten ent·*ver*·ten
valley Tal ⓝ tahl
valuable wertvoll *vert*·fol
value (price) Wert ⓜ vert
van Lieferwagen ⓜ *lee*·fer·vah·gen
veal Kalbfleisch ⓝ *kalp*·flaish
vegetable Gemüse ⓝ ge·*mü*·ze
vegetarian Vegetarier(in) ⓜ/ⓕ ve·ge·*tah*·ri·er/ve·ge·*tah*·ri·e·rin
vein Vene ⓕ *vay*·ne
venereal disease Geschlechts-krankheit ⓕ ge·*shlekhts*·krangk·hait
venue Veranstaltungsort ⓜ fer·*an*·shtal·tungks·ort
very sehr zair
view Aussicht ⓕ *ows*·zikht
village Dorf ⓝ dorf
vine Rebe ⓕ *ray*·be
vinegar Essig ⓜ *e*·sikh
vineyard Weinberg ⓜ *vain*·berk
virus Virus ⓜ *vee*·rus
visa Visum ⓝ *vee*·zum
visit besuchen be·*zoo*·khen
vitamins Vitamine ⓝ pl vi·ta·*mee*·ne
vodka Wodka ⓜ *vot*·ka

voice Stimme ① *shti*·me
volume (amount) Volumen ⑩ *vo·loo*·men
volume (book) Band ⑩ bant
volume (loudness) Lautstärke ① *lowt*·shter·ke
vomit brechen *bre*·khen
vote wählen *vay*·len

W

wage Lohn ⑩ lawn
wait warten *var*·ten
waiter Kellner(in) ⑩/① *kel*·ner/ *kel*·ne·rin
waiting room (doctor's) Wartezimmer ⑩ *var*·te·tsi·mer
waiting room (train station) Wartesaal ⑩ *var*·te·zahl
walk gehen *gay*·en
wall (outer) Mauer ① *mow*·er
want wollen *vo*·len
war Krieg ⑩ kreek
wardrobe Garderobe ① gar·*draw*·be
warm warm varm
warn warnen *var*·nen
wash (oneself) sich waschen zikh *va*·shen
wash (something) waschen *va*·shen
wash cloth (flannel) Waschlappen ⑩ *vash*·la·pen
washing machine Waschmaschine ① *vash*·ma·shee·ne
washing powder Waschpulver ⑩ *vash*·pul·ver
wasp Wespe ① *ves*·pe
watch Uhr ① oor
watch beobachten be·*aw*·bakh·ten
watch (TV) fernsehen *fern*·zay·en
water Wasser ⑩ *va*·ser
tap water Leitungswasser ⑩ *lai*·tungks·va·ser
water bottle Wasserflasche ① *va*·ser·fla·she
waterfall Wasserfall ⑩ *va*·ser·fal
watermelon Wassermelone ① *va*·ser·me·law·ne

waterproof wasserdicht *va*·ser·dikht
waterskiing Wasserskifahren ⑩ *va*·ser·shee·fah·ren
wave Welle ① *ve*·le
way Weg ⑩ vayk
we wir veer
weak schwach shvakh
wealthy reich raikh
weapon Waffe ① *va*·fe
wear tragen *trah*·gen
weather Wetter ⑩ *ve*·ter
wedding Hochzeit ① *hokh*·tsait
wedding cake Hochzeitstorte ① *hokh*·tsaits·tor·te
wedding present Hochzeitsgeschenk ⑩ *hokh*·tsaits·ge·shengk
Wednesday Mittwoch ⑩ *mit*·vokh
(this) week (diese) Woche ① (*dee*·ze) *vo*·khe
weekend Wochenende ⑩ *vo*·khen·en·de
weigh wiegen *vee*·gen
weight Gewicht ⑩ ge·*vikht*
welcome willkommen vil·*ko*·men
welfare Sozialhilfe ① zo·*tsyahl*·hil·fe
welfare state Sozialstaat ⑩ zo·*tsyahl*·shtaht
well gut goot
west Westen ⑩ *ves*·ten
wet nass nas
what was vas
wheel Rad ⑩ raht
wheelchair Rollstuhl ⑩ *rol*·shtool
when (adverb) wann van
when (conjunction) wenn ven
whenever wann immer van *i*·mer
where wo vaw
whisky Whisky ⑩ *vis*·ki
white weiß vais
who wer vair
whole ganz gants
why warum va·*rum*
wide breit brait
wife Ehefrau ① *ay*·e·frow
wild wild vilt
win gewinnen ge·*vi*·nen
wind Wind ⑩ vint

Y

window Fenster ⓝ *fens*·ter
windscreen Windschutzscheibe ⓕ *vint*·shuts·shai·be
windsurfing Windsurfen ⓝ *vint*·ser·fen
windy windig *vin*·dikh
wine Wein ⓜ vain
— red wine Rotwein ⓜ *rawt*·vain
— sparkling wine Schaumwein ⓜ *showm*·vain
— white wine Weißwein ⓜ *vais*·vain
winery Weinkellerei ⓕ *vain*·ke·le·rai
wings Flügel ⓜ pl *flü*·gel
winner Sieger(in) ⓜ/ⓕ *zee*·ger/*zee*·ge·rin
winter Winter ⓜ *vin*·ter
wire Draht ⓜ draht
wish wünschen *vün*·shen
with mit mit
within (an hour) innerhalb (einer Stunde) *i*·ner·halp (*ai*·ner *shtun*·de)
without ohne *aw*·ne
woman Frau ⓕ frow
wonderful wunderbar *vun*·der·bahr
wood Holz ⓝ holts
wool Wolle ⓕ *vo*·le
word Wort ⓝ vort
work Arbeit ⓕ *ar*·bait
work arbeiten *ar*·bai·ten
work permit Arbeitserlaubnis ⓕ *ar*·baits·er·lowp·nis
workout Training ⓝ *tray*·ning
workshop Werkstatt ⓕ *verk*·shtat
world Welt ⓕ velt
World Cup Weltmeisterschaft ⓕ *velt*·mais·ter·shaft
worms Würmer ⓜ pl *vür*·mer

worried besorgt be·*zorkt*
worse schlechter *shlekh*·ter
worship einen Gottesdienst besuchen *ai*·nen *go*·tes·deenst be·*zoo*·khen
write schreiben *shrai*·ben
writer Schriftsteller(in) ⓜ/ⓕ *shrift*·shte·ler/*shrift*·shte·le·rin
wrong falsch falsh

Y

(this) year (dieses) Jahr ⓝ (*dee*·zes) yahr
yellow gelb gelp
yen Yen ⓜ yen
yes ja yah
yesterday gestern *ges*·tern
yet schon shawn
not yet noch nicht nokh nikht
yoga Joga ⓝ *yaw*·ga
yoghurt Joghurt ⓜ *yaw*·gurt
you sg inf du doo
you sg&pl pol Sie zee
young jung yung
your sg inf dein dain
your sg&pl pol Ihr eer
youth hostel Jugendherberge ⓕ *yoo*·gent·her·ber·ge

Z

zero null nul
zipper Reißverschluss ⓜ *rais*·fer·shlus
zodiac Sternzeichen ⓝ *shtern*·tsai·khen
zoo Zoo ⓜ tsaw
zucchini Zucchini ⓕ tsu·*kee*·ni

Dictionary

GERMAN *to* ENGLISH

Deutsch–Englisch

Nouns in the dictionary, and adjectives affected by gender, have their gender indicated by ⓕ, ⓜ or ⓝ. If it's a plural noun, you'll also see pl. Where a word that could be either a noun or a verb has no gender indicated, it's a verb.

A

abbiegen *ap*·bee·gen turn
Abend ⓜ *ah*·bent evening
Abendessen ⓝ *ah*·bent·e·sen dinner
aber *ah*·ber but
Aberglaube ⓜ *ah*·ber·glow·be superstition
abfahren *ap*·fah·ren leave (depart)
Abfahrt ⓕ *ap*·fahrt departure
Abfall ⓜ *ap*·fal garbage
Abfertigungsschalter ⓜ ap·fer·ti·gungks·shal·ter check-in (desk)
Abflug ⓜ *ap*·flook take off
Abführmittel ⓝ *ap*·für·mi·tel laxatives
abgelegen *ap*·ge·lay·gen remote
Abgeordnete ⓜ&ⓕ *ap*·ge·ord·ne·te member of parliament
abgeschlossen *ap*·ge·shlo·sen locked
abhängig *ap*·heng·ikh addicted
Abholzung ⓕ *ap*·hol·tsung deforestation
Abkürzung ⓕ *ap*·kür·tsung shortcut
ablehnen *ap*·lay·nen refuse

Abschleppdienst ⓜ *ap*·shlep·deenst breakdown service
abseits *ap*·zaits offside
Abstrich ⓜ *ap*·shtrikh pap smear
Abtreibung ⓕ *ap*·trai·hung abortion
abwärts *ap*·verts downhill
Abzockerei ⓕ ap tso·ke·*rai* rip-off
Abzug ⓜ *ap*·tsook print (photography)
Adapter ⓜ a·*dap*·ter adaptor
Adressanhänger ⓜ a·dres·an·heng·er luggage tag
Adresse ⓕ a·*dre*·se address
Aerobics pl e·ro·biks aerobics
Aerogramm ⓝ air·ro·*gram* aerogram
Afrika ⓕ a·fri·kah Africa
Aftershave ⓝ *ahf*·ter·shayf aftershave
ähnlich *ayn*·likh similar
AIDS ⓝ aydz AIDS
Aktentasche ⓕ ak·ten·ta·she briefcase
Aktivist(in) ⓜ/ⓕ ak·ti·*vist*/ ak·ti·vis·tin activist
Aktuelles ⓝ ak·tu·e·les current affairs
Akupunktur ⓕ a·ku·pungk·*toor* acupuncture

Alkohol ⓜ *al*·ko·hawl alcohol
alkoholfreies Getränk ⓝ
al·ko·*hawl*/frai·es ge·*trengk* soft drink
Alkoholiker(in) ⓜ/ⓕ
al·ko·*haw*·li·ker/al·ko·*haw*·li·ke·rin
alcoholic
alkoholisch al·ko·*haw*·lish alcoholic
alle *a*·le all
Allee ⓕ *a·lay* avenue
allein a·*lain* alone
Allergie ⓕ a·lair·*gee* allergy
alles *a*·les everything
allgemein al·ge·*main* general
alltäglich al·*tayk*·likh every day
alt alt old · ancient
Altar ⓜ al·*tahr* altar
Alter ⓝ *al*·ter age
Amateur(in) ⓜ/ⓕ a·ma·*ter*/
a·ma·*ter*·in amateur
Ameise ⓕ *ah*·mai·ze ant
Ampel ⓕ *am*·pel traffic lights
sich amüsieren zikh a·mü·*zee*·ren
enjoy (oneself)
an an at · to
Anarchist(in) ⓜ/ⓕ a·nar·*khist*/
a·nar·*khis*·tin anarchist
anbaggern *an*·ba·gern chat up
andere *an*·de·re other · different
anfangen *an*·fang·en start
Anführer ⓜ *an*·fü·rer leader
Angel ⓕ *ang*·el fishing rod
Angestellte ⓜ&ⓕ *an*·ge·shtel·te
employee
Angst (haben) angkst (*hah*·ben)
(to be) afraid
anhalten *an*·hal·ten stop
Anhänger ⓜ pl *an*·heng·er
supporters
ankommen *an*·ko·men arrive
Ankunft ⓕ *an*·kunft arrivals
ansehen *an*·zay·en look at
(an)statt an·*shtat* instead of
Anti-Atom- *an*·ti·a·*tawm*·
antinuclear
Antibiotika ⓝ pl an·ti·bi·*aw*·ti·ka
antibiotics

Antiquariat ⓝ an·ti·kva·ri·*aht*
second-hand bookshop
Antiquität ⓕ an·ti·kvi·*tayt* antique
Antiseptikum ⓝ an·ti·*zep*·ti·kum
antiseptic
Antwort ⓕ *ant*·vort answer
antworten *ant*·vor·ten answer
Anzahlung ⓕ *an*·tsah·lung deposit
Anzeige ⓕ *an*·tsai·ge advertisement
Anzeigetafel ⓕ *an*·tsai·ge·tah·fel
scoreboard
Apfel ⓜ *ap*·fel apple
Apfelmost ⓜ *ap*·fel·most cider
Apotheke ⓕ a·po·*tay*·ke chemist ·
pharmacy
Aprikose ⓕ a·pri·*kaw*·ze apricot
Arbeit ⓕ *ar*·bait work
arbeiten *ar*·bai·ten work
Arbeiter(in) ⓜ/ⓕ *ar*·bai·ter/
ar·bai·te·rin worker · labourer
Arbeitgeber ⓜ *ar*·bait·gay·ber
employer
Arbeitserlaubnis ⓕ
ar·baits·er·lowp·nis work permit
arbeitslos *ar*·baits·laws unemployed
Arbeitslosengeld ⓝ
ar·baits·law·zen·gelt unemployment
benefit
Arbeitslosigkeit ⓕ
ar·baits·law·zikh·kait unemployment
Arbeitsstelle ⓕ *ar*·baits·shte·le job
archäologisch ar·khe·o·*law*·gish
archaeological
Architektur ⓕ ar·khi·tek·*toor*
architecture
Arm ⓜ arm arm
arm arm poor
Armut ⓕ *ar*·moot poverty
Arzt ⓜ artst doctor (medical)
Ärztin ⓕ *erts*·tin doctor (medical)
Aschenbecher ⓜ *a*·shen·be·kher
ashtray
Asien ⓝ *ah*·zi·en Asia
Asthma ⓝ *ast*·ma asthma
Asylant(in) ⓜ/ⓕ a·zü·*lant*/
a·zü·*lan*·tin asylum seeker

Atelier ⓝ a·tel·*yay* studio (art)
atmen *aht*·men breathe
Atmosphäre ⓕ at·mos·*fah*·re atmosphere
Atomenergie ⓕ a·tawm·e·ner·gee nuclear energy
Atommüll ⓜ a·*tawm*·mül nuclear waste
Aubergine ⓕ aw·ber·*zhee*·ne eggplant • aubergine
auch owkh too • also
auch nicht owkh nikht neither
auf owf on • at
auf ... zu owf ... tsoo towards
Aufführung ⓕ owf·*fü*·rung performance
aufheben owf·hay·ben pick up (object)
Aufnahme ⓕ owf·*nah*·me recording
aufpassen owf·pa·sen mind (object) • pay attention
Auftritt ⓜ owf·trit gig
aufwärts owf·verts uphill
Auge ⓝ ow·ge eye
Augenblick ⓜ ow·gen·blik moment
Augentropfen ⓜ pl ow·gen·trop·fen eye drops
aus ows from • out
aus (Baumwolle) ows (*bawm*·vo·le) made of (cotton)
Ausbeutung ⓕ ows·*boy*·tung exploitation
Ausgang ⓜ ows·gang exit
ausgebucht ows·ge·bookht booked out
ausgehen ows·gay·en go out • run out of
mit jemandem ausgehen mit *yay*·man·dem ows·gay·en date someone
ausgeschlossen ows·ge·shlo·sen excluded
ausgezeichnet ows·ge·*tsaikh*·net excellent
Auskunft ⓕ ows·kunft information
im Ausland im ows·lant abroad

ausländisch ows·len·dish foreign
Auspuff ⓜ ows·puf exhaust (car)
Ausrüstung ⓕ ows·rüs·tung equipment
Ausschlag ⓜ ows·shlahk rash
außer ow·ser apart from • besides
Aussicht ⓕ ows·zikht view
Aussichtspunkt ⓜ ows·zikhts·pungkt lookout
Ausstellung ⓕ ows·shte·lung exhibition
austeilen ows·tai·len deal (cards)
Auster ⓕ ows·ter oyster
Australien ⓝ ows·*trah*·li·en Australia
ausverkauft ows·fer·kowft sold out
Ausweis ⓜ ows·vais identification
Auto ⓝ ow·to car
Autobahn ⓕ ow·to·bahn motorway (tollway)
Autokennzeichen ⓝ ow·to·ken·tsai·khen licence plate number
automatisch ow·to·*mah*·tish automatic
Autor(in) ⓜ/ⓕ ow·tor/ow·*taw*·rin author
Autoverleih ⓜ ow·to·fer·*lai* car hire
Avokado ⓕ a·vo·*kah*·do avocado
Axt ⓕ akst axe

B

Baby ⓝ *bay*·bi baby
Babynahrung ⓕ *bay*·bi·nah·rung baby food
Babypuder ⓝ *bay*·bi·poo·der baby powder
Babysitter ⓜ *bay*·bi·si·ter babysitter
Bach ⓜ bakh stream
Bäckerei ⓕ be·ke·*rai* bakery
Backpflaume ⓕ bak·pflow·me prune
Bad ⓝ baht bath
Badeanzug ⓜ bah·de·an·tsook swimsuit
Badetuch ⓝ bah·de·tookh bath towel

B

Badezimmer ⓝ *bah*·de·tsi·mer bathroom

Bahn ⓕ bahn track (sports) • railway

Bahnhof ⓜ *bahn*·hawf railway station

Bahnsteig ⓜ *bahn*·shtaik platform

bald balt soon

Balkon ⓜ bal·*kawn* balcony

Ball ⓜ bal ball

Ballett ⓝ ba·*let* ballet

Banane ⓕ ba·*nah*·ne banana

Band ⓕ bent band (music)

Band ⓝ bant volume (book)

Bank ⓕ bangk bank

Bankauszug ⓜ *bangk*·ows·tsook bankdraft

Bankkonto ⓝ *bangk*·kon·to bank account

Bär ⓜ bair bear

Bargeld ⓝ *bahr*·gelt cash

Batterie ⓕ ba·te·*ree* battery

bauen *bow*·en build

Bauer ⓜ *bow*·er farmer

Bäuerin ⓕ *boy*·e·rin farmer

Bauernhof ⓜ *bow*·ern·hawf farm

Baum ⓜ bowm tree

Baumwolle ⓕ *bowm*·vo·le cotton

Bedienungszuschlag ⓜ be·*dee*·nungks·tsoo·shlahk service-charge

bedrohte be·*draw*·te endangered

beenden be·*en*·den finish

Beginn ⓜ be·*gin* beginning

beginnen be·*gi*·nen begin

Begleiter(in) ⓜ/ⓕ be·*glai*·ter/be·*glai*·te·rin companion

Begräbnis ⓝ be·*grayp*·nis funeral

behindert be·*hin*·dert disabled

bei bai at

Beichte ⓕ *baikh*·te confession (religious)

beide *bai*·de both

Bein ⓝ bain leg (body)

Beispiel ⓝ *bai*·shpeel example

Bekleidungsgeschäft ⓜ be·*klai*·dungks·ge·sheft clothing store

Belästigung ⓕ be·*les*·ti·gung harassment

Belichtungsmesser ⓜ be·*likh*·tungks·me·ser light meter

beliebt be·*leept* popular

Benzin ⓝ ben·*tseen* gas/petrol

Benzinkanister ⓜ ben·*tseen*·ka·nis·ter petrol can

beobachten be·*aw*·bakh·ten watch

bequem be·*kvaym* comfortable

berauben be·*row*·ben rob

Berg ⓜ berk mountain

Berghütte ⓕ *berk*·hü·te mountain hut

Bergsteigen ⓝ berk·*shtai*·gen mountaineering

Bergweg ⓜ *berk*·vayk mountain path

Beruf ⓜ be·*roof* occupation • profession

berühmt be·*rümt* famous

berühren be·*rü*·ren touch

beschäftigt be·*shef*·tikht busy (person)

beschützen be·*shü*·tsen protect

sich beschweren zikh be·*shvair*·en complain

besetzt be·*zetst* busy (phone)

Besitzer(in) ⓜ/ⓕ be·*zi*·tser/be·*zi*·tse·rin owner

besorgt be·*zorkt* worried

besser be·ser better

bestätigen be·*shtay*·ti·gen confirm (reservation)

beste *bes*·te best

bestechen be·*shte*·khen bribe

Besteck ⓝ be·*shtek* cutlery

besteigen be·*shtai*·gen board (plane, ship)

bestellen be·*shte*·len order

Bestellung ⓕ be·*shte*·lung order (restaurant)

bestrafen be·*shtrah*·fen punish

besuchen be·*zoo*·khen visit

Betäubung ⓕ be·*toy*·bung anaesthetic

B

sich beteiligen zikh be·*tai*·li·gen participate

Betrag m be·*trahk* amount

Betrüger(in) m/① be·*trü*·ger/be·*trü*·ge·rin cheat

betrunken be·*trung*·ken drunk

Bett ⓝ bet bed

Bettlaken ⓝ *bet*·lah·ken sheet (bed)

Bettler(in) m/① *bet*·ler/*bet*·le·rin beggar

Bettwäsche ① *bet*·ve·she linen (bed)

Bettzeug ⓝ *bet*·tsoyk bedding

Beutelmelone ① *boy*·tel·me·law·ne cantaloupe

bezahlen be·*tsah*·len pay

Beziehung ① be·*tsee*·ung relationship

BH m bay·*hah* bra

Bibel ① *bee*·bel bible

Bibliothek ① bi·bli·o·*tayk* library

Biene ① *bee*·ne bee

Bier ⓝ beer beer

Bildschirm m *bilt*·shirm screen (TV, computer)

Billard ⓝ *bil*·yart pool (game)

billig *bi*·likh cheap

Birne ① *bir*·ne pear

bis (Juni) bis (*yoo*·ni) until (June)

bis zu ... bis tsoo ... as far as ...

Biss m bis bite (animal)

ein bisschen ain bis·khen a little

bitte *bi*·te please

um etwas bitten um et·vas *bi*·ten ask for something

bitter *bi*·ter bitter

Blase ① *blah*·ze blister

Blasenentzündung ① *blah*·zen·en·tsün·dung cystitis

Blatt ⓝ blat leaf

blau blow blue

bleiben *blai*·ben stay (remain)

bleifrei *blai*·frai unleaded

Bleistift m *blai*·shtift pencil

blind blint blind

Blinddarm m *blint*·darm appendix

Blindenhund m *blin*·den·hunt guide dog

Blindenschrift ① *blin*·den·shrift Braille

Blinker m *bling*·ker indicator

Blitz m blits lightning • flash

blockiert blo·*keert* blocked

Blume ① *bloo*·me flower

Blumenhändler m *bloo*·men·hen·dler florist

Blumenkohl m *bloo*·men·kawl cauliflower

Blut ⓝ bloot blood

Blutdruck m *bloot*·druk blood pressure

Blutgruppe ① *bloot*·gru·pe blood group

Bluttest m *bloot* test blood test

Boden m *baw*·den floor

Bohne ① *baw*·ne bean

Bonbon m bong·*bong* candy

Boot ⓝ bawt boat

an Bord an bort aboard

Bordkarte ① *bort*·kar·te boarding pass

Botanischer Garten m bo·*tah*·ni·sher *gar*·ten botanic garden

Botschaft ① *bawt*·shaft embassy

Botschafter(in) m/① *bawt*·shaf·ter/*bawt*·shaf·te·rin ambassador

Boxen ⓝ *bok*·sen boxing

braten *brah*·ten fry

Bratpfanne ① *braht*·pfa·ne frying pan

brauchen *brow*·khen need

braun brown brown

brechen *bre*·khen vomit

breit brait wide

Bremsen ① pl *brem*·zen brakes

Bremsflüssigkeit ① *brems*·flü·sikh·kait brake fluid

Brennholz ⓝ *bren*·holts firewood

Brennstoff m *bren*·shtof fuel

Brett ⓝ bret board (plank)

Brief m breef letter

Briefkasten m *breef*·kas·ten mailbox

Briefmarke ① *breef*·mar·ke stamp

C

Briefumschlag ⓜ *breef*·um·shlahk envelope

brillant bril·*yant* brilliant

Brille ⓕ *bri*·le glasses (spectacles)

bringen *bring*·en bring • take

Brokkoli ⓜ pl *bro*·ko·li broccoli

Bronchitis ⓕ bron·*khee*·tis bronchitis

Broschüre ⓕ bro·*shū*·re brochure

Brot ⓝ brawt bread

Brötchen ⓝ *brert*·khen bread roll

Brücke ⓕ *brü*·ke bridge

Bruder ⓜ *broo*·der brother

Brunnen ⓜ *bru*·nen fountain

Brust ⓕ brust breast

Brustkorb ⓜ *brust*·korp chest

Buch ⓝ bookh book

buchen *boo*·khen book (reserve)

Buchhalter(in) ⓜ/ⓕ *bookh*·hal·ter/ *bookh*·hal·te·rin accountant

Buchhandlung ⓕ *bookh*·han·dlung bookshop

Buddhist(in) ⓜ/ⓕ bu·*dist*/bu·*dis*·tin Buddhist

Buffet ⓝ bü·*fay* buffet

bügeln *bü*·geln iron (clothes)

Bühne ⓕ *bü*·ne stage (theatre)

Bundeskanzler(in) ⓜ/ⓕ *bun*·des·kants·ler/ *bun*·des·kants·le·rin prime minister (Germany & Austria)

Burg ⓕ burk castle

Bürgermeister(in) ⓜ/ⓕ *bür*·ger·mais·ter/*bür*·ger·mais·te·rin mayor

Bürgerrechte ⓝ pl *bür*·ger·rekh·te civil rights

Büro ⓝ bü·*raw* office

Büroangestellte ⓜ&ⓕ bü·*raw*·an·ge·shtel·te office worker

Bus ⓜ bus bus (city)

Busbahnhof ⓜ *bus*·bahn·hawf bus station

Bushaltestelle ⓕ *bus*·hal·te·shte·le bus stop

Butter ⓕ *bu*·ter butter

C

Café ⓝ ka·*fay* cafe

Campingplatz ⓜ *kem*·ping·plats camping ground

Cashewnuss ⓕ *kesh*·yoo·nus cashew

CD ⓕ tsay·*day* CD

Celsius ⓜ *tsel*·zi·us centigrade

Cent ⓜ sent cent

Chancengleichheit ⓕ *shahng*·sen·glaikh·hait equal opportunity

charmant shar·*mant* charming

Chef(in) ⓜ/ⓕ shef/*she*·fin boss

chemische Reinigung *khay*·mi·she *rai*·ni·gung dry-cleaner

Chili(sauce) ⓕ *chi*·li(·*zaw*·se) chilli (sauce)

Christ(in) ⓜ/ⓕ krist/*kris*·tin Christian

Computerspiel ⓝ kom·*pyoo*·ter·shpeel computer game

Coupon ⓜ ku·*pong* coupon

Couscous ⓜ *kus*·kus couscous

Cousin(e) ⓜ/ⓕ ku·*zen*/ku·*zee*·ne cousin

Cracker ⓜ *kre*·ker cracker

Cricket ⓝ *kri*·ket cricket

Curry(pulver) ⓝ *ker*·ri(·*pul*·ver) curry (powder)

D

Dach ⓝ dakh roof

Dachboden ⓜ *dakh*·baw·den attic

Dachs ⓜ daks badger

Damenbinden ⓕ pl *dah*·men·bin·den sanitary napkins

Dämmerung ⓕ *de*·me·rung dawn • dusk

danken *dang*·ken thank

Datum ⓝ *dah*·tum date (day)

Decke ⓕ *de*·ke blanket

dein dain your sg inf

Demokratie ⓕ de·mo·kra·*tee* democracy

Demonstration ⓕ
de·mon·stra·tsyawn demonstration

denken deng·ken think

Denkmal ⓝ dengk·mahl monument

Deo ⓝ day·o deodorant

Detail ⓝ de·tai detail

Deutsch ⓝ doytsh German

Deutschland ⓝ doytsh·lant
Germany

Dia ⓝ dee·a slide (film)

Diabetis ⓕ di·a·bay·tis diabetes

Diät ⓕ di·ayt diet

Dichtung ⓕ dikh·tung poetry

dick dik thick • fat

Dieb ⓜ deep thief

Dienstag ⓜ deens·tahk Tuesday

dieser ⓜ dee·zer this (one)

direkt di·rekt direct

Diskette ⓕ dis·ke·te disk (computer)

Disko(thek) ⓕ dis·ko(·tayk) disco

Diskriminierung ⓕ
dis·kri·mi·nee·rung discrimination

Doktor(in) ⓜ/ⓕ dok·tor/dok·taw·rin
doctor (title)

Dokumentation ⓕ
do·ku·men·ta·tsyawn documentary

Dollar ⓜ do·lahr dollar

Dolmetscher(in) ⓜ/ⓕ
dol·met·sher/dol·met·she·rin
interpreter

Dom ⓜ dawm cathedral

Donner ⓜ do·ner thunder

Donnerstag ⓜ do·ners·tahk
Thursday

Dope ⓝ dawp/dohp dope (drugs)

Doppelbett ⓝ do·pel·bet double bed

doppelt do·pelt double

Doppelzimmer ⓝ do·pel·tsi·mer
double room

Dorf ⓝ dorf village

dort dort there

Dose ⓕ daw·ze can (tin)

Dosenöffner ⓜ daw·zen·erf·ner can
opener

Dozent(in) ⓜ/ⓕ do·tsent/
do·tsen·tin lecturer

Drachenfliegen ⓝ dra·khen·flee·gen
hang-gliding

Draht ⓜ draht wire

draußen drow·sen outside

dringend dring·ent urgent

dritte dri·te third

Droge ⓕ draw·ge drug

Drogenabhängigkeit ⓕ
draw·gen·ap·heng·ikh·kait drug
addiction

Drogenhändler ⓜ draw·gen·hen·dler
drug dealer

Druck ⓜ druk pressure • print (art)

Drüsenfieber ⓝ drü·zen·fee·ber
glandular fever

du doo you sg int

dumm dum stupid

dunkel dung·kel dark

dünn dün thin

durch durkh through

Durchfall ⓜ durkh·fal diarrhoea

Durchwahl ⓕ durkh·vahl direct-dial

durstig durs·tikh thirsty

Dusche ⓕ doo·she shower

Dutzend ⓝ du·tsent dozen

E

Ebene ⓕ ay·be·ne plain

Echse ⓕ ek·se lizard

Ecke ⓕ e·ke corner

egoistisch e·go·is·tish selfish

Ehe ⓕ ay·e marriage

Ehefrau ⓕ ay·e·frow wife

Ehemann ⓜ ay·e·man husband

ehrlich air·likh honest

Ei ⓝ ai egg

Eierstockzyste ⓕ ai·er·shtok·tsüs·te
ovarian cyst

eifersüchtig ai·fer·zükh·tikh jealous

(in) Eile in ai·le (in a) hurry

Eimer ⓜ ai·mer bucket

ein(s) ain(s) one

einfach ain·fakh simple

einfache Fahrkarte ⓕ ain·fa·khe
fahr·kar·te one-way ticket

einige ai·ni·ge some • several

E

E

einkaufen gehen *ain·kow·fen gay·en* go shopping

Einkaufszentrum ⓝ *ain·kowfs·tsen·trum* shopping centre

Einkommensteuer ⓕ *ain·ko·men·shtoy·er* income tax

einladen *ain·lah·den* invite

einlassen *ain·la·sen* admit (entry)

einlösen *ain·ler·zen* cash (a cheque)

einmal *ain·mahl* once

Einschreiben ⓝ *ain·shrai·ben* registered mail

eintreten *ain·tray·ten* enter

Eintrittsgeld ⓝ *ain·trits·gelt* cover charge

Eintrittskarte ⓕ *ain·trits·kar·te* (admission) ticket

Eintrittspreis ⓜ *ain·trits·prais* admission price

einzeln aufgeführt *ain·tseln owf·ge·fürt* itemised

Einzelzimmer ⓝ *ain·tsel·tsi·mer* single room

Eis ⓝ *ais* ice

Eiscreme ⓕ *ais·kraym* ice cream

Eisdiele ⓕ *ais·dee·le* ice cream parlour

Eisenwarengeschäft ⓝ *ai·zen·vah·ren·ge·sheft* hardware store

Eishockey ⓝ *ais·ho·ki* ice hockey

eislaufen *ais·low·fen* ice skating

Eispickel ⓜ *ais·pi·kel* ice axe

Ekzem ⓝ *ek·tsaym* eczema

Elektrizität ⓕ *e·lek·tri·tsi·tayt* electricity

Elektrogeschäft ⓝ *e·lek·tro·ge·sheft* electrical store

Eltern ⓝ *pl el·tern* parents

emotional *e·mo·tsyo·nahl* emotional

empfehlen *emp·fay·len* recommend

Empfindlichkeit ⓕ *emp·fint·likh·kait* film speed • sensitivity

(am) Ende *(am) en·de* (at the) end

Endstation ⓕ *ent·shta·tsyawn* terminal

Energie ⓕ *e·ner·gee* energy

eng *eng* tight

Englisch ⓝ *eng·lish* English

Enkelkind ⓝ *eng·kel·kint* grandchild

Ente ⓕ *en·te* duck

entscheiden *ent·shai·den* decide

sich entspannen *zikh ent·shpa·nen* relax

entwerfen *ent·ver·fen* design

entwerten *ent·ver·ten* validate (ticket)

Entzündung ⓕ *en·tsün·dung* infection • inflammation

Epilepsie ⓕ *e·pi·lep·see* epilepsy

er *air* he

erbrechen *er·bre·khen* vomit

Erbse ⓕ *erp·se* pea

Erdbeben ⓝ *ert·bay·ben* earthquake

Erdbeere ⓕ *ert·bair·re* strawberry

Erde ⓕ *er·de* Earth

Erdnuss ⓕ *ert·nus* peanut • ground nut

Erfahrung ⓕ *er·fah·rung* experience

erhalten *er·hal·ten* receive

erkältet sein *er·kel·tet zain* have a cold

Erlaubnis ⓕ *er·lowp·nis* permission

ermüden *er·mü·den* tire

ernst *ernst* serious

erstaunlich *er·shtown·likh* amazing

erste *ers·te* first

Erwachsene ⓜ&ⓕ *er·vak·se·ne* adult

erzählen *er·tsay·len* tell

Erziehung ⓕ *er·tsee·ung* education

Essen ⓝ *e·sen* food

essen *e·sen* eat

Essig ⓜ *e·sikh* vinegar

etwas *et·vas* something • anything

Euro ⓜ *oy·ro* euro

Europa ⓝ *oy·raw·pa* Europe

Euthanasie ⓕ *oy·ta·na·zee* euthanasia

Express- *eks·pres·* express

Expresspost ⓕ *eks·pres·post* express mail

F

Fabrik ① fa·*breek* factory
Faden ⓜ *fah*·den thread
fahren *fah*·ren travel by vehicle
Fahrgast ⓜ *fahr*·gast passenger (bus/taxi)
Fahrkarte ① *fahr*·kar·te ticket
Fahrkartenautomat ⓜ *fahr*·kar·ten·ow·to·maht ticket machine
Fahrkartenkontrolleur(in) ⓜ/① *fahr*·kar·ten·kon·tro·ler·(rin) ticket collector
Fahrkartenverkauf ⓜ *fahr*·kar·ten·fer·kowf ticket office
Fahrplan ⓜ *fahr*·plahn timetable
Fahrrad ⓝ *fahr*·raht bicycle
Fahrradkette ① *fahr*·raht·ke·te bicycle chain
Fahrzeugpapiere ⓝ pl *fahr*·tsoyk·pa·pee·re car owner's title (document)
Fallschirmspringen ⓝ *fal*·shirm·shpring·en parachuting
falsch falsh false · wrong
Familie ① fa·*mee*·li·e family
Familienname ⓜ fa·*mee*·li·en·nah·me family name
Familienstand ⓜ fa·*mee*·li·en·shtant marital status
Fan ⓜ fen fan (sports)
Farbe ① *far*·be colour
Farben ① pl *far*·ben paints
fast fast almost
Fastenzeit ① *fas*·ten·tsait Lent
faul fowl lazy
Fax ⓝ faks fax
Fechten ⓝ *fekh*·ten fencing (sports)
Feder ① *fay*·der spring (coil)
Fehler ⓜ *fay*·ler mistake
fehlerhaft *fay*·ler·haft faulty
Fehlgeburt ① *fayl*·ge·burt miscarriage
Feier ① *fai*·er celebration
Feige ① *fai*·ge fig

Feinkostgeschäft ⓝ *fain*·kost·ge·sheft delicatessen
Feld ⓝ felt field
Feldfrucht ① *felt*·frukht crop
Fels ⓜ fels rock
Fenster ⓝ *fens*·ter window
Ferien pl *fair*·ri·en holidays/vacation
Fern- fern· long-distance
Fernbedienung ① *fern*·be·dee·nung remote control
Fernbus ⓜ *fern*·bus bus (intercity)
Fernglas ⓝ *fern*·glahs binoculars
fernsehen *fern*·zay·en watch TV
Fernseher ⓜ *fern*·zay·er TV set
Fernsehserie ① *fern*·zay·zair·ri·e TV series
fertig *fer*·tikh ready · finished
Fest ⓝ fest festival · party
fest fest solid
fettarme Milch ① *fet*·ar·me milkh skimmed milk
feucht foykht damp
Feuchtigkeitscreme ① *foykh*·tikh·kaits·kraym moisturiser
Feuer ⓝ *foy*·er fire
Feuerzeug ⓝ *foy*·er·tsoyk cigarette lighter
Fieber ⓝ *fee*·ber fever
Filet ⓝ fi·*lay* fillet
Film ⓜ film movie · film (camera)
finden *fin*·den find
Finger ⓝ *fing*·er finger
Firma ① *fir*·ma company
Fisch ⓜ fish fish
Fischen ⓝ *fi*·shen fishing
Fitness-Studio ⓝ *fit*·nes·shtoo·di·o gym
flach flakh flat
Flagge ① *fla*·ge flag
Flasche ① *fla*·she bottle
Flaschenöffner ⓜ *fla*·shen·erf·ner bottle opener
Fleisch ⓝ flaish meat
Fliege ① *flee*·ge fly
fliegen *flee*·gen fly
Flitterwochen pl *fli*·ter·vo·khen honeymoon

G

Floh ⓜ flaw flea
Flohmarkt ⓜ flaw·markt flea-market
Flüchtling ⓜ flükht·ling refugee
Flug ⓜ flook flight
Flügel ⓜ pl flü·gel wings
Fluggast ⓜ flook·gast passenger (plane)
Flughafen ⓜ flook·hah·fen airport
Flughafengebühr ⓕ flook·hah·fen·ge·bür airport tax
Fluglinie ⓕ flook·lee·ni·e airline
Flugticket ⓝ flook·ti·ket plane ticket
Flugzeug ⓝ flook·tsoyk aeroplane
Fluss ⓜ flus river
folgen fol·gen follow
Forderung ⓕ for·de·rung demand
Form ⓕ form shape
formell for·mel formal
Foto ⓝ faw·to photo
Fotogeschäft ⓝ faw·to·ge·sheft camera shop
Fotograf(in) ⓜ/ⓕ fo·to·grahf/fo·to·grah·fin photographer
Fotografie ⓕ fo·to·gra·fee photograph · photography
fotografieren fo·to·gra·fee·ren take a photograph
Foul ⓝ fowl foul
Foyer ⓝ fo·a·yay foyer
Frage ⓕ frah·ge question
eine Frage stellen ai·ne frah·ge shte·len ask a question
Franc ⓜ frank franc
Frankreich ⓝ frangk·raikh France
Frau ⓕ frow woman
frei frai free (not bound) · vacant
Freibad ⓝ frai·baht (outdoor) swimming pool
Freigepäck ⓝ frai·ge·pek baggage allowance
Freitag ⓜ frai·tahk Friday
fremd fremt strange
Fremde ⓜ&ⓕ frem·de stranger
Fremdenverkehrsbüro ⓝ frem·den·fer·kairs·bü·raw tourist office

Freund ⓜ froynt male friend · boyfriend
Freundin ⓕ froyn·din female friend · girlfriend
freundlich froynt·likh friendly
Frieden ⓜ free·den peace
Friedhof ⓜ freet·hawf cemetery
frisch frish fresh (not stale)
Frischkäse ⓜ frish·kay·ze cream cheese
Friseur(in) ⓜ/ⓕ fri·zer/fri·zer·rin hairdresser
Frosch ⓜ frosh frog
Frost ⓜ frost frost
Frucht ⓕ frukht fruit
früh frü early
Frühling ⓜ frü·ling spring (season)
Frühstück ⓝ frü·shtük breakfast
Frühstücksflocke ⓕ frü·shtüks·flo·ke breakfast cereal
Frühstücksspeck ⓜ frü·shtüks·shpek bacon
fühlen fü·len feel
Führer ⓜ fü·rer guide · guidebook
Führerschein ⓜ fü·rer·shain driving licence
Führung ⓕ fü·rung guided tour
füllen fü·len fill
Fundbüro ⓝ funt·bü·raw lost property office
für für for
Fuß ⓜ foos foot
Fußball ⓜ foos·bal football · soccer
Fußgänger(in) ⓜ/ⓕ foos·geng·er/foos·geng·e·rin pedestrian
füttern fü·tern feed

G

Gabel ⓕ gah·bel fork
Gang ⓜ gang aisle
Gänge ⓜ pl geng·e gears
ganz gants whole
Garage ⓕ ga·rah·zhe garage
Garderobe ⓕ gar·draw·be wardrobe · cloakroom
Garnele ⓕ gar·nay·le prawn

Garten ⓜ *gar*·ten garden

Gas ⓝ gahs gas (for cooking)

Gasflasche ⓕ *gahs*·fla·she gas cylinder

Gaskartusche ⓕ *gahs*·kar·tu·she gas cartridge

Gastfreundschaft ⓕ *gast*·froynt·shaft hospitality

Gebäude ⓝ ge·*boy*·de building

geben *gay*·ben give

Gebet ⓝ ge·*bayt* prayer

Gebirgszug ⓜ ge·*birks*·tsook mountain range

gebraucht ge·*browkht* secondhand

Geburtsdatum ⓝ ge·*burts*·dah·tum date of birth

Geburtsort ⓜ ge·*burts*·ort place of birth

Geburtstag ⓜ ge·*burts*·tahk birthday

Geburtsurkunde ⓕ ge·*burts*·oor·kun·de birth certificate

gefährlich ge·*fair*·likh dangerous

Gefangene ⓜ&ⓕ ge·*fang*·e·ne prisoner

Gefängnis ⓝ ge·*fong*·nis prison

gefiltert ge·*fil*·tert filtered

gefrieren ge·*free*·ren freeze

Gefühle ⓝ pl ge·*fü*·le feelings

gegen *gay*·gen against

gegenüber gay·gen·*ü*·ber opposite

Gegenwart ⓕ *gay*·gen·vart present (time)

Gehacktes ⓝ ge·*hak*·tes mince

Gehalt ⓝ ge·*halt* salary

Geheimnis ⓝ ge·*haim*·nis secret

gehen *gay*·en walk

Gehweg ⓜ *gay*·vayk footpath

Geisteswissenschaften ⓕ pl *gais*·tes·vi·sen·shaf·ten humanities

geizig *gai*·tsikh stingy

gelangweilt ge·*lang*·vailt bored

gelb gelp yellow

Geld ⓝ gelt money

Geldautomat ⓜ *gelt*·ow·to·maht automatic teller machine (ATM)

Geldbuße ⓕ *gelt*·boo·se fine (money)

Geldschein ⓜ *gelt*·shain banknote

Geldwechsel ⓜ *gelt*·vek·sel currency exchange

Gelegenheitsarbeit ⓕ ge·*lay*·gen·haits·ar·bait casual work

Gemüse ⓝ ge·*mü*·ze vegetable

Genehmigung ⓕ ge·*nay*·mi·gung permit

genug ge·*nook* enough

Gepäck ⓝ ge·*pek* luggage

Gepäckaufbewahrung ⓕ ge·*pek*·owf·be·vah·rung left luggage

Gepäckausgabe ⓕ ge·*pek*·ows·gah·be luggage claim

gerade ge·*rah*·de straight (direction)

Gerechtigkeit ⓕ ge·*rekh*·tikh·kait justice

Gericht ⓝ ge·*rikht* court (legal)

Geruch ⓜ ge·*rookh* smell

Geschäft ⓝ ge·*sheft* shop • business

Geschäftsfrau ⓕ ge·*shefts*·frow businesswoman

Geschäftsmann ⓜ ge·*shefts*·man businessman

Geschäftsreise ⓕ ge·*shefts*·rai·ze business trip

Geschenk ⓝ ge·*shengk* present (gift)

Geschichte ⓕ ge·*shikh*·te story

Geschlechtskrankheit ⓕ ge·*shlekhts*·krangk·hait venereal disease

geschlossen ge·*shlo*·sen closed

geschützte (Tierarten) ⓕ pl ge·*shüts*·te (*teer*·ar·ten) protected (species)

Geschwindigkeit ⓕ ge·*shvin*·dikh·kait speed

Geschwindigkeitsbegrenzung ⓕ ge·*shvin*·dikh·kaits·be·gren·tsung speed limit

Gesetz ⓝ ge·*zets* law

Gesetzgebung ⓕ ge·*zets*·gay·bung legislation

H

Gesicht ⓝ ge·*zikht* face
gestern *ges*·tern yesterday
Gesundheit ⓕ ge·*zunt*·hait health
Getränk ⓝ ge·*trengk* drink
Getränkehandel ⓜ
ge·*treng*·ke·han·del liquor store
getrennt ge·*trent* separate (distinct)
Gewebe ⓝ ge·*vay*·be fabric
Gewicht ⓝ ge·*vikht* weight
Gewinn ⓜ ge·*vin* profit
gewinnen ge·*vi*·nen win
Gewürznelke ⓕ ge·*vürts*·nel·ke
clove (spice)
Gezeiten pl ge·*tsai*·ten tides
giftig *gif*·tikh poisonous
Giftmüll ⓜ *gift*·mül toxic waste
Gin ⓜ dzhin gin
Gipfel ⓜ *gip*·fel peak
Gitarre ⓕ gi·*ta*·re guitar
Glas ⓝ glahs glass • jar
glatt glat slippery
gleich dort glaikh dort right there
gleiche *glai*·khe same
Gleichheit ⓕ *glaikh*·hait equality
Gleis ⓝ glais platform
Gleitschirmfliegen ⓝ
glait·shirm·flee·gen paragliding
Gletscher ⓜ *glet*·sher glacier
Glück ⓝ glük luck • happiness
glücklich *glük*·likh lucky • happy
Glückwunsch ⓜ *glük*·vunsh
congratulations
Glühbirne ⓕ *glü*·bir·ne light bulb
Gold ⓝ golt gold
Golfplatz ⓜ *golf*·plats golf course
Gott ⓜ got god (general)
Gottesdienst ⓜ *go*·tes·deenst
church service
Grab ⓝ grahp grave • tomb
Grad ⓜ graht degree
grafische Kunst ⓕ *grah*·fi·she kunst
graphic art
Gramm ⓝ gram gram
Gras ⓝ grahs grass • pot (dope)
gratis *grah*·tis free (gratis)
grau grow grey

Grenze ⓕ *gren*·tse border
Grippe ⓕ *gri*·pe influenza
groß graws big • great • tall
Größe ⓕ *grer*·se size (general)
Großeltern ⓜ pl *graws*·el·tern
grandparents
Großmutter ⓕ *graws*·mu·ter
grandmother
Großvater ⓜ *graws*·fah·ter
grandfather
grün grün green
Grund ⓜ grunt reason
Gurke ⓕ *gur*·ke cucumber
Gürtel ⓜ *gür*·tel belt
gut goot good • well
gutaussehend *goot*·ows·zay·ent
handsome
Gymnastik ⓕ güm·*nas*·tik
gymnastics
Gynäkologe ⓜ gü·ne·ko·*law*·ge
gynaecologist
Gynäkologin ⓕ gü·ne·ko·*law*·gin
gynaecologist

H

Haar ⓝ hahr hair
Haarbürste ⓕ *hahr*·bürs·te
hairbrush
haben *hah*·ben have
Hafen ⓜ *hah*·fen port • harbour
Hafer(flocken) ⓜ pl
hah·fer(·flo·ken) oats
Hähnchenschenkel ⓜ
hayn·khen·sheng·kel chicken
drumstick
Halal- ha·*lal*· halal
Hälfte ⓕ *helf*·te half
Hallenbad ⓝ *ha*·len·baht (indoor)
swimming pool
hallo ha·lo/ha·*law* hello
halluzinieren ha·lu·tsi·*nee*·ren
hallucinate
Hals ⓜ hals throat
Halskette ⓕ *hals*·ke·te necklace
Halsschmerzen pl *hals*·shmer·tsen
sore throat

Halt ⓜ halt stop
Hammer ⓜ ha·mer hammer
Hamster ⓜ hams·ter hamster
Hand ⓕ hant hand
Handel ⓜ han·del trade
handgemacht hant·ge·makht handmade
Handschuh ⓜ hant·shoo glove
Handtasche ⓕ hant·ta·she handbag
Handtuch ⓝ han·tookh towel
Handwerk ⓝ hant·verk crafts
Handy ⓝ hen·di cell/mobile phone
Hang ⓜ hang slope
Hängematte ⓕ heng·e·ma·te hammock
hart hart hard (not soft)
Haschee ⓝ ha·shay hash
Hauptz howpt main
Hauptplatz ⓜ howpt·plats main square
Haus ⓝ hows house
Hausarbeit ⓕ hows·ar·bait housework
nach Hause nakh how·ze (go) home
Hausfrau ⓕ hows·frow homemaker
Hausmann ⓜ hows·man homemaker
Haut ⓕ howt skin
heilig hai·likh holy
Heiligabend ⓜ hai·likh·ah·bent Christmas Eve
Heilige ⓜ&ⓕ hai·li·ge saint
Heim ⓝ haim home
Heimweh haben haim·vay hah·ben to be homesick
heiraten hai·rah·ten marry
heiß hais hot
Heizgerät ⓝ haits·ge·rayt heater
helfen hel·fen help
hell hel light (weight)
Helm ⓜ helm helmet
Hemd ⓝ hemt shirt
Herausgeber(in) ⓜ/ⓕ he·rows·gay·ber/ he·rows·gay·be·rin editor
Herbst ⓜ herpst autumn • fall
Herd ⓜ hert stove

Hering ⓜ hay·ring herring
Heringe ⓜ pl hay·ring·e tent pegs
Heroin ⓝ he·ro·een heroin
Herz ⓝ herts heart
Herzleiden ⓝ herts·lai·den heart condition
Herzschrittmacher ⓜ herts·shrit·ma·kher pacemaker (heart)
Heuschnupfen ⓜ hoy·shnup·fen hay fever
heute hoy·te today
heute Abend hoy·te ah·bent tonight
hier heer here
Hilfe ⓕ hil·fe help
Himbeere ⓕ him·bair·re raspberry
Himmel ⓜ hi·mel sky
Hindu ⓜ&ⓕ hin·du Hindu
hinten hin·ten at the back • behind
Hintern hin·tern bum (body)
hinüber hi·nü·ber across (to)
historisch his·taw·rish historical
Hitze ⓕ hi·tse heat
HIV-positiv hah·ee·fow·paw·zi·teef HIV positive
hoch hawkh high (up)
Hochebene ⓕ hawkh·ay·be·ne plateau
Hochzeit ⓕ hokh·tsait wedding
Hochzeitsgeschenk ⓝ hokh·tsaits·ge·shenk wedding present
Hochzeitstorte ⓕ hokh·tsaits·tor·te wedding cake
Hockey ⓝ ho·ki hockey
Höhe ⓕ her·e altitude
Höhle ⓕ her·le cave
Holz ⓝ holts wood
homöopathisches Mittel ⓝ haw·mer·o·pah·ti·shes mi·tel homeopathic medicine
homosexuell haw·mo·zek·su·el homosexual
Honig ⓜ haw·nikh honey
hören her·ren hear • listen
Hörgerät ⓝ her·ge·rayt hearing aid

I

Horoskop ⓝ ho·ros·*kawp* horoscope
Hose ⓕ *haw*·ze trousers/pants
Hotel ⓝ ho·*tel* hotel
hübsch hüpsh pretty
Hüfttasche ⓕ *hüft*·ta·she bumbag
Hügel ⓜ *hü*·gel hill
Huhn ⓝ hoon chicken
Hühnerbrust ⓕ *hü*·ner·brust
chicken breast
Hülsenfrucht ⓕ *hül*·zen·frukht
legume
Hund ⓜ hunt dog
hundert *hun*·dert hundred
hungrig *hung*·rikh hungry
husten *hoos*·ten cough
Hustensaft ⓜ *hoos*·ten·zaft cough
medicine
Hut ⓜ hoot hat
Hütte ⓕ *hü*·te hut
Hüttenkäse ⓜ *hü*·ten·kay·ze cottage
cheese

I

ich ikh I
Idee ⓕ i·*day* idea
Idiot ⓜ i·di·*awt* idiot
ihr eer her • their
Ihr eer your (polite)
illegal i·le·*gahl* illegal
immer *i*·mer always • forever
Immigration ⓕ i·mi·gra·*tsyawn*
immigration
in in in • at
inbegriffen in·be·gri·fen included
Indien ⓝ *in*·di·en India
Industrie ⓕ in·dus·*tree* industry
Informationstechnologie ⓕ in·for·
ma·*tsyawns*·tekh·no·lo·gee IT
Ingenieur(in) ⓜ/ⓕ
in·zhe·*nyer*(·rin) engineer
Ingenieurwesen ⓝ
in·zhe·*nyer*·vay·zen engineering
Ingwer ⓜ *ing*·ver ginger
Injektion ⓕ in·yek·*tsyawn* injection
(medical)
injizieren in·yi·*tsee*·ren inject

innen *i*·nen inside
Innenstadt ⓕ *i*·nen·shtat city centre
innerhalb (einer Stunde) *i*·ner·halp
(*ai*·ner *shtun*·de) within (an hour)
Insekt ⓝ in·*zekt* insect
Insektenschutzmittel ⓝ
in·*zek*·ten·shuts·mi·tel insect repellant
Insel ⓕ *in*·zel island
Installateur(in) ⓜ/ⓕ in·sta·la·*ter*/
in·sta·la·*ter*·rin plumber
interessant in·tre·*sant* interesting
international in·ter·na·*tsyo·nahl*
international
Internet ⓝ *in*·ter·net internet
Interview ⓝ *in*·ter·vyoo interview
irgendein ir·gent·*ain* any
irgendetwas ir·gent·*et*·vas anything
irgendwo ir·gent·*vaw* anywhere
Irland ⓝ *ir*·lant Ireland

J

ja yah yes
Jacke ⓕ *ya*·ke jacket
Jagd ⓕ yahkt hunting
Jahr ⓝ yahr year
Jahreszeit ⓕ *yah*·res·tsait season
Japan ⓝ *yah*·pahn Japan
Jeans ⓕ pl dzheens jeans
jeder *yay*·der everyone
jeder ⓜ *yay*·der each • every
jemand *yay*·mant someone
Jetlag ⓜ *dzhet*·leg jet lag
jetzt yetst now
Jockey ⓜ *dzho*·ki jockey
Joga ⓝ *yaw*·ga yoga
Joggen ⓝ *dzho*·gen jogging
Joghurt ⓜ *yaw*·gurt yogurt
Journalist(in) ⓜ/ⓕ zhur·na·*list*/
zhur·na·*lis*·tin journalist
Juckreiz ⓜ *yuk*·raits itch
jüdisch *yü*·dish Jewish
Jugendherberge ⓕ
yoo·gent·*her*·ber·ge youth hostel
jung yung young
Junge ⓜ *yung*·e boy
Jura ⓝ *yoo*·ra law (subject)

K

Kabel ⓝ *kah*·bel cable
Kaffee ⓜ *ka*·fay coffee
Kakao ⓜ *ka*·kow cocoa
Kakerlake ① *kah*·ker·lah·ke cockroach
Kalbfleisch ⓝ *kalp*·flaish veal
Kalender ⓜ ka·*len*·der calendar
kalt kalt cold
Kamera ① *kah*·me·ra camera
Kamm ⓜ kam comb
Kampf ⓜ *kampf* fight
Kampfsport ⓜ *kampf*·shport martial arts
Kanada ⓝ *ka*·na·dah Canada
Kanarienvogel ⓜ ka·*nah*·ri·en·faw·gel canary
Kaninchen ⓝ ka·*neen*·khen rabbit
Kantine ① kan·*tee*·ne canteen
Kapelle ① ka·*pe*·le chapel • band (music)
Kapitalismus ⓜ ka·pi·ta·*lis*·mus capitalism
kaputt ka·*put* broken
Karte ① *kar*·te map • ticket
Karten ① pl *kar*·ten cards
Kartoffel ① kar·*to*·fel potato
Karton ⓜ kar·*tong* box • carton
Karwoche ① *kahr*·vo·khe Holy Week
Käse ⓜ *kay*·ze cheese
Kasino ⓝ ka·*zee*·no casino
Kasse ① *ka*·se cash register • checkout • ticket counter
Kassette ① ka·*se*·te cassette
Kassierer(in) ⓜ/① ka·*see*·rer/ ka·*see*·re·rin cashier
Katholik(in) ⓜ/① ka·to·*leek*/ ka·to·*lee*·kin Catholic
Kätzchen ⓝ *kets*·khen kitten
Katze ① *ka*·tse cat
kaufen *kow*·fen buy
Kaugummi ⓝ *kow*·gu·mi chewing gum
Kaviar ⓜ *kah*·vi·ahr caviar
Keilriemen ⓜ *kail*·ree·men fanbelt

keine *kai*·ne none
Keks ⓜ kayks biscuit • cookie
Keller ⓜ *ke*·ler cellar
Kellner(in) ⓜ/① *kel*·ner/*kel*·ne·rin waiter
kennen *ke*·nen know (a person)
Keramik ① ke·*rah*·mik ceramic
Kerze ① *ker*·tse candle
Kessel ⓜ *ke*·sel kettle
Ketchup ⓜ *ket*·chap ketchup
Kette ① *ke*·te chain
Kichererbse ① *ki*·kher·erp·se chickpea
Kiefer ⓜ *kee*·fer jaw
Kilogramm ⓝ *kee*·lo·gram kilogram
Kilometer ⓜ ki·lo·*may*·ter kilometre
Kind ⓝ kint child
Kinder ⓝ pl *kin*·der children
Kinderbetreuung ①
kin·der·be·troy·ung childminding
Kindergarten ⓜ *kin*·der·gar·ten kindergarten
Kinderkrippe ① *kin*·der·kri·pe creche
Kindersitz ⓜ *kin*·der·zits child seat
Kino ⓝ *kee*·no cinema
Kiosk ⓜ *kee*·osk convenience store
Kirche ① *kir*·khe church
Kissen ⓝ *ki*·sen pillow
Kissenbezug ⓜ *ki*·sen·be·tsook pillowcase
Kiwifrucht ① *kee*·vi·frukht kiwifruit
Klasse ① *kla*·se class
klassisch *kla*·sish classical
Klavier ⓝ kla·*veer* piano
Kleid ⓝ klait dress
Kleidung ① *klai*·dung clothing
klein klain little • small • short (height)
Kleingeld ⓝ *klain*·gelt loose change
klettern *kle*·tern climb
Klettern ⓝ *kle*·tern rock climbing
Klima ⓝ *klee*·ma climate
Klimaanlage ① *klee*·ma·an·lah·ge air-conditioning
klingeln *kling*·eln ring (of phone)
Klippe ① *kli*·pe cliff

K

Kloster ⓝ *klaws*·ter convent • monastery
Knappheit ⓕ *knap*·hait shortage
Kneipe ⓕ *knai*·pe pub
Knie ⓝ knee knee
Knoblauch ⓜ *knawp*·lowkh garlic
Knöchel ⓜ *kner*·khel ankle
Knochen ⓜ *kno*·khen bone
Knopf ⓜ knopf button
Knoten ⓜ *knaw*·ten lump (health)
Koch ⓜ kokh chef • cook
kochen *ko*·khen cook
Kocher ⓜ *ko*·kher camping stove
Köchin ⓕ *ker*·khin chef • cook
Köder ⓜ *ker*·der bait
Koffer ⓜ *ko*·fer suitcase
Kofferraum ⓜ *ko*·fer·rowm boot • trunk
Kohl ⓜ kawl cabbage
Kokain ⓝ ko·ka·*een* cocaine
Kollege ⓜ ko·*lay*·ge colleague
Kollegin ⓕ ko·*lay*·gin colleague
kommen *ko*·men come
Kommunion ⓕ ko·mun·*yawn* communion
Komödie ⓕ ko·*mer*·di·e comedy
Kompass ⓜ *kom*·pas compass
Konditorei ⓕ kon·dee·to·*rai* cake shop
Kondom ⓝ kon·*dawm* condom
König ⓜ *ker*·nikh king
Königin ⓕ *ker*·ni·gin queen
können *ker*·nen be able to • have permission to
konservativ kon·zer·va·*teef* conservative
Konsulat ⓝ kon·zu·*laht* consulate
Kontaktlinsen ⓕ pl kon·*takt*·lin·zen contact lenses
Kontostand ⓜ *kon*·to·shtant balance (account)
Kontrollstelle ⓕ kon·*trol*·shte·le checkpoint
Konzert ⓝ kon·*tsert* concert
Konzerthalle ⓕ kon·*tsert*·ha·le concert hall

Kopf ⓜ kopf head
Kopfsalat ⓜ *kopf*·za·laht lettuce
Kopfschmerzen pl *kopf*·shmer·tsen headache
Kopfschmerztablette ⓕ *kopf*·shmerts·ta·ble·te aspirin
Korb ⓜ korp basket
Körper ⓜ *ker*·per body
korrupt ko·*rupt* corrupt
koscher *kaw*·sher kosher
kosten *kos*·ten cost
köstlich *kerst*·likh delicious
Kraft ⓕ kraft power
Krampf ⓜ krampf cramp
krank krangk sick
Krankenhaus ⓝ *krang*·ken·hows hospital
Krankenpfleger ⓜ *krang*·ken·pflay·ger nurse
Krankenschwester ⓕ *krang*·ken·shves·ter nurse
Krankenwagen ⓜ *krang*·ken·vah·gen ambulance
Krankheit ⓕ *krangk*·hait disease
Kräuter ⓝ pl *kroy*·ter herbs
Krebs ⓜ krayps cancer
Kreditkarte ⓕ kre·*deet*·kar·te credit card
Kreisverkehr ⓜ *krais*·fer·kair roundabout
Kreuz ⓝ kroyts cross (religious)
Krieg ⓜ kreek war
Kritik ⓕ kri·*teek* review (arts)
Küche ⓕ *kü*·khe kitchen
Kuchen ⓜ *koo*·khen cake
Kuckucksuhr ⓕ *ku*·kuks·oor cuckoo clock
Kugelschreiber ⓜ *koo*·gel·shrai·ber pen (ballpoint)
Kuh ⓕ koo cow
Kühler ⓜ *kü*·ler radiator
Kühlschrank ⓜ *kül*·shrangk refrigerator
sich kümmern um zikh *kü*·mern um look after
Kunde ⓜ *kun*·de client

kündigen *kün*·di·gen resign
Kundin ① *kun*·din client
Kunst ① kunst art
Kunstgalerie ① *kunst*·ga·le·ree art gallery
Kunstgewerbe ⑩ *kunst*·ge·ver·be arts & crafts
Kunsthandwerk ⑩ *kunst* hant·verk handicrafts
Künstler(in) ⑩/① *künst*·ler/ *künst*·le·rin artist
Kunstsammlung ① *kunst*·zam·lung art collection
Kunstwerk ⑩ *kunst*·verk work of art
Kupplung ① *kup*·lung clutch (car)
Kürbis ⑩ *kür*·bis pumpkin
hurn hurts short
kurzärmelig *kurts*·er·me·likh short sleeved
Kuss ⑩ kus kiss
küssen *kü*·sen kiss
Küste ① *küs*·te coast

L

lächeln *le*·kheln smile
lachen *la*·khen laugh
Lachs ⑩ laks salmon
Lage ① *lah*·ge situation
Lager ⑩ *lah* ger lager
Lamm ⑩ lam lamb
Land ⑩ lant country • countryside
Landschaft ① *lant*·shaft scenery
Landwirtschaft ① *lant*·virt·shaft agriculture
lang lang long
langärmelig *lang*·er·me·likh long-sleeved
langsam *lang*·zahm slow • slowly
langweilig *lang*·vai·likh boring
Laptop ⑩ *lep*·top laptop
Lastwagen ⑩ *last*·vah·gen truck
Lauch ⑩ lowkh leek
laufen *low*·fen run
Läuse ① pl *loy*·ze lice
laut lowt loud • noisy

Lautstärke ① *lowt*·shter·ke volume (loudness)
Lawine ① la·*vee*·ne avalanche
leben *lay*·ben to live
Leben ⑩ *lay*·ben life
Lebenslauf ⑩ *lay*·bens·lowf CV • resume
Lebensmittelhändler ⑩ *lay*·bens·mi·tel·hen·dler greengrocer
Lebensmittelladen ⑩ *lay*·bens·mi·tel·lah·den grocery store
Lebensmittelvergiftung ① *lay* bens·mi·tel·fer·*gif*·tung food poisoning
Leber ① *lay*·ber liver
Leder ⑩ *lay*·der leather
ledig *lay*·dikh single (of person)
leer lair empty
legen *lay* gen put (horizontal)
Lehrer(in) ⑩/① *lair*·rer/*lair*·re·rin teacher • instructor
leicht laikht easy
Leichtathletik ① *laikht*·at·lay·tik athletics
leihen *lai*·en borrow
Leinen ⑩ *lai*·nen linen (fabric)
Leitungswasser ⑩ *lai*·tungks·va·ser tap water
Lenker ⑩ *leng*·ker handlebar
lernen *ler*·nen learn
Lesbierin ① *les*·bi·e·rin lesbian
lesen *lay*·zen read
letzte *lets*·te last
Licht ⑩ likht light
lieben *lee*·ben love
liebevoll *lee*·be·fol caring
Liebhaber(in) ⑩/① *leep*·hah·ber/ *leep*·hah·be·rin lover
Lied ⑩ leet song
liefern *lee*·fern deliver
Lieferwagen ⑩ *lee*·fer·vah·gen van
liegen *lee*·gen lie (not stand)
Lift ⑩ lift lift • elevator
lila *lee*·la purple
Limonade ① li·mo·*nah*·de lemonade
Limone ① li·*maw*·ne lime

M

Linie ① *lee*·ni·e line
links lingks left (direction)
linksgerichtet lingks·ge·rikh·tet left-wing
Linse ① *lin*·ze lentil
Lippen ① pl *li*·pen lips
Lippenbalsam ⑩ *li*·pen·bal·zahm lip balm
Lippenstift ⑩ *li*·pen·shtift lipstick
Liter ⑩ *lee*·ter litre
Löffel ⑩ *ler*·fel spoon
Lohn ⑩ lawn wage
Lohnsatz ⑩ *lawn*·zats rate of pay
Lokal ⑩ lo·*kahl* bar
Luft ① luft air
Luftkrankheit ① *luft*·krangk·hait airsickness
Luftpost ① *luft*·post airmail
Luftpumpe ① *luft*·pum·pe pump
Luftverschmutzung ① *luft*·fer·shmu·tsung air pollution
Lügner(in) ⑩/① *lüg*·ner/*lüg*·ne·rin liar
Lungen ① pl *lung*·en lungs
lustig *lus*·tikh funny
luxuriös luk·su·ri·*ers* luxury

M

machen *ma*·khen make
Mädchen ⑩ *mayt*·khen girl
Magen ⑩ *mah*·gen stomach
Magen-Darm-Katarrh ⑩ *mah*·gen·*darm*·ka·*tar* gastroenteritis
Magenschmerzen ⑩ pl *mah*·gen·shmer·tsen stomach ache
Magenverstimmung ① *mah*·gen·fer·shti·mung indigestion
Majonnaise ① ma·yo·*nay*·ze mayonnaise
Makler(in) ⑩/① *mahk*·ler/*mahk*·le·rin real estate agent
Maler(in) ⑩/① *mah*·ler/*mah*·le·rin painter
Malerei ① mah·le·*rai* painting (the art)
Mama ① *ma*·ma mum • mom

Mammogramm ⑩ ma·mo·*gram* mammogram
manchmal *mankh*·mahl sometimes
Mandarine ① man·da·*ree*·ne mandarin
Mandel ① *man*·del almond
Mann ⑩ man man
Mannschaft ① *man*·shaft team
Mantel ⑩ *man*·tel overcoat • cloak
Margarine ① mar·ga·*ree*·ne margarine
Marihuana ① ma·ri·hu·*ah*·na marijuana
Markt ⑩ markt market
Marktplatz ⑩ *markt*·plats market square
Marmelade ① mar·me·*lah*·de jam
Maschine ① ma·*shee*·ne machine
Masern pl *mah*·zern measles
Massage ① ma·*sah*·zhe massage
Masseur(in) ⑩/① ma·*ser*(·rin) masseur/masseuse
Material ⑩ ma·te·ri·*ahl* material
Matratze ① ma·*tra*·tse mattress
Matte ① *ma*·te mat
Mauer ① *mow*·er wall (outer)
Maurer(in) ⑩/① *mow*·rer/*mow*·re·rin bricklayer
Maus ① mows mouse
Mechaniker(in) ⑩/① me·*khah*·ni·ker/me·*khah*·ni·ke·rin mechanic
Medien pl *may*·di·en media
Meditation ① me·di·ta·*tsyawn* meditation
Medizin ① me·di·*tseen* medicine
Meer ⑩ mair sea
Meeresküste ① *mair*·res·küs·te seaside
Meerrettich ⑩ *mair*·re·tikh horseradish
Mehl ⑩ mayl flour
mehr mair more
nicht mehr nikht mair not any more
mein main mine • my
Meinung ① *mai*·nung opinion

Meisterschaften ① pl
mais·ter·shaf·ten championships
Melodie ① me lo *dee* tune
Melone ① me·*law*·ne melon
Mensch ⓜ mensh person
Menschen ⓜ pl *men*·shen people
Menschenrechte ⓝ pl
men·shen·rekh·te human rights
menschlich *mensh*·likh human
Menstruation ① mens·tru·a·*tsyawn*
menstruation
Menstruationsbeschwerden ① pl
mens·tru·a·*tsyawns*·be·shver·den
period pain
Messe ① *me*·se mass (Catholic) •
trade fair
Messer ⓝ *me*·ser knife
Metall ⓝ me·*tal* metal
Meter ⓜ *may*·ter metre
Metzgerei ① mets·ge·*rai* butcher shop
mieten *mee*·ten rent • hire
Mietvertrag ⓜ *meet*·fer·trahk lease
Migräne ① mi·*gray*·ne migraine
Mikrowelle ① *mee*·kro·ve·le
microwave
Milch ① milkh milk
Milchprodukte ⓝ pl
milkh·pro·duk·te dairy products
Militär ⓐ mi·li·*tair* military
Millimeter ⓜ mi·li·*may*·ter
millimetre
Million ① mi·*lyawn* million
Mineralwasser ⓝ mi·ne·*rahl*·va·ser
mineral water
Minute ① mi·*noo*·te minute
mischen *mi*·shen mix
mit mit with
Mitglied ⓝ *mit*·gleet member
Mittag ⓜ *mi*·tahk noon
Mittagessen ⓝ *mi*·tahk·e·sen lunch
Mitteilung ① *mi*·tai·lung message
Mitternacht ① *mi*·ter·nakht
midnight
Mittwoch ⓜ *mit*·vokh Wednesday
Möbel ⓝ pl *mer*·bel furniture
Modem ⓜ *maw*·dem modem

mögen *mer*·gen to like
möglich *merk*·likh possible
Mohrrübe ① *mawr*·rü·be carrot
Monat ⓜ *maw*·nat month
Montag ⓜ *mawn*·tahk Monday
Morgen ⓜ *mor*·gen morning (6am–
10am)
morgen *mor*·gen tomorrow
morgen früh *mor* gen frü tomorrow
morning
Moschee ① mo·*shay* mosque
Moskitospirale ①
mos·*kee*·to·shpi·rah le mosquito coil
Moslem ⓜ *mos*·lem Muslim
Moslime ① mos *lee*·me Muslim
Motor ⓜ *maw*·tor/mo·*tawr* engine
Motorboot ⓝ *maw*·tor·bawt
motor boat
Motorrad ⓝ *maw*·tor·raht motorcycle
Möwe ① *mer*·ve seagull
müde *mü*·de tired
Müll ⓜ mül rubbish
Mülleimer ⓜ *mül*·ai·mer rubbish bin
Mund ⓜ munt mouth
Mundfäule ① *munt* foy le thrush
(medical condition)
Münzen ① pl *mün*·tsen coins
Muschel ① *mu*·shel mussel
Museum ⓝ mu·*zay*·um museum
Musik ① mu·*zeek* music
Musiker(in) ⓜ/① *moo*·zi·ker/
moo·zi·ke·rin musician
Muskel ⓜ *mus*·kel muscle
Muskelzerrung ① *mus*·kel·tser·rung
sprain
Müsli ⓝ *müs* li muesli
mutig *moo*·tikh brave
Mutter ① *mu*·ter mother

N

nach nahkh after • towards
Nachkomme ⓜ *nahkh*·ko·me
descendant
Nachmittag ⓜ *nahkh*·mi·tahk
afternoon
Nachname ⓜ *nahkh*·nah·me surname

O

Nachrichten pl *nahkh·rikh·ten* news
nächste *naykhs·*te next • nearest
Nacht ① *nakht* night
Nadel ① *nah·*del sewing needle • syringe
Nagelknipser ⓜ pl *nah·*gel·knip·ser nail clippers
nahe *nah·*e close (nearby)
in der Nähe in dair *nay·*e nearby
nähen *nay·*en sew
Name ⓜ *nah·*me name
Nase ① *nah·*ze nose
nass nas wet
Natur ① na·*toor* nature
Naturheilkunde ①
na·*toor·*hail·kun·de naturopathy
Naturreservat ⓝ na·*toor·*re·zer·vaht nature reserve
neben *nay·*ben next to
neblig *nay·*blikh foggy
Neffe ⓜ *ne·*fe nephew
nehmen *nay·*men take
nein nain no
nett net nice • kind
Netz ⓝ nets net
neu noy new
Neujahrstag ⓜ *noy·*yahrs·tahk New Year's Day
Neuseeland ⓝ *noy·zay·*lant New Zealand
nicht nikht not
Nichte ① *nikh·*te niece
Nichtraucher- *nikht·*row·kher non-smoking
nichts nikhts nothing
nie nee never
Niederlande pl *nee·*der·lan·de Netherlands
niedrig *nee·*drikh low
noch nicht nokh nikht not yet
Nonne ① *no·*ne nun
Norden ⓜ *nor·*den north
normal nor·*mahl* ordinary
normale Post ① nor·*mah·*le *post* surface mail
Notfall ⓜ *nawt·*fal emergency

Notizbuch ⓝ no·*teets·*bookh notebook
notwendig *nawt·*ven·dikh necessary
Nudeln pl *noo·*deln noodles • pasta
null nul zero
Nummer ① *nu·*mer number
nur noor only
Nuss ① nus nut
nützlich *nüts·*likh useful

O

obdachlos op·dakh·laws homeless
oben *aw·*ben upstairs
Objektiv ⓝ op·yek·*teef* lens (camera)
Obsternte ① *awpst·*ern·te fruit picking
oder *aw·*der or
Ofen ⓜ *aw·*fen oven
offen *o·*fen open
offensichtlich o·fen·*zikht·*likh obvious
öffentlich *er·*fent·likh public
öffnen *erf·*nen open
Öffnungszeiten ① pl *erf·*nungks·tsai·ten opening hours
oft oft often
ohne *aw·*ne without
Ohr ⓝ awr ear
Ohrenstöpsel ⓜ *aw·*ren·shterp·sel earplugs
Ohrringe ⓜ pl *awr·*ring·e earrings
Öl ⓝ erl oil
Olive ① o·*lee·*ve olive
Olivenöl ⓝ o·*lee·*ven·erl olive oil
Olympische Spiele ⓝ pl o·*lüm·*pi·she *shpee·*le Olympic Games
Oma ① *aw·*ma grandmother
Onkel ⓜ *ong·*kel uncle
Opa ⓜ *aw·*pa grandfather
Oper ① *aw·*per opera
Operation ① o·pe·ra·*tsyawn* operation
Opernhaus ⓝ *aw·*pern·hows opera house
Optiker(in) ⓜ/① *op·*ti·ker/ *op·*ti·ke·rin optician
orange o·*rahngzh* orange (colour)
Orange ① o·*rahng·*zhe orange

Orangenmarmelade ①
o·*rahng*·zhen·mar·me·lah·de
marmalade

Orangensaft ⑩ o·*rahng*·zhen·zaft
orange juice

Orchester ⑪ or·*kes*·ter orchestra

organisieren or·ga·ni·*zee*·ren
organise

Orgasmus ⑩ or·*gas*·mus orgasm

Orgel ① *or*·gel organ (church)

Original- o·ri·gi·*nahl*· original (not
copied)

örtlich *ert*·likh local

Osten ⑩ *os*·ten east

der Nahe Osten ⑩ dair *nah*·e os·ten
Middle East

Ostern ⑪ *aws*·tern Easter

Österreich ⑪ ers·ter·*rikh* Austria

Ozean ⑩ *aw*·tse·ahn ocean

Ozonschicht ① o·*tsawn*·shikht
ozone layer

P

Paar ⑪ pahr pair (couple)

ein paar ain pahr a few

Packung ① *pa*·kung packet

Paket ⑪ pa·*kayt* package • parcel

Pampelmuse ① pam·pel·*moo*·ze
grapefruit

eine Panne haben ai·ne *pa*·ne
hah·ben break down

Papa ⑩ *pa*·pa dad

Papagei ⑩ pa·pa·*gai* parrot

Papier ⑪ pa·*peer* paper

Papiertaschentücher ⑪ pl
pa·*peer* ta·shen·tü·kher tissues

Paprika ① *pap*·ri·kah paprika •
capsicum • bell pepper

Parfüm ⑪ par·*füm* perfume

Park ⑩ park park

Parkplatz ⑩ *park*·plats car park

Parlament ⑪ par·la·*ment* parliament

Partei ① par·*tai* party (politics)

Pass ⑩ pas pass • passport

Passnummer ① *pas*·nu·mer
passport number

Pause ① *pow*·ze intermission

eine Pause machen ai·ne *pow*·ze
ma·khen rest

Pedal ⑪ pe·*dahl* pedal

Penis ⑩ *pay*·nis penis

Pension ① pahng·*zyawn* boarding
house • bed & breakfast

pensioniert pahng·zyo·*neert* retired

Person ① per·*zawn* person

Personalausweis ⑩
per·zo·*nahl*·ows·vais identification
card

persönlich per·*zern*·likh personal

Petersilie ① pay·ter·*zee*·li·e parsley

Petition ① pe·ti·*tsyawn* petition

Pfad ⑪ pfaht path • trail

Pfanne ① *pfa*·ne pan

Pfeffer ⑩ *pfe*·fer pepper

Pfefferminzbonbons ⑪ pl
pfe·fer *mints*·bong·bongs mints

Pfeife ① *pfai*·fe pipe

Pferd ⑪ pfert horse

Pfirsich ⑩ *pfir*·zikh peach

Pflanze ① *pflan*·tse plant

Pflaster ⑪ *pflas*·ter Band-aids

Pflaume ① *pflow*·me plum

pflücken *pflü*·ken pick (flowers)

Pfund ⑪ pfunt pound (weight)

Phantasie ① fan·ta·*zee* imagination

Physik ① fü·*zeek* physics

Picknick ⑪ *pik*·nik picnic

Pilgerfahrt ① *pil*·ger·fahrt
pilgrimage

Pille ① *pi*·le pill

die Pille ① dee *pi*·le the Pill

Pilz ⑩ pilts mushroom

Pinzette ① pin·*tse*·te tweezers

PKW-Zulassung ①
pay·kah·vay·*tsoo*·la·sung car
registration

Plakat ⑪ pla·*kaht* poster

Planet ⑩ pla·*nayt* planet

Plastik ① *plas*·tik plastic

Platz ⑩ plats place • seat (train,
cinema) • square (town) • court
(tennis)

Platz ⓜ **am Gang** plats am gang aisle seat
Poker ⓝ *paw*·ker poker (game)
Politik ⓕ po·li·*teek* politics • policy
Politiker(in) ⓜ/ⓕ po·*lee*·ti·ker/po·*lee*·ti·ke·rin politician
Polizei ⓕ po·li·*tsai* police
Polizeirevier ⓝ po·li·*tsai*·re·veer police station
Pollen ⓜ *po*·len pollen
Pony ⓝ *po*·ni pony
Porto ⓝ *por*·to postage
Post ⓕ post mail
Postamt ⓝ *post*·amt post office
Postkarte ⓕ *post*·kar·te postcard
postlagernd *post*·lah·gernt poste restante
Postleitzahl ⓕ *post*·lai·tsahl postcode
praktisch *prak*·tish practical
prämenstruelle Störung ⓕ *pray*·mens·tru·e·le *shter*·rung premenstrual tension
Präsident(in) ⓜ/ⓕ pre·zi·*dent*/pre·zi·*den*·tin president
Preis ⓜ prais price
Premierminister(in) ⓜ/ⓕ prem·*yay*·mi·nis·ter/prem·*yay*·mi·nis·te·rin prime minister
Priester ⓜ *prees*·ter priest
privat pri·*vaht* private
Privatklinik ⓕ pri·*vaht*·klee·nik private hospital
pro praw per
produzieren pro·du·*tsee*·ren produce
Programm ⓝ pro·*gram* program
Projektor ⓜ pro·*yek*·tor projector
Prosa ⓕ *praw*·za fiction
Prostituierte ⓕ pros·ti·tu·*eer*·te prostitute
Protest ⓜ pro·*test* protest
protestieren pro·tes·*tee*·ren protest
Prozent ⓝ pro·*tsent* percent
prüfen *prü*·fen check

Psychologie ⓕ psü·kho·lo·*gee* psychology
Pullover ⓜ pu·*law*·ver jumper • sweater
Pumpe ⓕ *pum*·pe pump
Punkt ⓜ pungkt point
Puppe ⓕ *pu*·pe doll

Q

Qualifikationen ⓕ pl kva·li·fi·ka·*tsyaw*·nen qualifications
Qualität ⓕ kva·li·*tayt* quality
Quarantäne ⓕ ka·ran·*tay*·ne quarantine
Querschnittsgelähmte ⓜ&ⓕ *kvair*·shnits·ge·laym·te paraplegic
Quittung ⓕ *kvi*·tung receipt

R

Rabatt ⓜ ra·*bat* discount
Rad ⓝ raht wheel
radfahren *raht*·fah·ren cycle
Radfahrer(in) ⓜ/ⓕ *raht*·fah·rer/*raht*·fah·re·rin cyclist
Radio ⓝ *rah*·di·o radio
Radsport ⓜ *raht*·shport cycling
Radweg ⓜ *raht*·vayk bike path
Rahmen ⓜ *rah*·men frame
Rallye ⓕ *re*·li rally
Rasiercreme ⓕ ra·*zeer*·kraym shaving cream
rasieren ra·*zee*·ren shave
Rasierer ⓜ ra·*zee*·rer razor
Rasierklingen ⓕ pl ra·*zeer*·kling·en razor blades
Rassismus ⓜ ra·*sis*·mus racism
Rat ⓜ raht advice
raten *rah*·ten advise • guess
Ratte ⓕ *ra*·te rat
Raub ⓜ rowp robbery
rauchen *row*·khen smoke
Raum ⓜ rowm space
realistisch re·a·*lis*·tish realistic
Rebe ⓕ *ray*·be vine
Rechnung ⓕ *rekh*·nung bill • check

rechts rekhts right (direction)
rechtsgerichtet rekhts·ge·rikh·tet right-wing
Rechtsanwalt ⓜ rekhts·an·valt lawyer
Rechtsanwältin ⓕ rekhts·an·vel·tin lawyer
recyceln ri·sai·keln recycle
Regal ⓝ re·gahl shelf
Regeln ⓟⓛ ray·geln rules
Regen ⓜ ray·gen rain
Regenmantel ⓜ ray·gen·man·tel raincoat
Regenschirm ⓜ ray·gen·shirm umbrella
Regierung ⓕ re·gee·rung government
Region ⓕ re·gyawn region
Regisseur(in) ⓜ/ⓕ re·zhi·ser/re·zhi·ser·rin director
reich raikh wealthy
Reifen ⓜ rai·fen tyre
Reifenpanne ⓕ rai·fen·pa·ne puncture
rein rain pure
Reinigung ⓕ rai·ni·gung cleaning
Reis ⓜ rais rice
Reise ⓕ rai·ze journey • trip
Reisebüro ⓝ rai·ze·bü·raw travel agency
Reiseführer ⓜ rai·ze·fü·rer guidebook
Reisekrankheit ⓕ rai·ze·krangk·hait travel sickness
reisen rai·zen travel
Reisende(r) ⓜ/ⓕ rai·zen·de passenger (train)
Reisepass ⓜ rai·ze·pas passport
Reiseroute ⓕ rai·ze·roo·te itinerary
Reisescheck ⓜ rai·ze·shek travellers cheque
Reiseziel ⓝ rai·ze·tseel destination
Reißverschluss ⓜ rais·fer·shlus zipper
Reiten ⓝ rai·ten horse riding
reiten rai·ten ride (horse)

Reitweg ⓜ rait·vayk bridle path
Religion ⓕ re·li·gyawn religion
religiös re·li·gyers religious
Reliquie ⓕ re·lee·kvi·e relic (religious)
Rennbahn ⓕ ren·bahn racetrack
rennen re·nen run
Rennen ⓝ re·nen race (sport)
Rennrad ⓝ ren·raht racing bike
Rentner(in) ⓜ/ⓕ rent·ner/rent·ne·rin pensioner
reparieren re·pa·ree·ren repair
Republik ⓕ re·pu·bleek republic
Reservereifen ⓜ re·zer·ve·rai·fen spare tyre
reservieren re·zer·vee·ren reserve
Reservierung ⓕ re·zer·vee·rung reservation
Restaurant ⓝ res·to·rahng restaurant
retten re·ten save (someone)
Rettich ⓜ re·tikh radish
R-Gespräch ⓝ air·ge·shpraykh collect call • reverse charge call
Rhythmus ⓜ rüt·mus rhythm
Richter(in) ⓜ/ⓕ rikh·ter/rikh·te·rin judge
richtig rikh·tikh right (correct)
riesig ree·zikh huge
Rindfleisch ⓝ rint·flaish beef
Ring ⓜ ring ring (on finger)
Risiko ⓝ ree·zi·ko risk
Ritt ⓜ rit ride
Rock ⓜ rok skirt
Rockgruppe ⓕ rok·gru·pe rock group
Rockmusik ⓕ rok·mu·zeek rock (music)
Rodeln ⓝ raw·deln tobogganing
Roggenbrot ⓝ ro·gen·brawt rye bread
roh raw raw
Rollschuhfahren ⓝ rol·shoo·fah·ren in-line skating
Rollstuhl ⓜ rol·shtool wheelchair
Rolltreppe ⓕ rol·tre·pe escalator

S

romantisch ro·*man*·tish romantic
rosa *raw*·za pink
Rosenkohl ⓜ *raw*·zen·kawl Brussels sprouts
Rosine ⓕ ro·*zee*·ne raisin
rot rawt red
Rotwein ⓜ *rawt*·vain red wine
Route ⓕ *roo*·te route
Rubel ⓜ *roo*·bel rouble
Rücken ⓜ *rü*·ken back (body)
Rückfahrkarte ⓕ *rük*·fahr·kar·te return (ticket)
Rucksack ⓜ *ruk*·zak backpack • knapsack
Rückzahlung ⓕ *rük*·tsah·lung refund
Rudern ⓝ *roo*·dern rowing
Rugby ⓝ *rag*·bi rugby
ruhig *roo*·ikh quiet
Ruinen ⓕ pl ru·*ee*·nen ruins
Rum ⓜ rum rum
rund runt round

S

Sabbat ⓜ *za*·bat Sabbath
Safe ⓜ sayf safe
Safe Sex ⓜ sayf seks safe sex
Saft ⓜ zaft juice
sagen *zah*·gen say
Sahne ⓕ *zah*·ne cream
Salami ⓕ za·*lah*·mi salami
Salat ⓜ za·*laht* salad
Salz ⓝ zalts salt
Samstag ⓜ *zams*·tahk Saturday
Sand ⓜ zant sand
Sandalen ⓕ pl zan·*dah*·len sandals
Sänger(in) ⓜ/ⓕ *zeng*·er/*zeng*·e·rin singer
Sardine ⓕ zar·*dee*·ne sardine
Sattel ⓜ *za*·tel saddle
sauber *zow*·ber clean
Sauce ⓕ *zaw*·se sauce
Sauerstoff ⓜ *zow*·er·shtof oxygen
Sauerteigbrot ⓝ *zow*·er·taik·brawt sourdough bread
Sauna ⓕ *zow*·na sauna
Schach ⓝ shakh chess

Schaf ⓝ shahf sheep
Schaffner(in) ⓜ/ⓕ *shaf*·ner/*shaf*·ne·rin conductor
Schal ⓜ shahl scarf
Schatten ⓜ *sha*·ten shade • shadow
einen Schaufensterbummel machen *ai*·nen *show*·fens·ter·bu·mel *ma*·khen go window-shopping
Schaumwein ⓜ *showm*·vain sparkling wine
Schauspiel ⓝ *show*·shpeel play (theatre) • drama
Schauspieler(in) ⓜ/ⓕ *show*·shpee·ler/*show*·shpee·le·rin actor
Scheck ⓜ shek cheque (bank)
einen Scheck einlösen *ai*·nen shek *ain*·ler·zen cash a cheque
Scheckkarte ⓕ *shek*·kar·te cheque card
Scheinwerfer ⓜ pl *shain*·ver·fer headlights
Schere ⓕ *shair*·re scissors
schieben *shee*·ben push
Schiedsrichter(in) ⓜ/ⓕ *sheets*·rikh·ter/*sheets*·rikh·te·rin referee
schießen *shee*·sen shoot (gun)
Schiff ⓝ shif ship
Schild ⓝ shilt sign
Schinken ⓜ *shing*·ken ham
schlafen *shlah*·fen sleep
schläfrig *shlayf*·rikh sleepy
Schlafsack ⓜ *shlahf*·zak sleeping bag
Schlaftabletten ⓕ pl *shlahf*·ta·ble·ten sleeping pills
Schlafwagen ⓜ *shlahf*·vah·gen sleeping car
Schlafzimmer ⓝ *shlahf*·tsi·mer bedroom
Schläger ⓜ *shlay*·ger racquet
Schlamm ⓜ shlam mud
Schlange ⓕ *shlang*·e queue • snake
Schlauch ⓜ shlowkh tube (tyre)
schlecht shlekht bad • off (of food)

schlechter *shlekh·*ter worse

schließen *shlee·*sen close (shut)

Schließfächer ⓝ pl *shlees·*fe·kher luggage lockers

Schloss ⓝ shlos lock • palace

Schlucht ⓕ shlukht gorge

Schlüssel ⓜ *shlü·*sel key

schmackhaft *shmak·*haft tasty

Schmalz ⓜ shmalts lard

Schmand ⓜ shmant sour cream

Schmerz ⓜ shmerts pain

schmerzhaft *shmerts·*haft sore • painful

Schmerzmittel ⓝ *shmerts·*mi·tel painkillers

Schmetterling ⓜ *shme·*ter·ling butterfly

Schmiermittel ⓝ *shmeer·*mi·tel lubricant

Schminke ⓕ *shming·*ke make-up

Schmuck ⓜ shmuk jewellery

schmutzig *shmu·*tsikh dirty

Schnecke ⓕ *shne·*ke snail

Schnee ⓜ shnay snow

Schneefeld ⓝ *shnay·*felt snowfield

schneiden *shnai·*den cut

Schneider/in ⓜ/ⓕ *shnai·*der/ *shnai·*de·rin tailor

schnell shnel quick

Schnorcheln ⓝ *shnor·*kheln snorkelling

Schnuller ⓜ *shnu·*ler dummy • pacifier

Schnur ⓕ shnoor string

Schokolade ⓕ sho·ko·*lah·*de chocolate

schon shawn yet • already

schön shern beautiful

Schönheitssalon ⓜ *shern·*haits·za·long beauty salon

Schottland ⓝ *shot·*lant Scotland

Schramme ⓕ *shra·*me bruise

Schrank ⓜ shrangk cupboard

Schraubenzieher ⓜ *shrow·*ben·tsee·er screwdriver

schrecklich *shrek·*likh terrible

Schreibarbeit ⓕ *shraip·*ar·bait paperwork

schreiben *shrai·*ben write

Schreibwarenhandlung ⓕ *shraip·*vah·ren·han·dlung stationer

schreien *shrai·*en shout

Schrein ⓜ shrain shrine

Schreiner(in) ⓜ/ⓕ *shrai·*ner/ *shrai·*ne·rin carpenter

Schriftsteller(in) ⓜ/ⓕ *shrift·*shte·ler/*shrift·*shte·le·rin writer

schüchtern *shükh·*tern shy

Schuhe ⓜ pl *shoo·*e shoes

Schuld ⓕ shult (someone's) fault

schulden *shul·*den owe

schuldig *shul·*dikh guilty

Schule ⓕ *shoo·*le school

Schulter ⓕ *shul·*ter shoulder

Schüssel ⓕ *shü·*sel bowl

Schutzimpfung ⓕ *shuts·*im·pfung vaccination

schwach shvakh weak

schwanger *shvang·*er pregnant

Schwangerschaftserbrechen ⓝ *shvang·*er·shafts·er·bre·khen morning sickness

Schwangerschaftstest ⓜ *shvang·*er·shafts·test pregnancy test kit

Schwanz ⓜ shvants tail

schwarz shvarts black

schwarzer Pfeffer ⓜ *shvar·*tser *pfe·*fer black pepper

schwarzweiß shvarts-*vais* B&W (film)

Schwein ⓝ shvain pig

Schweinefleisch ⓝ *shvai·*ne·flaish pork

Schweiz ⓕ shvaits Switzerland

schwer shvair difficult (task) • heavy

Schwester ⓕ *shves·*ter sister

Schwiegermutter ⓕ *shvee·*ger·mu·ter mother-in-law

Schwiegersohn ⓜ *shvee·*ger·zawn son-in-law

Schwiegertochter ⓕ *shvee·*ger·tokh·ter daughter-in-law

S

Schwiegervater ⓜ *shvee·ger·fah·ter* father-in-law

schwierig *shvee·rikh* difficult

Schwimmbad ⓝ *shvim·baht* swimming pool

schwimmen *shvi·men* swim

Schwimmweste ⓕ *shvim·ves·te* lifejacket

schwindelig *shvin·de·likh* dizzy

schwul *shvool* gay

schwül *shvül* muggy

Secondhandgeschäft ⓝ *se·kend·hend·ge·sheft* secondhand shop

See ⓜ *zay* lake

seekrank *zay·krangk* seasick

Segeln ⓝ *zay·geln* sailing

segnen *zayg·nen* bless

sehen *zay·en* see • look

sehr *zair* very

Seide ⓕ *zai·de* silk

Seife ⓕ *zai·fe* soap

Seifenoper ⓕ *zai·fen·aw·per* soap opera

Seil ⓝ *zail* rope

Seilbahn ⓕ *zail·bahn* cable car

sein *zain* his

sein *zain* be

seit (Mai) *zait (mai)* since (May)

Seite ⓕ *zai·te* side • page

Sekretär(in) ⓜ/ⓕ *ze·kre·tair/ ze·kre·tair·rin* secretary

Sekundarschule ⓕ *ze·kun·dahr·shoo·le* high school

Sekunde ⓕ *ze·kun·de* second

Selbstbedienung ⓕ *zelpst·be·dee·nung* self-service

selbstständig *zelpst·shten·dikh* self-employed

selten *zel·ten* rare

senden *zen·den* send

Senf ⓜ *zenf* mustard

Serie ⓕ *zair·ri·e* series

Serviette ⓕ *zer·vye·te* napkin

Sessellift ⓜ *ze·se·lift* chairlift (skiing)

Sex ⓜ *seks* sex

Sexismus ⓜ *sek·sis·mus* sexism

sexy *sek·si* sexy

Shampoo ⓝ *sham·poo* shampoo

Shorts pl *shorts* shorts • boxer shorts

Show ⓕ *shoh* show

sicher *zi·kher* safe

Sicherheit ⓕ *zi·kher·hait* safety

Sicherheitsgurt ⓜ *zi·kher·haits·gurt* seatbelt

Sicherung ⓕ *zi·khe·rung* fuse

sie *zee* she • they

Sie *zee* you sg&pl pol

Sieger(in) ⓜ/ⓕ *zee·ger/zee·ge·rin* winner

silbern *zil·bern* silver

Silvester ⓝ *zil·ves·ter* New Year's Eve

Singapur ⓐ *zing·a·poor* Singapore

singen *zing·en* sing

Single ⓜ *singl* single (of person)

sinnlich *zin·likh* sensual

Sitz ⓜ *zits* seat (car)

sitzen *zi·tsen* sit

Skateboarden ⓝ *skayt·bor·den* skateboarding

Skibrille ⓕ *shee·bri·le* goggles (skiing)

skifahren *shee·fah·ren* ski

Skulptur ⓕ *skulp·toor* sculpture

Slipeinlage ⓕ *slip·ain·lah·ge* panty liner

Snack ⓜ *snek* snack

Snowboarden ⓝ *snoh·bor·den* snowboarding

Socken ⓕ pl *zo·ken* socks

sofort *zo·fort* immediately

Sohn ⓜ *zawn* son

Sojamilch ⓕ *zaw·ya·milkh* soy milk

Sojasauce ⓕ *zaw·ya·zaw·se* soy sauce

Sommer ⓜ *zo·mer* summer

Sonne ⓕ *zo·ne* sun

Sonnenaufgang ⓜ *zo·nen·owf·gang* sunrise

Sonnenbrand ⓜ *zo·nen·brant* sunburn

Sonnenbrille ① zo·nen·bri·le sunglasses

Sonnencreme ① zo·nen·kraym sunblock

Sonnenuntergang ⑩ zo·nen·un·ter·gang sunset

sonnig zo·nikh sunny

Sonntag ⑩ zon·tahk Sunday

Soße ① zaw·se sauce

Souvenir ⑪ zu·ve·neer souvenir

Souvenirladen ⑩ zu·ve·neer·lah·den souvenir shop

Sozialhilfe ① zo·tsyahl·hil·fe welfare

sozialistisch zo·tsya·lis·tish socialist

Sozialstaat ⑩ zo·tsyahl·shtaht welfare state

Spanien ⑪ shpah·ni·en Spain

sparen shpah·ren save (money)

Spargel ⑩ shpar·gel asparagus

Spaß ⑩ shpahs fun

Spaß haben shpahs hah·ben have fun

spät shpayt late

Spaten ⑩ shpah·ten spade

Speichen ① pl shpai·khen spokes

Speisekarte ① shpai·ze·kar·te " menu

Speisewagen ⑩ shpai·ze·vah·gen dining car

Spezialist(in) ⑩/① shpe·tsya·list/ shpe·tsya·lis·tin specialist

speziell shpe·tsyel special

Spiegel ⑩ shpee·gel mirror

Spiel ⑪ shpeel match (sport)

spielen shpee·len play (game) • play (instrument)

Spielzeug ⑪ shpeel·tsoyk toy

Spinat ⑩ shpi·naht spinach

Spinne ① shpi·ne spider

Spitze ① shpi·tse lace

Spitzhacke ① shpits·ha·ke pickaxe

Spitzname ⑩ shpits·nah·me nickname

Sport ⑩ shport sport

Sportler(in) ⑩/① shport·ler/ shport·le·rin sportsperson

Sprache ① shprah·khe language

Sprachführer ⑩ shprahkh·fü·rer phrasebook

sprechen shpre·khen speak

springen shpring·en jump

Spritze ① shpri·tse syringe

Spülung ① shpü·lung conditioner

Staat ⑩ shtaht state

Staatsangehörigkeit ① shtahts·an·ge·her·rikh·kait nationality

Staatsbürgerschaft ① shtahts·bür·ger·shaft citizenship

Stadion ⑪ shtah·di·on stadium

Stadium ⑪ shtah·di·um stage

Stadt ① shtat city • town

Standby-Ticket ⑪ stend·bai·ti·ket stand-by ticket

stark shtark strong

Start ⑩ shtart start (sport)

statt shtat instead of

Statue ① shtah·tu·e statue

Steak ⑪ stayk steak (beef)

Stechmücke ① shtekh·mü·ke mosquito

Stecker ⑩ shte·ker plug (electricity)

stehlen shtay·len steal

Stehplatz ⑩ shtay·plats standing room

steil shtail steep

Stein ⑩ shtain stone

stellen shte·len put (vertical)

sterben shter·ben die

Stereoanlage ①
shtair·re·o·an·lah·ge stereo

Sterne ⑩ pl shter·ne stars

Sternzeichen ⑪ shtern·tsai·khen star sign • zodiac

Steuer ① shtoy·er tax

Stich ⑩ shtikh bite (insect)

Stickerei ① shti·ke·rai embroidery

Stiefel ⑩ shtee·fel boot (footwear)

Stil ⑩ shteel style

stilles Wasser ⑪ shti·les va·ser still water

Stimme ① shti·me voice

Stock ⑩ shtok floor (storey)

stoned stohnd stoned (drugged)

T

stoppen *shto*·pen stop
Stöpsel ⓜ *shterp*·sel plug (bath)
stornieren shtor·*nee*·ren cancel
Strand ⓜ shtrant beach
Straße ⓕ *shtrah*·se street • road
Straßenbahn ⓕ *shtrah*·sen·bahn tram
Straßenkarte ⓕ *shtrah*·sen·kar·te road map
Straßenkinder ⓝ pl *shtrah*·sen·kin·der street kids
Straßenmusiker(in) ⓜ/ⓕ *shtrah*·sen·moo·zi·ker/*shtrah*·sen·moo·zi·ke·rin busker
Streichhölzer ⓝ pl *shtraikh*·herl·tser matches
streiken *shtrai*·ken (to be) on strike
Streit ⓜ shtrait quarrel
streiten *shtrai*·ten argue
Strom ⓜ shtrawm current (electricity)
Stromschnellen ⓕ pl *shtrawm*·shne·len rapids
Strümpfe ⓜ pl *shtrümp*·fe stockings
Strumpfhose ⓕ *shtrumpf*·haw·ze pantyhose
Stück ⓝ shtük piece
Student(in) ⓜ/ⓕ shtu·*dent*/shtu·*den*·tin student
Studentenausweis ⓜ shtu·*den*·ten·ows·vais student card
studieren shtu·*dee*·ren study
Studio ⓝ shtoo·di·o studio
Stufe ⓕ *shtoo*·fe step (stairs)
Stuhl ⓜ shtool chair
stumm shtum mute
stur shtoor stubborn
Sturm ⓜ shturm storm
suchen nach *zoo*·khen nahkh look for
Süchtige ⓜ/ⓕ *zükh*·ti·ge addict
Süden ⓜ *zü*·den south
Supermarkt ⓜ *zoo*·per·markt supermarket
Suppe ⓕ *zu*·pe soup
Surfbrett ⓝ *serf*·bret surfboard

surfen *ser*·fen surf
süß züs sweet/candy
Süßigkeiten ⓕ pl *zü*·sikh·kai·ten lollies
Synagoge ⓕ zü·na·*gaw*·ge synagogue
synthetisch zün·*tay*·tish synthetic

T

Tabak ⓜ *ta*·bak tobacco
Tabakladen ⓜ *ta*·bak·lah·den tobacconist
Tag ⓜ tahk day
Tagebuch ⓝ *tah*·ge·bookh diary (journal)
täglich *tayk*·likh daily
Tal ⓝ tahl valley
Tampons ⓜ pl *tam*·pons tampons
Tankstelle ⓕ *tangk*·shte·le service station
Tante ⓕ *tan*·te aunt
tanzen *tan*·tsen dance
Tasche ⓕ *ta*·she bag • pocket
Taschenbuch ⓝ *ta*·shen·bookh paperback
Taschenlampe ⓕ *ta*·shen·lam·pe torch • flashlight
Taschenmesser ⓝ *ta*·shen·me·ser penknife
Taschenrechner ⓜ *ta*·shen·rekh·ner calculator
Tasse ⓕ *ta*·se cup
Tastatur ⓕ tas·ta·*toor* keyboard
taub towp deaf
Tauchen ⓝ *tow*·khen diving
Taufe ⓕ *tow*·fe baptism • christening
tausend *tow*·zent thousand
Taxi ⓝ *tak*·si taxi
Taxistand ⓜ *tak*·si·shtant taxi stand
Technik ⓕ *tekh*·nik technique
Tee ⓜ tay tea
Teelöffel ⓜ *tay*·ler·fel teaspoon
Teil ⓝ tail part
teilen *tai*·len share
Teilzeit ⓕ *tail*·tsait part-time
Telefon ⓝ te·le·*fawn* telephone

Telefonauskunft ① te·le·*fawn*·ows·kunft directory enquiries
Telefonbuch ⑪ te·le·*fawn*·bookh phone book
telefonieren te·le·fo·*nee*·ren phone
Telefonkarte ① te·le·*fawn*·kar·te phone card
Telefonzelle ① te·le·*fawn*·tse·le phone box
Telefonzentrale ①
te·le·*fawn*·tsen·trah·le telephone centre
Telegramm ⑪ te·le·*gram* telegram
Teleskop ⑪ te·les·*kawp* telescope
Teller ⑩ te·ler plate
Tempel ⑩ *tem*·pel temple
Temperatur ① tem·pe·ra·*toor* temperature (weather)
Tennis ⑪ te·nis tennis
Tennisplatz ⑩ te·nis·plats tennis court
Teppich ⑩ te·pikh rug
Termin ⑩ ter·*meen* appointment
Terminkalender ⑩
ter·*meen*·ka·len·der diary (for appointments)
Terrasse ① te·*ra*·se patio
Test ⑩ test test
teuer toy·er expensive
Theater ⑪ te·*ah*·ter theatre
Theaterkasse ① te·*ah*·ter·ka·se ticket office (theatre)
Theke ① *tay*·ke counter (at bar)
Thermosflasche ① ter·mos·fla·she thermos
Thunfisch ⑩ *toon*·fish tuna
tief teef deep
Tier ⑪ teer animal
Tisch ⑩ tish table
Tischdecke ① tish·de·ke tablecloth
Tischtennis ⑪ tish·te·nis table tennis
Toast ⑩ tawst toast
Toaster ⑩ *taws*·ter toaster
Tochter ① tokh·ter daughter

Tofu ⑩ *taw*·fu tofu
Toilette ① to·a·le·te toilet
Toilettenpapier ⑪
to·a·le·ten·pa·peer toilet paper
toll tol terrific
Tomate ① to·*mah*·te tomato
Tomatensauce ① to·*mah*·ten·zaw·se tomato sauce
Topf ⑩ topf pot (ceramics)
Töpferwaren ① pl *terp*·fer·vah·ren pottery
Tor ⑪ tawr gate • goal
Torhüterin ① *tawr*·hü·te·rin goalkeeper
Torwart ⑩ *tawr*·vart goalkeeper
ein Tor schießen ain *tawr* shee·sen score a goal
tot tawt dead
töten ter·ten kill
Tour ① toor tour
Tourist(in) ⑩/① tu·*rist*/tu·*ris*·tin tourist
Touristenklasse ① tu·*ris*·ten·kla·se economy class
tragen *trah*·gen carry • wear
Training ⑪ *tray*·ning workout
trampen trem·pen hitchhike
Transitraum ⑩ tran·*zeet*·rowm transit lounge
Transport ⑩ trans·*port* transport
trauen *trow*·en trust
träumen *troy*·men dream
traurig *trow*·rikh sad
treffen tre·fen meet
Treppe ① *tre*·pe stairway
treten *tray*·ten kick
trinken *tring*·ken drink
Trinkgeld ⑪ *tring*k·gelt tip (gratuity)
trocken tro·ken dry
Trockenobst ⑪ tro·ken·awpst dried fruit
trocknen trok·nen dry (clothes)
Truthahn ⑩ *troot*·hahn turkey
T-Shirt ⑪ tee·shert T-shirt
tun toon do
Tür ① tür door

T

U

Turm ⓜ turm tower
Türsteher ⓜ *tür*·shtay·er bouncer (club heavy)
Tüte ⓕ *tü*·te carton (milk)
Typ ⓜ tüp type
typisch *tü*·pish typical

U

U-Bahn ⓕ *oo*·bahn subway (underground)
U-Bahnhof ⓜ *oo*·bahn·hawf metro station
Übelkeit ⓕ *ü*·bel·kait nausea
über *ü*·ber about • above • over
Überbrückungskabel ⓝ *ü*·ber·*brü*·kungks·kah·bel jumper leads
Überdosis ⓕ *ü*·ber·daw·zis overdose
überfüllt *ü*·ber·*fült* crowded
Übergepäck ⓝ *ü*·ber·ge·pek excess baggage
übermorgen *ü*·ber·*mor*·gen day after tomorrow
übernachten ü·ber·*nakh*·ten stay (at a hotel)
Überraschung ⓕ ü·ber·*ra*·shung surprise
Überschwemmung ⓕ ü·ber·*shve*·mung flooding
übersetzen ü·ber·ze·tsen translate
Uhr ⓕ oor clock • watch
Ultraschall ⓜ *ul*·tra·shal ultrasound
umarmen um·*ar*·men hug
Umfrage ⓕ *um*·frah·ge polls
Umkleideraum ⓜ *um*·klai·de·rowm changing room
Umsatzsteuer ⓕ *um*·zats·shtoy·er sales tax
umsteigen *um*·shtai·gen change (trains)
Umtausch ⓜ *um*·towsh exchange
Umwelt ⓕ *um*·velt environment
Umweltverschmutzung ⓕ *um*·velt·fer·shmu·tsung pollution
unbequem *un*·be·kvaym uncomfortable
und unt and

unfair *un*·fair unfair
Unfall ⓜ *un*·fal accident
ungefähr un·ge·*fair* approximately
ungewöhnlich *un*·ge·vern·likh unusual
Ungleichheit ⓕ *un*·glaikh·hait inequality
Uniform ⓕ u·ni·*form* uniform
Universität ⓕ u·ni·ver·zi·*tayt* university
Universum ⓝ u·ni·*vair*·zum universe
unmöglich un·*merk*·likh impossible
unschuldig *un*·shul·dikh innocent
unser *un*·zer our
unten *un*·ten down • at the bottom
unter *un*·ter among • below • under
Unterhemd ⓝ *un*·ter·hemt singlet
Unterkunft ⓕ *un*·ter·kunft accommodation
Unterschrift ⓕ *un*·ter·shrift signature
Untertitel ⓜ pl *un*·ter·tee·tel subtitles
Unterwäsche ⓕ *un*·ter·ve·she underwear
Urlaub ⓜ *oor*·lowp holiday

V

Vagina ⓕ va·*gee*·na vagina
Vater ⓜ *fah*·ter father
Vegetarier(in) ⓜ/ⓕ ve·ge·*tah*·ri·er/ve·ge·*tah*·ri·e·rin vegetarian
Vene ⓕ *vay*·ne vein
Ventilator ⓜ ven·ti·*lah*·tor fan (machine)
Verabredung ⓕ fer·*ap*·ray·dung date (appointment)
Veranstaltungskalender ⓜ fer·*an*·shtal·tungks·ka·len·der entertainment guide
Veranstaltungsort ⓜ fer·*an*·shtal·tungks·ort venue
Verband ⓜ fer·*bant* bandage
Verbandskasten ⓜ fer·*bants*·kas·ten first-aid kit
Verbindung ⓕ fer·*bin*·dung connection (person)

verbrennen fer·*bre*·nen burn
verdienen fer·*dee*·nen earn
Vergangenheit ⓕ fer·*gang*·en·hait past
Vergaser ⓜ fer·*gah*·zer carburettor
vergessen fer·*ge*·sen forget
vergewaltigen fer·ge·*val*·ti·gen rape
Verhaftung ⓕ fer·*haf*·tung arrest
verhindern fer·*hin*·dern prevent
Verhütungsmittel ⓝ
fer·*hü*·tungks·mi·tel contraceptives
verkaufen fer·*kow*·fen sell
Verkehr ⓜ fer·*kair* traffic
Verlängerung ⓕ fer·*leng*·e·rung
extension (visa)
verlegen fer·*lay*·gen embarrassed
verletzen fer·*le*·tsen hurt
Verletzung ⓕ fer·*le*·tsung injury
verlieren fer·*lee*·ren lose
Verlobte ⓜ&ⓕ fer·*lawp*·te fiance •
fiancee
Verlobung ⓕ fer·*law*·bung
engagement (marriage)
verloren fer·*law*·ren lost
Vermieter(in) ⓜ/ⓕ fer·*mee*·ter/
fer·*mee*·te·rin landlord/landlady
vermissen fer·*mi*·sen miss (feel
absence of)
Vermittlung ⓕ fer·*mit*·lung operator
vernünftig fer·*nünf*·tikh sensible
verpassen fer·*pa*·sen miss (the bus)
Verpflegung ⓕ fer·*pflay*·gung
provisions
verrückt fer·*rükt* crazy
Versicherung ⓕ fer·*zi*·khe·rung
insurance
Verspätung ⓕ fer·*shpay*·tung delay
versprechen fer·*shpre*·khen promise
verstehen fer·*shtay*·en understand
Verstopfung ⓕ fer·*shtop*·fung
constipation
versuchen fer·*zoo*·khen try (attempt)
Vertrag ⓜ fer·*trahk* contract
Verwaltung ⓕ fer·*val*·tung
administration
Verwandte ⓜ&ⓕ fer·*van*·te relation
(family)

verzeihen fer·*tsai*·en forgive
viel feel a lot (of) • plenty
viele *fee*·le many
vielleicht fi·*laikht* maybe
Viertel ⓝ *feer*·tel quarter
vierzehn Tage ⓜ pl *feer*·tsayn *tah*·ge
fortnight
Virus ⓜ *vee*·rus virus (health) • virus
(computer)
Visum ⓝ *vee*·zum visa
Vitamine ⓝ pl vi·ta·*mee*·ne vitamins
Vogel ⓜ *faw*·gel bird
Volksentscheid ⓜ *folks*·ent·shait
referendum
voll fol full
Vollkornbrot ⓝ *fol*·korn·brawt
wholemeal bread
Vollkornreis ⓜ *fol*·korn·rais brown
rice
Vollzeit ⓕ *fol*·tsait full-time
Volumen ⓝ vo·*loo*·men volume
von fon from
vor fawr in front of • before
vor kurzem fawr *kur*·tsem recently
vor uns fawr uns ahead
vorbereiten *fawr*·be·rai·ten prepare
vorgestern *fawr* ges·tern day before
yesterday
Vorhängeschloss ⓝ
fawr·heng·e·shlos padlock
Vormittag ⓜ *fawr*·mi·tahk morning
(10am–12pm)
Vorname ⓜ *fawr*·nah·me Christian/
given name
Vorort ⓜ *fawr*·ort suburb
Vorrat ⓜ *fawr*·raht stock
vorsichtig fawr·*zikh*·tikh careful
Vorwahl ⓕ *fawr*·vahl area code
vorziehen *fawr*·tsee·en prefer

W

wachsen *vak*·sen grow
sich waschen zikh *va*·shen wash
(oneself)
Waffe ⓕ *va*·fe weapon
Wagen ⓜ *vah*·gen carriage (train)

wählen *vay*·len choose • vote
Wahlen ① pl *vah*·len elections
Wählton ⓝ *vayl*·tawn dial tone
wahr vahr true
während *vair*·rent during
Währung ① *vair*·rung currency
Wald ⓜ valt forest
wandern *van*·dern hike
Wanderstiefel ⓜ pl
van·der·shtee·fel hiking boots
Wanderweg ⓜ *van*·der·vayk hiking
route
wann van when
wann immer van *i*·mer whenever
Warenhaus ⓝ *vah*·ren·hows department
store
warm varm warm
warnen *var*·nen warn
warten *var*·ten wait
Wartesaal ⓜ *var*·te·zahl waiting
room (train station)
Wartezimmer ⓝ *var*·te·tsi·mer
waiting room (doctor's)
warum va·*rum* why
was vas what
Wäscheleine ①*ve*·she·lai·ne
clothesline
waschen *va*·shen wash (something)
Wäscherei ① *ve*·she·rai laundrette
Waschküche ① *vash*·kü·khe laundry
(room)
Waschlappen ⓜ *vash*·la·pen wash
cloth (flannel)
Waschmaschine ①
vash·ma·shee·ne washing machine
Waschpulver ⓝ *vash*·pul·ver
washing powder
Wasser ⓝ *va*·ser water
wasserdicht *va*·ser·dikht waterproof
Wasserfall ⓜ *va*·ser·fal waterfall
Wasserflasche ① *va*·ser·fla·she
water bottle
Wasserhahn ⓜ *va*·ser·hahn
faucet • tap
Wassermelone ① *va*·ser·me·law·ne
watermelon

Wasserskifahren ⓝ
va·ser·shee·fah·ren waterskiing
Watte-Pads pl *va*·te·pedz cotton
balls
Wechselgeld ⓝ *vek*·sel·gelt change
(coins)
Wechselkurs ⓜ *vek*·sel·kurs
exchange rate
wechseln *vek*·seln exchange
(money)
Wecker ⓜ *ve*·ker alarm clock
Weg ⓜ vayk track (path) • way
wegen *vay*·gen because of
Wegweiser ⓜ *vayk*·vai·zer signpost
sich weh tun zikh *vay* toon hurt
(yourself)
Wehrdienst ⓜ *vair*·deenst military
service
Weihnachten ⓝ *vai*·nakh·ten
Christmas
Weihnachtsbaum ⓜ
vai·nakhts·bowm Christmas tree
Weihnachtsfeiertag ⓜ
vai·nakhts·fai·er·tahk Christmas Day
weil vail because
Wein ⓜ vain wine
Weinberg ⓜ *vain*·berk vineyard
Weinbrand ⓜ *vain*·brant brandy
Weintrauben ① pl *vain*·trow·ben
grapes
weiß vais white
Weißbrot ⓝ *vais*·brawt white bread
weißer Pfeffer ⓜ *vai*·ser *pfe*·fer
white pepper
weißer Reis ⓜ *vai*·ser *rais* white
rice
Weißwein ⓜ *vais*·vain white wine
weit vait far
Welle ① *ve*·le wave
Welt ① velt world
Weltmeisterschaft ①
velt·mais·ter·shaft World Cup
wenig *vay*·nikh (a) little
wenige *vay*·ni·ge few
weniger *vay*·ni·ger less
wenn ven when • if

wer *vair* who

Werkstatt ① *verk*·shtat garage (car repair)

Werkzeug ⑩ *verk*·tsoyk tools

Wert ⑩ *vert* value (price)

wertvoll *vert*·fol valuable

Wespe ① *ves*·pe wasp

Westen ⑩ *ves*·ten west

Wette ① *ve*·te bet

Wetter ⑪ *ve*·ter weather

Whisky ⑩ *vis*·ki whisky

wichtig *vikh*·tikh important

wie vee how

wie viel vee feel how much

wieder vee·der again

wiederverwertbar
vee·der·fer·vert·bahr recyclable

wiegen vee·gen weigh

wild vilt wild

willkommen vil·ko·men welcome

Wind ⑩ vint wind

Windel ① *vin*·del nappy (diaper)

Windeldermatitis ①
vin·del·der·ma·tee·tis nappy rash

windig vin·dikh windy

Windschutzscheibe ①
vint·shuts·shai·be windscreen

Windsurfen ⑪ vint·ser·fen
windsurfing

Winter ⑩ vin·ter winter

winzig *vin*·tsikh tiny

wir veer we

wissen vi·sen know (something)

Wissenschaft ① vi·sen·shaft science

Wissenschaftler(in) ⑩/①
vi·sen·shaft·ler/vi·sen·shaft·le·rin
scientist

Witz ⑩ vits joke

wo vaw where

Wochenende ⑪ vo·khen·en·de
weekend

Wodka ⑩ vot·ka vodka

Wohlfahrt ① vawl·fahrt social welfare

wohnen vaw·nen reside

Wohnung ① vaw·nung apartment
(flat)

Wohnwagen ⑩ vawn·vah·gen
caravan

Wolke ① vol·ke cloud

wolkig vol·kikh cloudy

Wolle ① vo·le wool

wollen vo·len want

Wort ⑪ vort word

Wörterbuch ⑪ ver·ter·bookh
dictionary

wunderbar vun·der·bahr wonderful

wünschen vün·shen wish

Würfel ⑩ vür·fel dice

Würmer ⑩ pl vür·mer worms

Wurst ① vurst sausage

würzig vür·tsikh spicy

Wüste ① vüs·te desert

wütend vü·tent angry

Y

Yen ⑩ yen yen

Z

Zahl ① tsahl number

zählen tsay·len count

Zahlung ① tsah·lung payment

Zahn ⑩ tsahn tooth

Zahnarzt ⑩ tsahn·artst dentist

Zahnärztin ① tsahn·erts·tin dentist

Zahnbürste ① tsahn·bürs·te
toothbrush

Zähne ⑩ pl tsay·ne teeth

Zahnfleisch ⑪ tsahn·flaish gum
(mouth)

Zahnpasta ① tsahn·pas·ta toothpaste

Zahnschmerzen pl
tsahn·shmer·tsen toothache

Zahnseide ① tsahn·zai·de dental
floss

Zahnstocher ⑩ tsahn·shto·kher
toothpick

Zauberer(in) ⑩/①
tsow·be·rer/tsow·be·re·rin magician

Zaun ⑩ tsown fence

Zehe ① tsay·e toe • clove (of garlic)

zehn tsayn ten

Z

zeigen *tsai*·gen show • point
Zeit ① tsait time
Zeitschrift ① *tsait*·shrift magazine
Zeitung ① *tsai*·tung newspaper
Zeitungshändler ⓜ
tsai·tungks·hen·dler newsagency
Zeitungskiosk ⓜ
tsai·tungks·kee·osk newsstand
Zeitunterschied ⓝ
tsait·un·ter·sheet time difference
Zelt ⓝ tselt tent
zelten *tsel*·ten camp
Zeltplatz ⓜ *tselt*·plats campsite
Zentimeter ⓜ tsen·ti·*may*·ter
centimetre
Zentralheizung ①
tsen·*trahl*·hai·tsung central heating
Zentrum ⓝ *tsen*·trum centre
zerbrechen tser·*bre*·khen break
zerbrechlich tser·*brekh*·likh fragile
Zertifikat ⓜ tser·ti·fi·*kaht* certificate
Zeugnis ⓝ *tsoyk*·nis reference
(work)
Ziege ① *tsee*·ge goat
ziehen *tsee*·en pull
Ziel ⓝ tseel target • finish (sport)
Zigarette ① tsi·ga·*re*·te cigarette
Zigarre ① tsi·*gar*·re cigar
Zimmer ⓝ *tsi*·mer room
Zimmernummer ① *tsi*·mer·nu·mer
room number
Zirkus ⓜ *tsir*·kus circus
Zitrone ① tsi·*traw*·ne lemon

Zoll ⓜ tsol customs
Zoo ⓜ tsaw zoo
zu tsoo too • at
zu Hause tsoo *how*·ze (at) home
Zucchini ① tsu·*kee*·ni zucchini •
courgette
Zucker ⓜ *tsu*·ker sugar
Zuckererbse ① *tsu*·ker·erp·se
snow pea
Zufall ⓜ *tsoo*·fal chance
Zug ⓜ tsook train
zugeben *tsoo*·gay·ben admit (accept
as true)
Zukunft ① *tsoo*·kunft future
Zulassung ① *tsoo*·la·sung car
registration
zum Beispiel tsum *bai*·shpeel for
example
Zündung ① *tsün*·dung ignition
zurück tsu·*rük* back (return)
zurückkommen tsu·*rük*·ko·men
return
zusammen tsu·*za*·men together
Zusammenstoß ⓜ
tsu·*za*·men·staws crash
zustimmen *tsoo*·shti·men agree
Zutat ① *tsoo*·taht ingredient
zweimal *tsvai*·mahl twice
zweite *tsvai*·te second
Zwerchfell ⓝ *tsverkh*·fel diaphragm
Zwiebel ① *tsvee*·bel onion
Zwillinge ⓜ pl *tsvi*·ling·e twins
zwischen *tsvi*·shen between

Index

Register

For topics that are covered in several sections of this book, we've indicated the most relevant page number in bold.

INDEX

10 Ways to Start a Sentence

When's (the next flight)?	Wann ist (der nächste Flug)?	van ist (dair *naykhs*·te fl ook)
Where's (the station)?	Wo ist (der Bahnhof)?	vaw ist (dair *bahn*·hawf)
Where can I (buy a ticket)?	Wo kann ich (eine Fahrkarte kaufen)?	vaw kan ikh (*ai*·ne *fahr*·kar·te *kow*·fen)
Do you have (a map)?	Haben Sie (eine Karte)?	*hah*·ben zee (*ai*·ne *kar*·te)
Is there (a toilet)?	Gibt es (eine Toilette)?	gipt es (*ai*·ne to·a·*le*·te)
I'd like (a coffee).	Ich möchte (einen Kaffee).	ikh *merkh*·te (*ai*·nen ka·fay)
I'd like (to hire a car).	Ich möchte (ein Auto mieten).	ikh *merkh*·te (ain *ow*·to *mee*·ten)
Can I (enter)?	Darf ich (hereinkommen)?	darf ikh (her·*ein*·ko·men)
Could you please (help me)?	Könnten Sie (mir helfen)?	*kern*·ten zee (meer *hel*·fen)
Do I have to (book a seat)?	Muss ich (einen Platz reservieren lassen)?	mus ikh (*ai*·nen plats re·zer·*vee*·ren *la*·sen)